The Company States Keep

This book argues that investor risk in emerging markets hinges on the company a country keeps. When a country signs on to an economic agreement with states that are widely known to be stable, it looks less risky. Conversely, when a country joins a group with more unstable members, it looks more risky. Investors use the company a country keeps as a heuristic in evaluating that country's willingness to honor its sovereign debt obligations. These heuristics, however, tend not to reflect the realities on the ground in the country in question. This has important implications for the study of international cooperation as well as of sovereign risk and credibility at the domestic level.

Julia Gray is an assistant professor of political science at the University of Pennsylvania. Her work in international political economy and international organization has appeared or is forthcoming in the *American Journal of Political Science*, *Comparative Political Studies*, *International Studies Quarterly*, the *European Journal of Political Research*, *Political Science Research Methods*, and the *Review of International Organizations*. Prior to her career in academia, she worked for five years as a journalist, editor, and program officer in Prague and Budapest.

For Roy and Natalie Gray, and Bess and Jack Slaughter

The Company States Keep

International Economic Organizations and Investor Perceptions

JULIA GRAY
University of Pennsylvania

CAMBRIDGE
UNIVERSITY PRESS

CAMBRIDGE
UNIVERSITY PRESS

32 Avenue of the Americas, New York, NY 10013-2473, USA

Cambridge University Press is part of the University of Cambridge.

It furthers the University's mission by disseminating knowledge in the pursuit of education, learning, and research at the highest international levels of excellence.

www.cambridge.org
Information on this title: www.cambridge.org/9781107030886

First published 2013

Printed in the United States of America

A catalog record for this publication is available from the British Library.

Library of Congress Cataloging in Publication data
Gray, Julia, 1974–
The company states keep: international economic organizations and investor perceptions / Julia Gray, University of Pennsylvania.
    pages cm
Includes bibliographical references and index.
ISBN 978-1-107-03088-6 (hardback)
1. Debts, Public – Developing countries.   2. International organizations.
I. Title.
HJ8899.G73   2013
336.3'435091724 – dc23   2013009529

ISBN 978-1-107-03088-6 Hardback

Contents

List of Figures

List of Tables

Acknowledgments

This project came out of a paper I wrote for Geoff Garrett and Ron Rogowski's survey in political economy. Thanks to Geoff for noting that the concept was "a fine idea, worth pursuing," and then guiding me through that pursuit. I'm grateful to Ken Schultz for taking on the project in its early stages and pushing me to think clearly about the foundations as well as the execution. And thanks to Ron Rogowski for providing vital advocacy at the first iteration of the paper as well as rigorous thinking thereafter. James Honaker provided patience, ideas, and endless methodological guidance. John Zaller got no official credit for extending to me his time, good humor, and encouragement – but he receives profuse thanks here. Thanks as well to Barbara Geddes, Jeff Lewis, Dan Posner, Michael Ross, Art Stein, and Mike Thies. My cohort, broadly defined, also provided invaluable support and comments, especially Alex Baturo, Nancy Brune, Daniela Campello, Cari Coe, Kim Dionne, Katja Favretto, Erica Frantz, Desha Girod, Ashley Jester, Mark Kayser, Moonhawk Kim, Phil Potter, Rachel Potter, Rob Salmond, Jon Slapin, Jana von Stein, Jessica Weeks, Joe Wright, Dan Young, and Cesar Zucco. And my gratitude goes to David Stasavage and Andrew Walter for originally putting me on the IPE track.

Versions of this project benefited from valuable feedback that I received from talks at Columbia, Harvard Business School, Princeton, Stanford, Yale, the University of Colorado at Boulder, the University of Michigan, the University of Virginia, and Washington University in St. Louis. I received particularly helpful comments from Rawi Abdelal, Bill Clark, Christina Davis, Matt Gabel, Judy Goldstein, Joanne Gowa, Raymond Hicks, John Ikenberry, Nate Jensen, Bob Jervis, Joe Jupille, David Leblang, Ed Mansfield, Helen Milner, Sunita Parikh, Jack Snyder, Andy Sobel, Allan Stam, Kathryn Stoner-Weiss, Mike Tomz, and Jim Vreeland. Special thanks to Bill Bernhard and Ken Scheve for providing insight and comments at my book conference, hosted at the University of Pittsburgh. Thanks to the faculty then in the political science department at Pitt, especially Despina Alexiadou, Barry Ames, David Bearce, Chuck Gochman, Michael Goodhart, Scott Morgenstern, Daniela Donno Panayides, Anibal Perez-Liñan, Nita Rudra, Burcu Savun, and Alberta Sbragia. Thanks as well to colleagues in the political science department at the University of Pennsylvania for their support in the final stages of this project. Two anonymous reviewers also provided valuable and through feedback, for which I'm grateful. Thanks to Juliet Whelan at Jibe Design for giving the book a far more interesting cover than it deserves.

This manuscript would not have been possible without funding from many sources. The Institute for Humane Studies provided support throughout my graduate career; particular thanks to Nigel Ashford for his many comments and guidance. At UCLA, I'm grateful for funding from the Burkle Center for International Studies, the Graduate Division, the Center for European and Eurasian Studies, and the Office for Summer Research Mentorship. A Foreign Language Area Studies grant, funding from the National Council for Eurasian and Eastern European Research, and the American Council of Learned Societies Summer Language Training Grant helped me develop language skills for the interviews and case studies. The Institute for European Studies at UC-Berkeley and the Institute of Global Conflict and Cooperation also provided support. A year-long residency at Stanford's Center on Democracy, Development and the Rule of Law gave me time to write and valuable interactions. A postdoctoral fellowship at the Woodrow Wilson Center for International Studies also provided me with time, resources, and ideas. At the University of Pittsburgh, the European Union Center for Excellence as well as the Department of Political Science provided generous support for the book conference and for fieldwork. Thanks as well to interview subjects in Ankara, Budapest, Bratislava, Brussels, Buenos Aires, Gaborone, Istanbul, Johannesburg, Lima, Lusaka, Montevideo, New York, Prague, Tbilisi, and Zagreb for their time and insights.

And I'm grateful to Keri Allison, Sasha Baturo, Sascha Beicken, Emily Byers, Valerie Crowell, Erik d'Amato, Carolina Garriga, Brian Glover, Brigid Gorski, Sujata Gosalia, Emaline Gray, Hallie Gray, John Gray, the Roy Grays II and III, Janet Haven, Mary Henderson, Lukas Kendall, Julia Kent, Karen Lautanen, Ryan Marshall, Betsy and VJ Maury, Becky Mingo, Emma Nilsson, Aaron Panofsky, Kelly Reid, Joanna Rohozinska, Eli Rykoff, John Sharpless, Bess and Jack Slaughter, Mary Frank Slaughter, Sue Vilushis, Brian Warner, Natalie Wilkerson, and Harris Wulfson for their support and encouragement at various stages of this project.

I

Introduction: The Company You Keep

Emerging markets the world over struggle for political as well as economic legitimacy on the international stage. Risk perceptions are an important component of their image, because access to credit on international markets can provide cash-strapped governments with much-needed financing. What can developing countries do to make themselves look attractive to private international creditors? How – in the absence of enforcement by third parties or truly binding contracts – can a country assure markets that it is a trustworthy investment, that it is both willing and able to service the loans it incurs? Emerging markets have a long history of shirking their foreign debt obligations; nearly half of the defaults in the last century occurred in developing countries. How can these countries convince investors of their intentions to make good on their debt obligations?

This book argues that regional economic organizations (REOs) can help solve cooperation problems in international credit markets. But perhaps counterintuitively, the rules and enforcement within those organizations tend to be not so important to investors. Rather than design, investors pay particular attention to the other member states in those organizations – that is, the company a country keeps. If emerging markets announce formal ties with other countries, investors look to whether those associated countries have low political risk, which gives clues as to their willingness to service their debt. International organization with responsible countries makes emerging markets look less risky – and by the same token, organizing with ill-behaved countries will make a new member look like more of a risky investment. Specifically, sovereign spreads – the risk premium that portfolio investors demand for holding a country's debt – fluctuate as a function of the other members of groups a country joins on the international stage. When uncertainty is high, investors use the company a country keeps as a way of making inferences about other investors' perceptions of a country's trajectory.

Examples of this phenomenon abound in world politics. After the 1993 split of Czechoslovakia – four years after the fall of the Berlin Wall – Slovakia seemed ready to sink. It featured crumbling, Soviet-era industries as its economic base, and it was isolated from the international community by the authoritarian Vladimir Mečiar. Despite many market-friendly reforms – liberalizing trade and prices and privatizing formerly state-owned industries – the country was largely ignored by short- and long-term investors alike. All that changed in 1999, after voters dumped Mečiar and the European Union formally opened negotiations for entry with Slovakia. Within hours of the initial announcement of EU talks, the extra premium that investors demanded to hold Slovak debt – essentially, insurance against the possibility of default – plummeted. "Once we were validated by the talks with the EU, investor perception shifted radically, and this changed everything for our country," says one official in the Slovak central bank.[1] Slovakia was not alone. For those postcommunist countries that managed to open talks with the European Union in the 1990s, the cost of borrowing abroad dropped 33 percent, giving those once-closed economies unprecedented access to capital on international financial markets.

But as the 2007 financial crisis has demonstrated, portfolio investors can take flight as quickly as they rush in, and punish as severely as they reward. In the mid-2000s, Venezuela was flush with oil money and should have been a welcome member of any economic organization. During that period, Venezuelan President Hugo Chávez positioned himself for regional influence by opening talks with South America's biggest regional organization, the Common Market for the South (Mercosur), as well as proposing a new regional economic alternative of his own, the Bolivarian Alternative for the Americas (ALBA). But as Chávez's acts at home became more and more erratic – such as nationalizing several industries, firing the well-regarded head of the central bank – investors began to look less kindly not only on Venezuela, but also on the countries that were preparing to link themselves to it. Investment risk for the other members of Mercosur spiked in concert with Chávez's anti-market behavior, even though those members traded relatively less with Venezuela than did many of that country's neighbors.

What do these two stories tell us about perceptions of risk and their consequences? For one thing, they show the power of cognitive shortcuts in information processing. Developing countries across the globe strive to convince markets of their creditworthiness. If they fail, they remain marginalized, aid-dependent, and poor, with their only options being loans from international financial institutions – and those loans typically come with many strings attached. The prize, however, is private investment capital that can further economic growth. Countries can gain legitimacy in the eyes of creditors through gestures great and small, both domestically and abroad. They might vote in forward-looking leaders who adopt bold policy reforms or fly in

---

[1] Interview, L'udovit Ódor, National Bank of Slovakia, 23 July 2006.

decorated international consultants. But economic development is full of false starts, incomplete reforms, political falls from grace, and policy reversals. If emerging markets have a history of uncertainty, how do investors know what to believe? More specifically, what acts do investors most closely monitor? The 2007 financial crisis has demonstrated amply that investors in financial markets are not shy about taking inferential shortcuts, and international agreements – specifically, the nature of the other members in those agreements – can serve as a powerful signal to investors about a country's intentions, even about its perceived identity (Anderson, 1991).

Investors use the company a country keeps as an important heuristic, or speculative formulation, through one central mechanism. Portfolio investors coordinate on public pronouncements that are easily generalizable across situations.[2] Investors may not know about the details of an organization's structure, the degree to which rules are enforced, or the speed at which attendant policies are implemented (if, in fact, they are implemented at all). But bond traders make inferences based on the already visible attributes of the better-known members of the organization, and the announcement of economic ties is a visible and public way for emerging markets to link to those countries. In an environment of high uncertainty, the peer effect of international economic organization is a commonly relatable and publicly observable way for market actors to arrive at similar assessments – even if those assessments subsequently turn out to be flawed, and even if, as is often the case, the proposed economic ties never materialize. Indeed, herd behavior may drive markets to over-rely on international organization as a heuristic in shaping their views on the risk associated with a given country.[3] But in the short term, the company a country keeps can have a big impact on a government's ability to borrow on international capital markets.

Individual bond traders can arrive at a whole host of different assessments, of course, based on their own judgments or on the differing weight they might put on various indicators. In the last fifty years, with not only the improvement of computer processing power but the availability of data to crunch, algorithms can digest scores of variables and spit out a proposed price of an asset. But bond traders also act on their own personal judgment, which stems from experience, sentiment, or their own appetites for risk. Bond traders work in environments where there is a glut of information about countries that they themselves have likely never visited; thus, they must sort through a variety of secondhand information to make their assessments about the level of risk. They must make what in decision theory is called a decision under uncertainty – a case when

---

[2] Behavioral finance (Thaler, 1993, 1994) and prospect theory (Kahneman and Tversky, 1979) have long argued that investors evaluate assets using interesting shortcuts; Zuckerman (2004) shows that although investors rely on classifications, these classiciations are imperfect.

[3] This phenomenon has been widely noted in many types of investment; see Kindleberger (2005) and Benartzi and Thaler (2001, 2007).

each possible alternative is associated with a probability distribution, but those distributions are unknown (Ben-Haim, 1998).

Investors' assessments can be particularly subjective in high-uncertainty environments such as emerging markets. Eichengreen and Mody (1998) demonstrated empirically that, particularly in emerging markets, bond spreads are more a function of market sentiment than of economic fundamentals. In fact, bond traders who deal particularly with emerging markets have been accused of having "too much money and too little local knowledge or power."[4] This is in part a function of the unreliability of statistics in emerging markets and those countries' vulnerability to political or economic shocks. In such high-uncertainty circumstances, investors are particularly sensitive to overall market sentiment on particular assets, as well as to how other investors interpret the actions of emerging markets. International economic organizations, I argue, can be a powerful driver of market sentiment in high-uncertainty environments – and markets use the known members of those organizations as shorthands in their estimations of less-known members.

The argument advanced in this book makes a distinct contribution to the debate on international cooperation. International relations scholars have long advanced the importance of international institutions as a means of promoting stability and coordination among nations. This book tests that claim using a measure of uncertainty in countries from financial markets: the risk associated with sovereign bonds, a measure that is of substantive as well as theoretical interest to social scientists. The argument offers a new mechanism – the company a country keeps – through which institutions matter. In contrast to previous research, I find that the effect of the company a country keeps has little to do with the legalistic design of the organization (Koremenos, 2001, 2005; Rosendorff, 2005; McCall Smith, 2000) or the policy reform that countries undertake in order to enter (Schimmelfennig and Sedelmeier, 2005), or the unobserved factors that might drive countries both to enter certain types of organizations and to have certain kinds of risk profiles (Vreeland, 2001; von Stein, 2005), or rule enforcement in the organization (Fearon, 1998; Abbott and Snidal, 1998). Nor is the effect simply a function of being in the same neighborhood (Simmons and Elkins, 2004; Gleditsch and Ward, 2006). The argument advanced here is a new and independent mechanism through which international institutions can matter. Because these effects are independent of policy change, the inferences about a new member's quality may be undeserved – witness the severe market corrections of risk assessments in Greece, Spain, and Portugal during the eurozone crisis. But these changes in risk perception are an empirical reality.

This argument comes at a time when international agreements are on the rise, particularly regional trade agreements (Mansfield and Milner, 1997, 2012; Mattli, 1999; Solingen, 2002; Pevehouse, 2002; Donno, 2010; Goertz and Powers, 2012). The number of international and regional organizations has

---

[4] "A nasty spillage," *The Economist,* 10 June 2006.

grown steadily in the past decades, but their effects are far from understood. With multilateral trade talks in crisis, and with purchasing power in Asia on the rise, the accession of Russia, Vietnam, and Ukraine to the WTO may be less formative than the possible creation of a deep trade agreement that would include Australia, India, Southeast Asia, and China,[5] or the Trans-Pacific Partnership – a regional trade agreement that includes the United States, Australia, Malaysia, Singapore and Vietnam.[6] In November 2011, Vladimir Putin announced the formation of a new Eurasian Union; commentators noted that Russia would use this regional organization as a way of projecting its power in the east.[7] Realizing the assumptions that markets make about members enables a better understanding of these organizations' effects.

This book offers two important contributions to the literature on international cooperation. The first is theoretical: I argue that portfolio investors pay attention primarily to the reputation of other members of an organization in determining a country's *willingness*, not its ability, to uphold its debt. Taking insights from management theory and sociology as well as political science, I posit that investors' private expectations about particular countries coordinate around those countries' public affiliations within international organizations. When an emerging market announces close ties with a given group of nations, investors take the reputation of those member countries into account as indicators of a new member's willingness to cooperate in international bond markets. This focus on peer effects contrasts with much of the research that places particular emphasis on institutional design in international organizations (Koremenos, Lipson, and Snidal, 2001; McCall Smith, 2000). It also stands apart from claims on how regime type and domestic institutions influence investor perceptions (Schultz and Weingast, 2003; Li and Resnick, 2003; Saiegh, 2005). This book suggests that a focus on domestic factors alone is incomplete; investors' uncertainty coordinates on the company a country keeps in addition to what its domestic institutions look like.

The second is empirical: through data analysis as well as qualitative field research and case illustrations, I show that institutions matter to markets and also address the questions of "when" and "how" they do so. Firsthand interviews with portfolio investors, finance ministers, central bankers, and trade officials, from Brussels to Istanbul to Lima to Johannesburg, supplement the empirical findings. This on-the-ground research helps give support to the theory at all levels.

This book focuses on the credibility that REO membership can give to emerging markets in particular, but the basics of the argument can also extend

---

[5] "Asian Leaders Plan Free-Trade Area from India to New Zealand," *Bloomberg*, 15 January 2007.

[6] "At APEC, President Obama welcomes Asian trade agreement, warns Iran," *Politico*, 12 November 2011.

[7] "Russia's Putin dreams of sweeping Eurasian Union," *Associated Press*, 3 January 2012.

to the developed world. They have resonance in any situation where information is poor and where investors take mental shortcuts to arrive at their assessments. "The company you keep" tends to operate as a heuristic device that is independent of actual changes that occur in a country as a result of international organization – that is, the reaction is often disproportionate to the reality. Given the recent crisis of asset-backed securities throughout the world, this argument has particular relevance.

The findings presented here are also of importance to the research on international development. The terms on which countries borrow can make or break emerging markets' attempts to attract international capital. Countries in that category account for 80 percent of the world's population, all but a quarter of its landmass, 66 percent of its foreign-exchange reserves, and 50 percent of its purchasing-power-parity adjusted GDP. Currently, more than 40 percent of developing-country debt is investment grade – up from just 3 percent in 1997. As governments in developing countries issue their debt on international markets, the interest rates associated with their sovereign debt have big impacts on their ability to raise revenue. And sovereign debt – government-issued debt securities, also known as government bonds – is a fast-growing category of asset; by the end of 2011, there were $31 trillion worth of government bonds in issue, up from $11 trillion in 2001.[8] Thus, the arguments and results in this book are of concern for countries hoping to raise money on international capital markets.

Is paying attention to the company a country keeps a rational response on the part of investors? That is, does joining an organization with good members really promote better behavior on the part of the new member? Conversely, do countries of ill repute infect their international partners? The answer is nuanced. Deep trade ties do leave countries exposed to economic or political shocks in their neighbors, repeated interactions may bring countries' preferences closer together, and adoption of group rules may bring members' policies more in line with one another. I give evidence that the extent of investor reaction is usually not justified by the observable changes in countries, not least because the actual level of integration achieved in these arrangements often falls short of the level of proposed integration. Members of all sorts of organizations break supposedly strict rules; bailouts are extended to countries regardless of their formal international ties; and countries do not necessarily mimic the behavior, good or bad, of their international partners. However, because investors traffic not only in countries' actual performance, but in other investors' perceptions of that performance, the changes in risk levels may still be rational. That is, investors can benefit in the short term from acting on these heuristics, even if the herd's perceptions do not match the fundamentals on the ground, because investors have an incentive to act in tandem with market sentiment. Of course, what is rational for one investor can create systemic risk when

---

[8] "Oat cuisine," *The Economist*, 11 February 2012.

compounded; investor positions become serially correlated, and a given fixed-income instrument can become systematically over- or undervalued, but it can still make sense for investors to follow the herd in the short run.[9]

1.1 INTERNATIONAL COOPERATION AND UNCERTAINTY

This topic intersects with a broader research question that has shaped academic debate for years: how do institutions matter, and to whom? Political scientists have grappled with this topic for decades. The initial stages of the debate were theoretical, with realists arguing that powerful states behaved as they pleased (Mearsheimer, 1994; Krasner, 1991). Liberal institutionalists, by contrast, argued that international organizations were pivotal in ensuring cooperation among states. The list of possible mechanisms behind how IOs might encourage cooperation among states was broad and inclusive. International organizations, it has been argued, spread norms of behavior (Finnemore, 1996b), reduce transaction costs (North, 1990), ensure punishment of bad behavior (Axelrod, 1984), provide information about other actors' behavior (Milgrom, North, and Weingast, 1990), and establish frameworks for litigation and enforcement of rules (Goldstein et al., 2000; McCall Smith, 2000). These many distinct mechanisms, in the early stages of IO research, were rarely assumed to be mutually exclusive; indeed, many writers on this topic claimed that all these forces were in effect simultaneously (Keohane, 1984; Ikenberry, 1988; North, 1990). When researchers on international organizations turned to the empirical, then, they faced a daunting task. How would it be possible to disentangle these many different potential mechanisms?

I put forward and test the independent effects of a mechanism that is novel in this literature. This argument about "the company you keep" is relatively new to the field of international organizations,[10] but it has a long-standing history in other areas of research. Disciplines throughout the social science have studied and theorized about so-called neighborhood effects. Researchers have observed the effects of peer groups in education and crime, of endorsements in management and finance; of labeling in sociology, of self-fulfilling prophecies in psychology, and of group ritualization in anthropology.[11] Management theory has examined the influence of an underwriters' reputation on the price of an

---

[9] On the irrationality of markets generally, see Kindleberger (2005) and Aspara (2010). One study shows that past experience and existing beliefs tend to guide investors, rather than logical thinking and rational decision making (Knauff et al., 2010).

[10] See Dreher and Voigt (2008); Gray (2009).

[11] For just a few examples, one study in sociology focuses on how criminal activity and drug abuse patterns tend to be replicated within neighborhoods, as a result of "collective socialization" and "contagion"(Case and Katz, 1991). Mead (1934) gives a sociological account of how the self is socially constructed and reconstructed through individuals' interactions with their community. Psychologists have studied how labeling can have negative impacts on the mentally ill (Scheff, 1966). Becker (1963) studies the effects of deviance from social groups on the behavior of an individual.

asset (Carter and Manaster, 1990) and the self-fulfilling power of stereotypes (Chen and Bargh, 1997).

Those studies all point to the critical importance of actors' relationships to a variety of outcomes. But the mechanisms of influence are often either ill-defined, contradictory, or both. If peer groups matter, is it because the individuals within those groups actually change their behavior as a function of being in that group? Or do others make unfair inferences about the propensities of individuals in those groups, even if those individuals' nature is fundamentally unchanged? Or is the chain of causality more complex, such that individuals modify their behavior as a result of their new (deserved or undeserved) reputations – or even that the types of individuals who join certain groups are only acting on propensities that were previously unobserved?

This book examines all those possible mechanisms from both a theoretical and an empirical perspective. My key argument is that, in assessing the risk premia on sovereign debt, investors are looking for two types of information. One is on a country's ability to service its debt. This information can be gleaned relatively easily, by looking at macroeconomic indicators and past performance. But governments change; new policies are enacted; and reading the tea leaves for developing countries can be a difficult task, particularly when getting solid priors on the second type of information: a country's willingness to service its debt. This is where "the company you keep" comes in. Visibly bad behavior among a developing country's closest friends can make financial markets skittish about the reliability of that country by extension, because markets assume that countries form ties with nations they hope to emulate. Conversely, investors cut slack to emerging markets that themselves have histories of behaving badly if they join groups of countries that have upstanding reputations. Joining different groups can potentially affect a country's *ability* to service its debt, through the economic benefits where trade integration occurs – but the company it keeps fills in the blanks about its *willingness* to honor its debt obligations. This peer effect is distinct from the material benefits that may emerge as a result of international organization. Markets may not get this right, as the current financial crisis in the eurozone shows: simply being, for example, in the same club as Germany does not mean that every other country adopted fiscal discipline. But this heuristic was nonetheless a powerful driver of European sovereign spreads for years.

By looking at the role of international organizations on investor confidence, and by parsing out many different aspects of those organizations and their members that might influence third parties, this book makes important theoretical and empirical distinctions that enhance our understanding of what matters in institutions. I show how being in the same neighborhood is *not* equivalent to being in the same club – and how, to extend the metaphor, the requirements for entry, the rules of membership and the structure of the building are less important than the quality of the members in a particular club. In more technical terms, I demonstrate that the impacts of international organization on a country's perceived creditworthiness are not a function of selection (the underlying propensity of an actor to choose like-minded groups). Nor can those impacts be explained away by the policy reform that countries undertake either before or during membership in a particular organization. The quality of members can have substantial effects, particularly when those members give their blessing to policy reform in new members, as in the case of the European Union. In the context of international organization, the company you keep has an impact on a country's standing in financial markets. The rational expectations hypothesis hinges on the assumption that all market participants have equal access to the same data, and that those actors also share one model of how the world works. Because IO membership is elective, unlike geography, it makes a strong statement about the types of countries that a country considers its peers, and thus serves as a potential expression of willingness to pay. Regions are static across time, whereas IO membership is dynamic – not only at the moment when countries themselves join, but also when the addition or exit of still other countries either dilute or reinforce the brand.

1.2 WHY EMERGING MARKETS? WHY SOVEREIGN DEBT?

The claims about international organization and international cooperation are vast ones, and what I present here is an examination of these claims along a relatively narrow dimension. Drawn fine, this argument focuses on a somewhat limited sample (emerging markets) and a fairly specialized measure of credibility (sovereign debt), which is merely the collective evaluations of one set of private actors at a given time. Furthermore, the argument extends most powerfully to one particular type of international organization (economic agreements). This focus inevitably limits the scope of the claims I am able to make. Yet these are powerful test cases for many of the theories about international organizations and their welfare implications.

Taking those components in turn, why focus specifically on emerging markets, a category that excludes both the more developed countries and the very poorest? Richer countries have other indicators from which investors can make inferences about their debt; those deeper markets are better understood, and there is less need for heuristic shortcuts in assessing their creditworthiness. The poorest countries do not issue their debt on international markets, because their levels of risk are so great that an insufficient number of international creditors are willing to lend to them. By contrast, emerging markets occupy a middle ground – not so poor that they are fundamentally untrustworthy and not creditworthy, and not so rich that it is easy for investors to gather information about them. They are still at the stage where investors want to give them credit but have differing opinions about the risks of doing so.[12] Particularly

[12] Many articles on diffusion and persuasion use this logic, where new countries or new issue areas are those most likely to be influenced by external forces. See Johnston (2001) and Finnemore and Sikkink (1998).

for countries with a patchy track record in the global marketplace, keeping good international company will give them a credibility boost in the eyes of investors. This is not an argument that applies to countries that are experiencing such low economic growth that their main sources of revenue are from aid. The countries under consideration here are not ravaged by war or suffering widespread famine or disease. Rather, they are all at stages of economic development where they might have buyers for their debt on international markets. Thus, they are at a point where their future may be uncertain, but there is an opportunity for investors to bet on that future – and possibly reap rewards from the risk. Elucidating the mechanism that describes why this might be the case can help us gain an understanding of how institutions work, and which aspects of them carry weight in specific settings.

In terms of the second component, spreads on sovereign debt – the gap between the risk associated with one country relative to a comparable more stable security, such as U.S. Treasury bills – is but one way of operationalizing reputation. Scholars in the social sciences are increasingly turning to financial market data for empirical work on a number of topics relating to international behavior and domestic policy.[13] What can this measure of government capability and willingness to repay its debt tell political scientists, and how does it differ from other economic indicators? I offer three main justifications for my choice of dependent variable: one is theoretical, the second is practical, and the third is the substantive implication. Spreads on sovereign debt are superior as a measure of uncertainty to many other indicators; its level of detail and relative availability give it an edge over other economic indicators; and finally, a country's cost of borrowing can have important implications for its ability to raise capital on international markets.

Countries can gain international legitimacy by running military demonstrations, winning wars, throwing summits, or hosting international sporting events.[14] This is admittedly a very specific claim about how a particular audience (international bond traders) regards international organization. Yet sovereign debt (and market measures more generally) have gained great traction in political science as a means of measuring and operationalizing otherwise elusive concepts, such as uncertainty (Root, 2005), reputation (Tomz, 2007), and credibility (Jensen and Schmith, 2005). Many of the propositions about the power of institutions center on how they decrease uncertainty, a concept that is difficult to measure directly. Investment data are particularly useful in testing such claims, because measuring and pricing uncertainty is one of the market's fundamental operating principles. Especially in volatile emerging markets, investors stand to gain or lose vast sums of money on the basis of their

---

[13] See, for example, Ferguson and Schularick (2006); Tomz (2007); Stasavage (2007); Mitchener and Weidenmier (2008).

[14] See O'Neill (2006) on prestige in international relations, and Kurscheidt and Rahmann (2006) on the reputational benefits of hosting the FIFA world cup in Germany.

bets on the security as well as the potential return of an investment. The trick, however, lies in grappling with a lack information by changing it into measurable probabilities; in other words, translating uncertainty into risk, risk into opportunity, and opportunity into profit (Root, 2005). This is of tremendous importance to developing countries, who strive to break free from development traps and gain access to international finance.

In finance, calculating risk associated with governments is a common practice, but social scientists have only recently begun to take advantage of these data. Sovereign debt – the measure employed in this book – is increasingly in use in political science as a means of measuring third-party expectations. In the past ten years, researchers have used market data – including stock market returns and sovereign paper of various maturities – to test various hypotheses.[15] Sovereign debt in particular has served as a stand-in for state credibility on international markets. Because sovereign debt often has maturities that extend past the lifespan in office of any given leader, it is a useful indicator of the reputation that countries have irrespective of who is in office.

Theoretically, sovereign debt offers a summary of how markets rate government stability as well as the future levels of development in a country. Unlike other forms of investment, such as foreign direct investment in plants and long-term projects, bondholders have little interest in the promotion of any one good, in historical ties to a country, or in current-day alliances.[16] Bondholders seek profit – and relatively quick profit at that – and they profit from seeking relatively high rates of return in environments with varying degrees of risk. As such, the yields and spreads on bonds reflect *perceptions* of that economy, both in terms of other investors' assessments as well as in future returns on investment (later in the book I discuss in further detail how those perceptions work). Thus, they are themselves a measure of collective uncertainty about the ability as well as the willingness of a country's government to

---

[15] See Mosley (2003); Jensen and Schmith (2005); Stasavage (2007); Bernhard and Leblang (2002, 2006); Mosley and Singer (2009). Tomz (2007) has effectively harnessed the rates at which countries can borrow abroad as an indicator of reputation. My focus here, however, is different. Where Tomz was concerned with leveraging data on international interest rates as a proxy for a country's reputation, I examine how that reputation changes as a function of membership in international organizations. In technical terms, then, although this concerns the same outcome (dependent variable), the main explanatory factors (independent variables) differ. Tomz provided convincing empirical evidence that yields on countries' sovereign debt are a strong indicator of a country's reputation on international credit markets, and that yields are elastic to bad behavior on the part of those countries. That is, when countries give indication of defaulting on their debt, markets treat them as more risky investments. However, I show that developing countries need not behave badly themselves in order to be treated as risky investments. If they form close ties with *other* countries who engage in risky behavior, investors will treat them as risky, too. Thus, my argument takes a different theoretical tack: I show that countries' reputations are a function not only of their own behavior but of the behavior of their friends. This implies that investors piece together their assessments of countries' reputations through what are at times inefficient means.

[16] See Biglaiser and DeRouen (2007) on how FDI tends to track military alliances or colonial ties.

uphold its obligations to service its debt. Yields on sovereign debt are therefore an obvious theoretical choice in testing the claims about expectations of future behavior found in the literature on international institutions, which claims that institutions should regularize behavior and encourage cooperation.

Utilizing sovereign debt yields for research purposes also provides substantial practical advantages. Particularly in developing countries, where data are only as reliable as the governments that collect them, this type of financial market data offers significant benefits to researchers. For one thing, there is a lot of it, and at high levels of detail. Although trading of emerging-market sovereign debt only became widespread in the 1990s, the years for which data are available represent a full cycle of operations for bond investors, including the heady days of enthusiasm for emerging-market debt in the mid-1990s and the investment backlash following the Latin American and East Asian debt crises (Erb, Harvey, and Viskanta, 2000). Though coverage of sovereign debt varies across region, in many cases it is available in weekly and daily increments. This is far more substantial and detailed coverage than can be had for many other economic indicators in emerging markets. The level of detail afforded by sovereign debt allows us to examine the impact of particular events as well as trends over time.

Finally, and importantly, there is a considerable substantive reason that social scientists – and indeed, governments – should be concerned with estimating the determinants of sovereign risk. The volume of money traded in sovereign debt is huge. The 2008 financial crisis and its aftermath initially dampened investors' tolerance for risk, but portfolio investment will not rebound cyclically, and emerging economies will have ever greater access to international capital. The Institute for International Finance estimated capital flows to emerging markets totaled $435 billion in 2009, down from $667 billion in 2008.[17] But in 2010, emerging market debt trade reached a record high of $6.765 trillion.[18] More and more countries are turning to sovereign bond markets as a form of financing; even Angola, one of the most risky sovereign investments, took advantage of the increasing appetite for emerging market sovereign debt by issuing a bond in January of 2011.[19] Sovereign debt is thus an increasingly important part of international capital flows.

Therefore, risk levels in sovereign debt are rightfully making headway in political science and public policy for theoretical and practical reasons, as well as for the growing importance these debt instruments play in emerging economies' fortunes. In addition to the relative quality and availability of these indicators compared with other types of economic data in developing countries, they also serve as an independent measure of uncertainty – a concept that is extremely important in much of the literature on the consequences of

---

[17] "IIF Sees $720 billion Emerging Market Capital Flows In 2010," *Financial Times*, 26 January 2010.

[18] "Emerging market debt volumes dip 4 pct in 2011," *Reuters*, 2 March 2012.

[19] "Angolan Eurobond Yield May Be Near Nigeria's on Oil Boost, Standard Says," *Bloomberg*, 21 April 2011.

membership in international institutions – and provide us with leverage in operationalizing difficult-to-measure concepts such as risk and uncertainty. They are also in and of themselves an increasingly important means of financing in emerging markets. Previous research (Mosley, 2003) has shown the powerful effect that market forces can have on governments. The cost at which a country can borrow on international markets has immense impact on its ability to raise revenue. For an emerging market, prohibitively high interest rates on international capital markets effectively cuts them off from that source of financing, so it is important to determine the factors that make emerging markets seem less risky to investors.

1.3 CHAPTER OUTLINE

This book proceeds in the following manner. Chapter 2 lays out the theoretical underpinnings of the central hypothesis: that "the company you keep" on the international stage can make an emerging market look more or less risky, depending on the nature of that company. Organizations that promote economic links among members with strong political quality seem less risky to investors; conversely, membership in organizations with countries of poor political quality will increase perceived risk. Investors make inferences about a country's *willingness* (not its ability) to repay its debt based on the company it keeps. This is a function of both the public nature of economic agreements and a relative commonality of its interpretation. This chapter also examines rival explanations in the form of hypotheses to be tested in subsequent chapters. These hypotheses include the possibility that creditworthy countries "select" into good institutions; that countries undergo changes either in the run-up to entering the organization; or that investors are anticipating the enforcement of rules once countries join an organization.

Chapter 3 extends the argument to a global scale. I test the argument on all emerging markets that issue debt on international markets, and examine the effects of membership in a wide variety of international organizations. I demonstrate evidence for the central hypothesis – that risk decreases when emerging markets integrate closely with good-quality members – for a sample of more than 100 developing countries, both on quarterly data from 1993 to 2008 and on annual data from 1980 to 2008. This finding holds up against the three alternate hypotheses described earlier. Economic and political indicators as well as metrics for policy reform do not cancel out the evidence for "the company a country keeps." The central finding is robust to the possibility of enforcement, as indicated by greater legalization and dispute settlement in the agreement, and of economic changes in member states. The effect of proposed integration with good-quality countries is substantial; its magnitude trumps many of the variables indicating economic fundamentals on the ground.

Chapter 4 focuses on a single organization, to test the argument that the institution itself matters more than what you do to get in. I demonstrate that candidacy for the European Union leads to a decrease in perceived default risk. I find that the drop in risk is strongest when the EU puts its "seal of approval" on candidates' economic policy reform in the negotiation stage. I also test three alternative hypotheses for the mechanism behind the drop in risk. First, I use instrumental variables to measure the cultural factors that drive states to open negotiations with the EU, while controlling for the unobservable factors that affect market perceptions. Additionally, I test whether this effect is the result of preexisting policy reform taken either within or outside the process of EU accession. I also look at enforcement records of the EU, by examining violations of the Stability and Growth pact as well as budget crises in Hungary and bailouts of both EU and non-EU members. I find little evidence for any of the alternate mechanisms: the "seal of approval" has the strongest effect.

Chapter 5 looks at the underbelly of the company a country keeps – when joining groups with risky partners will lead to increases in perceived risk and uncertainty. I focus in particularly on membership patterns in ALBA, which was founded by Cuba and Venezuela to serve as a leftist counterpart to other integration schemes; the organization is strongly identified with Hugo Chávez and his anti-Western rhetoric. Although for some countries, the news of their accession was no surprise – Bolivia's Evo Morales had already identified strongly with socialism when his country joined, for example – for other countries their membership gave new information about increased risk to investors. I show the changes in perception that accompanied their joining. For Russia – the country most in flux at the time of the announcement of the Eurasian Union – risk perceptions increased once it proclaimed closer ties with Belarus and Kazakhstan. I also show how risk levels changed for Tanzania once it pulled out of COMESA, a poorly functioning trade agreement in Africa. Finally, I examine the impact of China's free-trade areas in emerging markets, demonstrating that although risk for those countries has not increased systematically, the variance surrounding investor perceptions has increased.

Chapter 6 looks at the effects of new entrants to organizations on core members. This chapter explicitly focuses on the effects of enlargement to existing institutions, a topic that is understudied in political science. Taking the example of Germany, I show that the drop in risk levels for emerging markets entering good organizations are echoed by slight *increases* in risk for the stable members at that organization's core. I look at investor reaction to defaults in the Mercosur countries; an illustration of Uruguay's debt restructuring following the Argentine crisis demonstrates that investors were overly skittish about Uruguay's prospects based on the company it kept. I also show how opening Mercosur entry to Venezuela – an oil-rich country with a high level of political risk – was associated with increases in risk for core Mercosur members. But, under what conditions does the company a country keep begin to lose its sway? I demonstrate how letting in too many risky members can degrade the brand of a good organization, by looking at changes in risk as countries negotiated with a larger EU after the 2007 enlargement. This demonstrates that risk for core members can actually increase by letting in new members – evidence that challenges the view of research in endogenous cooperation, which holds that heads of state will only form institutions where compliance is likely, and therefore do not take risks (Downs, Rocke, and Barsoom, 1996).

Chapter 7 concludes by expanding on the implications of the central argument, that investors react decisively to membership in international institutions at two extremes: they reward membership in agreements with high-quality members, and they punish those who join agreements with poor-quality members. This is an important finding for the study of international cooperation and comparative development. In addition to its contribution to the academic literature, this book has implications for public policy as well as for future studies of the merits and demerits of international economic ties and international agreements. Currently, international organizations of all variety are in flux. Debate rages in the EU over the consequences of opening negotiations with Turkey, which likely played a part in France's recent rejection of the constitution. While the effects of NAFTA are still a subject of controversy, the United States' attempt to create a comprehensive trade agreement in Central America has stalled, in favor of pursuing bilateral trade agreements with developing countries. At the same time, the Doha round of negotiations in the WTO is at a standstill, and the future of institutionalized multilateral trade is unclear. Crucial to these discussions is whether and how the institution can maintain its clout among international audiences, providing benefits to developed and developing members alike. By disentangling the characteristics of international institutions that matter to financial markets, this project will contribute to discussions of effective institutional design, as well as regional integration and economic cooperation. Furthermore, it sheds light on one of the most common claims of the literature on international institutions – the claim of reduced uncertainty – and provides a theoretical as well as an empirical elaboration of the conditions that contribute to that uncertainty.

2

International Institutions and Sovereign Risk

Turkey has long been an important member of several prestigious international organizations; it was one of the first members of NATO, and has long been included in the Organization for Economic Cooperation and Development (OECD). On the multilateral stage, it joined the UN at its inception in 1945 and the GATT in 1951, and it was a founding member of the Council of Europe in 1949. Yet why did investors demand an extra premium to hold Turkish debt after its 1985 formation of the Economic Cooperation Organization with Iran and Pakistan?[1] And why is the holdup of its negotiations with the European Union such a cause for concern among portfolio investors – particularly given the country already has a customs union with the EU in place since 1995 and already undertook significant economic liberalization (under the stewardship of the IMF) in 2001?

This chapter lays out a theory of how membership in international trade agreements ought to matter to markets. What causes investors to take countries more seriously if they are members of good clubs, or less seriously if they are members of bad clubs? Formally, why might a separating equilibrium prevail, in which different types of organizations engender different reactions, instead of a pooling equilibrium, where membership in different types of organizations invokes the same response from investors? In high-uncertainty environments, traders look to clear signals of a country's likelihood of default.

Macroeconomic and other indicators can tell much about a country's *ability* to pay back its debt. The company one keeps, however, communicates information about a county's potential *willingness* to honor its debt obligations. Even rich countries can decide to forego their debt obligations for political or ideological reasons, and investors evaluate this likelihood – and anticipate other investors' reactions – by taking cues from the company a country keeps

[1] Interview, Istanbul Stock Exchange, 14 July 2008.

on the international stage. When a country announces intended close ties with other countries, it absorbs to some extent the reputations of those states.

Many scholars have theorized that membership in institutions can reduce uncertainty about the credibility of commitments, and thus help actors' expectations converge around some cooperative outcome (Martin, 1997; Dai, 2005; Thompson, 2006; Fang, 2009; Johns, 2008).[2] Here, however, the organizations do not serve as a credible commitment, but rather as a shorthand for a country's intentions. Membership in international trade agreements is one of the more frequently observed international acts in which countries engage. Well-publicized international affiliations – the closure of negotiating chapters in the EU accession process, the proposed creation of a left-leaning agreement to counteract Western neoliberal ideology – serve as widely visible pieces of knowledge that can enable investors to process information about those states. Thus, once countries proclaim close ties with countries of particularly good or ill repute, investors – rightly or wrongly – use membership in those organizations as heuristics not because of their design features or their rules, but because they are public signals of the types of countries a new member wishes to emulate. This coordination of investor perceptions results in changed levels of risk for emerging markets.

Put in another context, international ties help investors resolve a certain kind of uncertainty about the trajectory of an emerging market. The rational design literature (Koremenos, Lipson, and Snidal, 2001) delineates uncertainty pertaining to three different factors: about behavior, the state of the world, and others' preferences. Within this framework, IOs help resolve uncertainty not about behavior (because many economic organizations – even the most rigid, such as the EU – have a hard time enforcing their own rules, and countries can make promises for integration that they do not end up fulfilling) or about the state of the world (this is separate from the domain of an organization). Rather, IOs decrease uncertainty about preferences. Even if states do not end up adhering to the commitments they make, for better or for worse, their membership in IOs is still an expression of their intentions in terms of the company they keep and the types of countries with which they would like to be associated. This signal's importance is not in its costliness or in the level of commitment implied – in fact, many agreements do not actually achieve their stated goals, and members frequently backslide on their pledges – but in its public nature (Lupia, 1994).

Investment data – increasingly in use in political science (Mosley, 2000; Stasavage, 2004; Tomz, 2008) – are particularly useful in testing these claims, because finance is based on measuring and trading uncertainty. Investors have

---

[2] Other work in political science points to this phenomenon. For example, Lupia and McCubbins (1998) describe how external forces can clarify beliefs about the knowledge and trustworthiness of actors. Franck (1990) describes how actors can receive "symbolic validation" in international institutions. Thompson (2006) and Chapman (2009) have already studied how IOs can help publics take "informational shortcuts."

differing and private information on governments' intentions and future performance. However, they can use the observation of membership in international agreements to make inferences about not only a nation's future behavior, but also other investors' perceptions of that nation's future behavior. Thus,
sovereign paper is itself a measure of collective uncertainty about the ability and
willingness of a country's government to uphold its obligations in servicing its
debt. Sovereign spreads (the difference between the interest rate of a given country and a comparable, less risky security) are therefore a good vehicle through
which to examine the arguments about expectations of future behavior found in
the literature on international institutions, which claims that institutions should
regularize behavior and encourage cooperation. Investor risk stems from uncertainty, and for countries with erratic histories on international debt markets,
membership in some agreements create a more predictable environment that
observers interpret consistently, for better or worse. In an environment of nonstrategic information aggregation, international institutions can provide public
information that unifies investors' expectations.

Before laying out the details of the central theory and hypothesis, the next
section goes into greater detail on how these debt instruments work and the role
of perceptions in risk, and how important concepts from the finance literature
on the determinants of risk can be linked to the study of international organizations. The risk of default stems from investor assessments of a country's ability
as well as its willingness to service its debt. I then draw up expectations, based
on literature in political science, business, and finance, for how sovereign debt
in middle-income countries would behave in the face of international integration, arguing that in high-uncertainty environments, international institutions
can change investor perceptions of countries' *willingness* to honor their debt
obligations. I set up conditions for the type of organization that ought to matter
to investors. Specifically, I argue that two conditions – proposed closeness of
ties and political risk of members – are critical for investor perceptions of international organization among emerging markets. I discuss alternate hypotheses,
drawing from literature in economics as well as political science. I then restate
the components of the theory to set up expectations for empirical testing.

2.1 WHAT MARKETS TELL US ABOUT INSTITUTIONS, AND WHAT INSTITUTIONS TELL MARKETS

Why is sovereign debt a suitable metric for examining perceptions related to
international affiliations? Investors trade government securities through numerous instruments covering a variety of time periods; the most common are fixed-
interest rate instruments such as treasury bills with maturities that span from
six months to ten years, though longer-term securities exist as well (Broker,
1993). Debt instruments' levels change according to the risk of the currency in
which the bond is issued, and the risk associated with lending to the country
itself. Higher yields on sovereign bonds indicate a higher perceived likelihood

that a government will default on its debt. Spreads on sovereign debt are essentially a function of a country's perceived default risk (as described earlier, its ability and willingness to service its debt) as well as the liquidity of the trading instrument.[3] Though sovereign spreads do not perfectly capture levels of risk on the ground in countries – in fact, investors frequently over- or undervalue certain assets, as the 2007 financial crisis has demonstrated – they do reflect the perceptions of investors, which has an important feedback mechanism to countries' access to financing. Market sentiment can be volatile, and the collective consensus of the risks associated with lending can change in minutes (recall, for example, the swift falls from grace that dot-com stocks suffered in the late 1990s, or the speed with which the 1997 East Asian financial crisis took place). Once overall risk perceptions shift, individual investors have a huge incentive to "follow the herd," even if their own particular assessments of a country's worth may differ from that of the herd.

As developing countries mature, more and more of them have issued public debt as a means of financing, making these data ever more available for analysis. Developing countries have historically alternated between drawing on bank lending or bonds for financing. Emerging markets have issued bonds since the early 1800s, but those did not play an important part in international bond trade until relatively recently, picking up in 1989 with the Brady plan to restructure bad Latin American bank debt.[4] Since the 1990s, markets for government debt have stabilized, becoming more commercially oriented and more sophisticated. A 2000 World Bank report noted that stock markets in emerging markets were generally underdeveloped, with low market capitalization and turnover (Claessens, Djankov, and Klingebiel, 2000). But those numbers have increased, and the past decade in particular has seen huge amounts of emerging-market activity.

Emerging-market sovereign debt structurally differs from that in more developed countries. Even though maturities are shorter on average, long-term debt is almost always issued in foreign currency. This structure is what some economists have called "original sin" (Eichengreen and Hausmann, 1999; Eichengreen and Panizza, 2003). Both the need to service that debt in hard currency (which can be in short supply) and the relatively longer periods of time that the interest must be serviced make emerging-market debt fundamentally risk-prone. In fact, high levels of dollar-denominated debt have left many emerging economies badly exposed to the global credit crunch.[5]

---

[3] Bond traders pay a lower price for assets that are illiquid, meaning that they cannot be resold on secondary markets, making it more difficult to hedge risk; see Amihud and Mendelson (1986); Glosten and Milgrom (1984); Lo, Mamayski, and Wang (2004).

[4] "Private Debt Finance for Developing Countries," Global Development Finance 2004 report, p. 49.

[5] Nonetheless, even in the presence of a relatively high risk of default, it can still be possible for investors to reap significant gains, thanks to high yields that those bonds offer compared with securities in developed countries. In the roughly seventy-five years before World War I,

It is perhaps understandable that in developing countries, investors are sensitive to overall market sentiment about those economies and thus more prone to herd behavior. Information in emerging markets – including the political situation or state of public finance – is often of low quality and reliability, which leads investors to demand a risk premium (Fabozzi, 2001; Akemann and Kanczuk, 2005; Levine and Zervos, 1998; MacGregor et al., 2000). Wright (2005) emphasizes the limited efficiency in emerging markets attributable to the impossibility of guaranteeing that a sovereign debt contract will be upheld. In the absence of third-party enforcement, the specter of default looms large in emerging markets – and history bears this fear out. For example, since 1800 (or since the year of their independence), Latin American countries spent an average of around 35 percent of their time in default, with an average of nine defaults per country. Venezuela, with ten defaults since independence, holds the record not just in Latin America but for emerging markets overall. This contrasts with an average of 3.5 defaults in the same time period for Western Europe (Reinhart and Rogoff, 2009). So the threat of default is a real concern for investors in emerging-market securities.

2.1.1 Ability and Willingness to Repay Debt

At their most basic level, yields on sovereign debt are a collective estimate of the likelihood that a government will either fail to make interest payments or default altogether on its debt obligations. This estimate has two main components. The first is a government's *ability* to make its debt payments – that is, whether it has the financial means to service its debt. A country's ability to pay back its debt can be tracked by many easily available indicators. Because this is simply a question of a country's solvency, investors can monitor a country's fiscal pressures in contrast to its revenues. For example, if a government has enough hard currency coming into its coffers, relatively low public debt, and a favorable exchange rate, those factors all point to its having enough cash to make its interest rate payments on schedule and ultimately to repay the principal. Most of those indicators are directly observable and widely available, and there is very little ambiguity in the role those factors play in calculating risk. Increases in global commodity prices, for example, will mean big economic gains for exporters of oil, copper, or steel, and thus an increased confidence in those countries' ability to make their debt payments.

However, a country's relative wealth is only part of the story. A government can have ample resources, but it can still decide to forego making its debt payments for ideological or political reasons. Thus, a government's *willingness*

even though Argentina, Brazil, and Chile defaulted or partially defaulted at least once, investors holding those countries' sovereign debt instruments would have still made money, even taking those defaults into account. In the same period, investors in Egyptian debt reaped the benefits of high yields and debt obligations made good after the 1882 British invasion (Sturzenegger and Zettelmeyer, 2005).

to pay back its debt is the second major component of sovereign risk. Even when they have the ability to do so, throughout history many emerging-market countries have shown themselves to be unwilling to service their foreign debt. This unwillingness to repay debts, which is sometimes referred to as political risk, represents a significant chunk of emerging-market spreads. Empirical research in finance acknowledges that political risk plays a far greater role in yields in emerging markets compared with those in developing countries. Some estimates put political risk as the main driver of the cost of borrowing in emerging markets (Baily and Chung, 1995; Diamonte, Liew, and Stevens, 1996; Perotti and van Oijen, 2001) – in fact, the International Crisis and Risk Group considers political risk to be twice as important as economic and financial risk in emerging markets. Recent studies in economics have shown that debt history, domestic institutions, and political factors are the primary factors in a country's willingness to honor its payment schedule for its debt (Kray and Nehru, 2004). This illustrates how critical it is for investors to have some way of estimating a government's intentions to pay back its debt. Easily available indicators of a government's ability to make its debt payments – that is, the revenues that a country is bringing in, compared with its expenditures – can only tell markets so much. Investors are constantly on the lookout for signals of a government's *willingness* to repay its debt.

History abounds with examples of countries that were perfectly capable of servicing their debt but failed to do so. After the 1917 revolution, Russia abrogated on nearly $30 billion in sovereign debt to Western countries, rather than be beholden to the bourgeois nations. More recently, in 2007, Ecuador defaulted on nearly $11 billion worth of foreign arrears, despite maintaining consistently high growth rates thanks to the commodity boom in the 2000s. A Goldman Sachs economist noted at the time, "They seem to have a dogmatic and ideological view on debt, and they will act on it irrespective of the significant capacity to pay."[6] "With Ecuador, it is almost always an issue of willingness to pay, not ability," another analyst noted.[7] Similarly, after a 2007 referendum in Venezuela that would extend the presidential term limits, investors and rating agencies alike became jittery, specifically citing doubts over the government's willingness – not ability – to service its debt obligations. "Given current and expected high oil prices and sizable, if opaque, government financial assets, Venezuela's current rating is constrained by policy and political concerns and not by doubts about the country's capacity to pay its debt," a Moody's analyst was quoted as saying following the referendum.[8]

The idea of a government's unwillingness to meet its foreign debt obligations is illustrated by the comments of one Peruvian investor, who was speaking

---

[6] "Ecuador Credit Rating Cut by Standard & Poor's to CCC," *Bloomberg*, 19 January 2007.
[7] "Ecuador Defaults on Its Foreign Debt," *Wall Street Journal*, 12 December 2008.
[8] "Moody's: Effects of Venezuelan Vote Will Play Out Over Long Term," *InfoProd*, 5 December 2007.

about the risk associated with lending to Hugo Chávez's Venezuela (the particulars of which are examined in detail in Chapter 5). Following a string of events that spooked investors – including the nationalization of the central bank, the governmental capture of the country's main independent television station, and the government takeover of one of the main resort hotels – Venezuela's cost of borrowing on international markets increased, even though the country was still reaping considerable profits from the high price of oil. This particular investor explained the increased sovereign risk as follows:

> The guy had plenty of money, but this was basically his way of showing the world what his intentions were. I don't care how much money he has; I'd never buy any Venezuelan paper. That guy is crazy. It has nothing to do with whether he *can* pay, it's whether he wants to. [Peruvian President] Alan García did the same thing in the 1980s; he had plenty of money to service his debt, he just decided that he didn't want to.[9]

To compensate for uncertainty in a country's ability as well as its willingness to honor its credit obligations, debt issued by governments of emerging economies tends to command much higher interest rates than treasury bills issued by the United States, Eurobonds, or investment-grade corporate debt. Compared with interest rates on those securities, which tend to run well below 3 percent, government debt in emerging markets can have interest rates in the double digits; in times of economic crisis, such as the Argentine default of 2001, interest rates even have soared up into the hundreds of percents. Such extremes result from the combination of a demonstrated lack of ability *and* willingness to pay back debt.

2.1.2 Other Ways of Measuring Risk

Investors also express their confidence in a country in other measurable ways – such as through foreign direct investment (FDI), credit ratings, and currency risk – but these are less well suited for testing the propositions laid out in this book. FDI already receives considerable attention in political science.[10] FDI refers to the acquisition of a lasting interest in enterprises operating outside of an investor's home country, either as a purchase of a majority share of a company or as a "greenfield" project in which a factory or plant is built from scratch. The amount of foreign direct investment a country receives reflects in part the political risk associated with a country. Indeed, Büthe and Milner (2008) have examined how membership in PTAs as well as in the WTO increases FDI flows, arguing that those agreements provide mechanisms for reassuring foreign investors that they treat their assets well.

---

[9] Interview, Alberto Araspe, Kallpa Securities-Lima, 7 July 2009.
[10] See, for example, Jensen (2005); Chakrabarti (1999) for an exhaustive review of the empirical literature; Oneal (1994) and Harms and Ursprung (2002) on whether direct investors prefer repressive regimes.

There are reasons to expect that the risk associated with FDI is distinct from and to some extent incomparable with risk in portfolio investment. Unlike portfolio investors, direct investors have an effective voice in the management of the enterprise. Their investment is also of the "bricks and mortar" type – factories or plants physically located in the country. Direct investors would have more tangible concerns: whether property rights are respected (Li and Resnick, 2003) so that they could be assured that their investment would not be expropriated, as well as the status of labor markets in that country. They are making a medium- to long-term investment in a country and sink considerable costs into that investment.

These are not comparable to the concerns of portfolio investors. Indeed, one study has shown that in developing countries, portfolio investors respond to past government behavior and fiscal policy outcomes, where FDI does not (Ahlquist, 2006). Like portfolio investment, FDI acts as a bet on the future worth of a particular asset, and in order for an asset to realize its potential, an investor should be able to put money into it without fear of abrogation.[11] But unlike those who deal in FDI, bond traders need not ever lay eyes on the capitals from which their securities are issued. They are buying assets whose returns reflect primarily the perceived likelihood that an issuing government will be unable to make scheduled interest payments on time or default on its debt altogether, as well as the supply of and demand for that asset. Portfolio investors rarely interact with the citizens or governments of a country whose bonds they hold and can offload that paper on secondary markets in an instant, if the market is sufficiently liquid.

The differing nature of those investments, and particularly in the type of investor behind them, means that the two are not interchangeable in terms of examining the theory put forward in this book. FDI is much less driven by perceptions and overall market sentiment than is portfolio investment. While membership in international institutions may play into one set of concerns for foreign direct investors, their utility functions would be less responsive to the heuristic element of the company states keep.

Another indicator of investor risk are credit ratings compiled by private agencies, such as Standard and Poor's and Moody's. However, these measures also fall short of the many theoretical and practical advantages of portfolio investment per se. Credit ratings tend not to reflect closely actual investor activity in emerging economies. In OECD countries, credit ratings and bond yields are very highly correlated; less so in developing countries, where market activity tends to break from the recommendations of creditors (Cantor and Packer, 1996; Kaminsky and Schmukler, 2002). In emerging markets in particular, most traders of sovereign debt agree that Moody's and S&P are

---

[11] This taps the literature on the importance of property rights in economic development generally (de Soto, 2001).

typically several steps behind the market.[12] Indeed, the current financial crisis has brought to light the fact that even in developed countries, ratings did not reflect the actual level of risk of various assets.

Another, more practical problem with credit ratings is that, while they are relatively easy to compare across countries, their degree of within-country variance over time is slight. Rating agencies – which gave the East Asian economies as well as the many mortgage-backed securities clean bills of health in the run-up to the crises in both those markets – are now especially conservative in emerging markets. They tend to give those economies relatively low credit ratings and adjust those scores only occasionally. Croatia's rating from Standard and Poor and Moody's, for example, has only been changed once since the country first started receiving the ratings. For practical reasons, they are not well suited for this analysis.

Currency risk is a third potential measure of investor risk. A country's currency can be relatively stronger or weaker itself, but risk associated with that currency measures the probability that the purchasing power of a given currency will deviate in the future from the value that was originally anticipated. Even though there are common factors in currency and sovereign debt markets, researchers usually treat those two variables as separate: movements in the first anticipate inflation, where the second primarily takes into account political risk (Baily and Chung, 1995). Although traders can invest in currencies themselves as an asset, currency risk is a particular concern for multinational corporations, where unanticipated changes in exchange rates would upset contracts or trade flows that were denominated in a foreign currency. Some researchers have calculated currency risk by comparing yields on local currency bonds and dollar-denoted bonds, and used those as indicators of the credibility of a country (Mitchener and Weidenmier, 2008). Currency risk particularly takes into account a given currency's deviation from purchasing power parity within that country, or the cost of a basket of goods and services that is comparable across states (Adler and Dumas, 1984). But there are many factors, both domestic (Frieden, 1991) and international, that could predict the levels of a country's currency, and a strong currency is not necessarily a sign of a country with no political risk; in 2012, both Venezuela's and Brazil's currencies were considered to be overvalued, but so were currencies of countries with far less political risk, including Norway, Switzerland, and Australia.[13] Thus, sovereign debt is a more direct way of measuring political risk in a country.

2.2 THEORIES OF INTERNATIONAL INSTITUTIONS

How do international economic organizations help resolve the types of uncertainty that are commonplace in financial markets, and what room exists in

---

[12] Author interview, Tom Lockhard, Stone & Youngberg LLC, 25 April 2006.
[13] "Big Mac Index," *The Economist*, 26 July 2012.

the cooperation literature for thinking about how international organizations might influence perceptions? Some researchers have demonstrated that the member content of an organization has effects that are internal to the countries within the organization (Pevehouse, 2002). For the most part, this literature does not make explicit predictions about how membership might affect perceptions of investor risk.[14] But I argue that the membership can also have an impact on third-party perceptions of members – a claim that has deep roots in IO scholarship but is as of yet underexplored.

The claims of how institutions might matter are so vast that empiricists often address them one at a time. Researchers in economics have fruitfully examined how institutions originate informally in emerging markets.[15] A subset of the literature on international institutions looks specifically at risk. If formal institutions do not exist, rational actors will turn to informal institutions, or governance structures, to help them manage and hedge against risk (Williamson, 1985; Putterman, 1986). Scholars in economic development, international relations, and international political economy alike have long championed the importance of institutions in ensuring all sorts of positive outcomes, from successful policy reform to economic growth to international cooperation. International institutions are also thought to have broad domestic ramifications for those countries that sign onto them. Constraining international institutions help executives push through policies that would otherwise be domestically unpopular (Putnam, 1988), internalize norms of mutual respect and tolerance (Moravcsik, 1997; Finnemore, 1996a, 1996b; Barnett and Finnemore, 2004), and use issue linkage to ensure outcomes that are otherwise unattainable on their own (Hafner-Burton, 2005; Boas, 2000; Gosovic and Ruggie, 1976; Keohane, Macedo, and Moravcsik, 2009).

One early and influential argument describes institutions as sets of formal and informal constraints that reduce transaction costs and enforce norms (North, 1990). The cooperation that ensues after repeated interactions are, for North, the stuff of international institutions, encompassing member concerns about reputation, codes of conduct, and the legacy of history, language, mental models, and ideologies. Those constraints make individual decision making more reflexive, creating regularized behavior and stability over time. Thus, institutions can be a form of credible commitment to a pattern of future behavior – in other words, uncertainty surrounding the behavior of members of IOs should decrease.

Indeed, the claim that international institutions reduce uncertainty has permeated much of the literature on international institutions (Axelrod, 1981;

---

[14] But see Dreher and Voigt (2008), who argue that risk premia decrease when countries join international organizations with a high degree of delegation; similarly, Dreher, Gaston and Martens (2008) use a count of the number of organizations to which a country is a member as a measure of integration that they say should increase credibility.

[15] See Grief (1993) for a formal analysis of contract enforcement in a coalition that enabled overseas agents to be employed by eleventh-century Maghribi traders.

Keohane, 1984; Morrow, 1994; Koremenos, Lipson, and Snidal, 2001). Institutions, it has been argued, can stabilize expectations of members' future behavior and therefore promote more stable patterns of behavior among members. This argument has been the bedrock of liberal institutionalism. Game-theoretic work has shown how institutions can ensure the repeated interaction necessary for future cooperation (Axelrod, 1981, 1984). In a repeated game with perfect monitoring, by having their future employment conditional on past conduct, agents have an incentive to be honest even without a legal system (Grief, 1993).

But these propositions have not been thoroughly tested, in part because there are few widespread empirical measures of uncertainty in political science. Even separate from the question of whether behavior actually converges, would *expectations* of countries' behavior converge once they join international institutions? Testing this latter claim involves not an examination of countries' actual behavior as a function of membership in institutions, but of third-party assessment of those countries' prospects once they join an institution – and no work thus far has systematically done so. Additionally, perceptions do not necessarily map the actual realities of a particular actor. Rodrik (2003) points to sentiments on protection of investor rights in China and Russia in the late 1990s. Even though China did not even have a formal system of property rights at that time, investors still claimed to feel more secure there than in Russia, which at least nominally had adopted all the institutions associated with democracy. Thus, the perceptions themselves – if they can be credibly linked to subsequent investment – might have more bearing on the country's fortunes than the institutions actually in place.

Thus, no work has yet examined in detail the perceptions of third parties as they relate to international institutions, yet this is a major observable implication of many of the literature's most cited arguments. Other researchers have established the effect of regional IO membership on various outcomes within member states, including the consolidation of democracy (Pevehouse, 2002), government repression (Hafner-Burton, 2005), and electoral misconduct (Donno, 2010). But the literature has not yet systematically considered the effect of regional IOs on uncertainty. Investor perceptions are a good place to start in terms of evaluating these claims, and the next section discusses how those perceptions can be fit into the literature on international organizations.

2.3 COLLECTIVE ASSESSMENTS OF RISK

The behavior of other investors is a key component of asset prices generally, but particularly in emerging markets. Bond traders depend on the perceptions of other actors in the market for two reasons. First, they need a liquid secondary market, so that if they do not want to hold onto an asset up to its listed date of maturity, they can easily find a buyer who will take over that country's paper. This is common in emerging-market finance: around 60 percent of the total volume of trade in junk bonds takes place on secondary markets. Traders remain aware of how the market at large values a particular asset, so that they can estimate the interest of potential secondary buyers for a bond at any given moment.

Second, and more importantly, there is the possibility of speculative attack or capital flight, which can kick in as a result of what is often described as herd behavior (Scharfstein and Stein, 1990; Banerjee, 1992; Avery and Zamsky, 1998). The value of a particular issue remains steady as long as other investors are consistent in their estimation of a country's risk. But particularly in emerging markets, where trading is relatively shallow, it only takes a relatively small number of bond traders losing confidence in a country to cause the whole market to collapse. Speculative attacks can quickly degrade a country's currency and assets. Then the probability that a country is able to service its foreign-currency debt plummets, driving up the risk premium on that country's sovereign debt and making it even harder for a country to honor its interest rate payment schedule.

Once herd behavior goes into effect, it acquires a force of its own that proceeds irrespective of what may actually be happening on the ground. Bikchandi and Welch (1992) call these processes "informational cascades," noting that after a certain point in the trend, adoptees stop accumulating new information and simply mimic others' behavior blindly. These processes occur in financial markets frequently, at the apexes of both the boom and the bust cycles (Wang, 1993). The same mentality that drove the dot-com rage of the late 1990s and the surge in housing prices in this century also prompted the currency selloffs that triggered the East Asian financial crisis in 1997. Indeed, such booms and busts have persisted throughout the centuries, and historical evidence shows that the pattern is remarkably similar across time and place (Reinhart and Rogoff, 2009).

Faced with the possibility of severe fluctuation in market sentiment, bond traders must not only come up with their own evaluations of an asset's worth. Crucially, they must also be mindful of other investors' perceptions of that asset. Keynes famously described this phenomenon as a beauty contest in which "it is not a case of choosing those which, to the best of one's judgment, are really the prettiest, nor even those which average opinion genuinely thinks the prettiest. We have reached the third degree where we devote our intelligences to anticipating what average opinion expects the average opinion to be. And there are some, I believe, who practise the fourth, fifth, and higher degrees" (Keynes, 1936, p. 157).

Thus, any portfolio investor must at any given time know not only what he thinks of a particular asset. He also must have a sense of what other traders think of that asset. This requires processing a vast amount of information. Indeed, Ganzach (2001) found that for stocks of unfamiliar companies, even professional analysts based their assessments of risk and potential return on global attitudes toward those companies. Similarly, in a 2007 survey of market actors (Schindler, 2007), many investors claimed that they assessed the credibility of market rumors primarily on the basis of the source of that rumor. Interestingly, in the same survey, 30 percent of traders surveyed claimed the truth of the rumor was irrelevant. "If I want to be longer-term invested in that security, I better want to know very much what the chances are of the rumor being true. However, if I am a short-term investor just interested in a quick profit, I don't care at all what happens in the end," one investor was quoted as saying. Another states, "Ninety percent of what we do is based on perception. It doesn't matter if that perception is right or wrong or real. It only matters that other people in the market believe it. I may know it's crazy. I may think it's wrong. But I lose my shirt by ignoring it" (Schindler, 2007).

So how do market actors figure this out? As noted, especially in emerging markets, domestic data are often unreliable, and government intention is often difficult to interpret based solely on reports in international news. Data on economic fundamentals for those countries may be easy enough to obtain, even if the quality may be suspect, but interpreting political events is trickier. According to Cheong Chan, Chui and Kwok (2001), political news is difficult for markets to make sense of for several reasons. Not only are most analysts trained in economics and finance rather than politics, but politicians tend to mask the informational content of the news. How, then, do investors form their own judgments of a developing country, as well as anticipate how markets will assess that country?

2.3.1 IOs and Perceptions of Ability to Service Debt

One way investors form judgments is to place value on membership in international institutions. Given the high degree of uncertainty in emerging markets, international institutions can help markets make sense of developing nations. In terms of policy reform, a country can give out all the signals it wants – appointing new economic ministers, privatizing previously state-owned industries,[16] adopting flat taxes – but if the relevant actors do not read its signals the way a country wants them read, there is no effect.[17] Therefore, in order for membership in an institution to give a viable signal, that institution must contain some elements that are not just signals but constitute a shared perspective by all. That is, there must be either some reality that implies stability and that is shared by many, or there must be some reason for the commonality of interpretation of the significance of joining an institution.

Easily interpretable signals may have little to do with economics. Rather, they may center on things that a country does on the world stage. For example, Sussman and Yafeh (2000) note that the only two events that improved Japan's

---

[16] See Perotti and van Oijen (2001), who show that when a government announces and sticks to a privatization program, it can resolve uncertainty over political commitment to a market-oriented policy, and thus political risk decreases.

[17] This phenomenon is widely discussed in the game theoretic literature on cheap talk; see Spence (1973).

country risk prior to World War II were adopting the gold standard in October 1897 and Japan's victory against Russia in 1905. Those two occurrences – observable to all and unambiguously positive – did more to make Japan seem a credible borrower than any number of domestic economic reforms. Although domestic institutional reforms played an important role in economic growth, they only affected borrowing costs when incorporated into well-understood "'summary indicators'... [used] to evaluate the creditworthiness of faraway Japan"(Sussman and Yafeh, 2000). Because of Japan's remoteness and the lack of consistent information, nineteenth-century investors relied on widely visible, international heuristics to assess Japan's risk.

Similarly, Ferguson and Schularick (2006) show that being a British colony – the "empire effect" – allowed less developed nations to borrow at a discount of 175 basis points (hundredths of a percentage point). They point out that this was more an effect of reputation than of any observed policy changes that those countries enacted. They speculate that the mechanism behind the "empire effect" that allowed British colonies to borrow at tighter spreads than other countries was that "British rule may have reduced the endemic contract enforcement problems associated with cross-border lending." But there is no evidence that the Brits actually enforced contracts – instead, markets shared a *perception* that London would intervene in the event of a crisis.[18]

Political scientists have focused on domestic political or institutional factors in explaining sovereign risk. These usually center on institutions that might offer credible commitments to sound policy, such as fiscal institutions (Hallerberg and Wolff, 2008) or democracy (North and Weingast, 1989; Stasavage, 2002; Schultz and Weingast, 2003). The "democratic advantage" in attracting finance has been noted in both foreign direct investment (Li and Resnick, 2003) as well as portfolio investment and bond ratings (Saiegh, 2005; Biglaiser and Staats, 2012; Beaulieu, Cox, and Saiegh, 2012). But I argue that this explanation is incomplete. Democracy and domestic institutions do capture elements of uncertainty, but when a state joins up with another country about whom investors have strong priors, that country's assumed risk dominates. This dovetails with claims about an economic institution's ability to impart credibility on the countries that sign onto it (Maxfield, 1998; Stone, 2002; Hallenberg and Wolf, 2008).

The importance of prior beliefs in a world of incomplete information has been well documented with respect to developing countries. For many economic policies – including central-bank independence and pegged exchange rates – publicizing a commitment to fiscal discipline is an important psychological component of that policy's effectiveness (Posen, 1995; Lohmann, 1992). Again,

---

[18] But see Soydemir (2000), who shows that where economic linkages exist between countries, stock market responses are consistent with differences in trade flows, indicating that markets respond rationally to underlying economic fundamentals rather than irrationally assuming contagion.

this situation is particularly extreme in emerging markets; Rodrik (1989) has pointed out that in developing countries, where information is often poor and uncertainty is high, governments may have to rely on signals that communicate their intentions for policy reform. Currency boards, which legally require that countries cannot print local fiat without backing in hard-currency reserves, are designed to offer the same kind of assurance to investors (Hanke, 1994).

Similarly, even when the affiliations appear to be economic, there is evidence that investor sentiment tracks the affiliations rather than the outcomes. That is, investors can be more interested in the de jure commitments that emerging markets make, rather than how those commitments actually play out on the ground. Bordo and Rockoff (1996) argue that at the turn of the nineteenth century, signing onto the gold standard operated as a "seal of approval" for peripheral countries, and that "markets attached nearly as much weight to close shadowing of the gold standard as actual adherence" – implying, then, that the record of policy change mattered less to investors than nominal membership. They estimate that membership in the gold standard tightened spreads by forty basis points. Thus, it is clear that investors take shortcuts in evaluating the risk associated with particular assets.

2.3.2 Affiliations and Reputation

New borrowers' affiliations can substantially change the risk levels associated with their assets. The finance and business literature has shown that the reputations of the actors affiliated with a given asset are paramount in situations where investors do not have enough reliable information to form their own judgments – particularly in the early days of a security or company, or in volatile environments. Researchers have shown empirically how the reputation of the underwriter – that is, the financial institution that administers the public issuance and distribution of a given security – can influence the outcome of initial public offerings (IPOs); equivalent securities with more reliable underwriters do far better in their IPOs (Beatty and Ritter, 1986; Carter and Manaster, 1990; Carter, Dark, and Singh, 1998; Higgins and Gulati, 2003). Other research demonstrates that new business ventures can gain credibility by appointing a new director to the board, depending on the reputation of the director and the quality of information (Deutsch and Ross, 2003). When information is poor, the credibility and history of the director carries significant weight. Further research in business has demonstrated that for new ventures, interorganizational endorsements can have a huge effect on their ultimate success (Stuart, Hoang, and Hybels, 1999). In pharmaceutical research, the reputation of a firm can positively impact the success of research endeavors (Henderson and Cockburn, 1994). Another study shows that the choices of influential third parties to serve on boards of organizations can boost the prominence of the organization in the minds of stakeholders, which subsequently plays a role in the price premium (Rindova et al., 2005). The impact of third parties has also been applied to the study of politics; Bernhard and Sulkin (2009) examine the effects of cosponsorship of bills on the floors of the U.S. Congress.

In all of these papers, it is understood that the endorsements of third parties act in large part as a heuristic that allows investors to process information quickly and perhaps efficiently. Although those endorsements do carry some substance behind them, the scale and speed of market reaction to their presence signifies that investors are using them as shorthand for arriving at a price for an asset in the absence of other information. New directors, for example, can certainly have medium- and long-run effects on the operations of a particular venture, but this does not explain the initial boost in reputation that those firms receive. Thus, the affiliations of a venture can have a strong impact on the rate at which that venture has access to credit, particularly in the short term and in the absence of other reliable information on that venture.

The assessments of reputation described above go beyond simply responding to news about the future, which happens frequently in financial markets.[19] What is important is that the affiliations that investors observe help them organize their beliefs about an asset where there may not be much other information, or where the given information may be unreliable. These third-party affiliations take a known quantity and apply it to an asset whose future trajectory is relatively uncertain, and thus allow investor perceptions to converge. In sociology the concept of social identity theory (Tajfel and Turner, 1979) builds in part off the concept of "basking in reflected glory" by Cialdini et al. (1976). These theories show that individuals often deliberately choose to take on at least the appearance of the characteristics of others in a group, whether or not they themselves possess those attributes.[20]

There is evidence that investors treat countries in the same manner as the types of assets described earlier, and that they lump countries into categories. In bond markets, joint perceptions are amassed by lumping countries into what are described as "peer groups." There are broader peer groups, such as those that include emerging markets more generally (Mosley and Brooks, 2012). Indeed, when valuing a company's stock, financial market actors usually compare "peer firms" from the same industry (Aspara, 2009; Zuckerman, 2004). Regions constitute one simple peer group that is relatively easy to define, and indeed many investment indices are grouped on a regional basis (JP Morgan's Latin America index, for example). However, regions are limited in their utility as a heuristic, namely because they do not change over time. Once a country is in a region, it is there to stay, and many changes can occur in a country that cannot be predicted simply by knowing the region it is in.

[19] See Jaimovich and Rebelo (2005) on how news about future total factor productivity spurs recessions, Bussie and Mulder (2000) on how elections impact investment flows, and Beaudry and Portier (2006) on stock market sensitivity to news.

[20] This is a huge area of research in sociology; for just a few examples, see Tajfel (1978); Turner et al. (1987); Reicher, Spears, and Postmes (1995); Oakes (1987).

Many peer groups, however, are defined not by geography but by macro-economic conditions and overall performance. This creates a shorthand for the types of countries most likely to behave in similar ways, with similar levels of uncertainty. Gelos, Sahay, and Sandleris (2004) find that market perceptions of creditworthiness, as well as vulnerability to shocks, are crucial in determining whether countries even pass the threshold where international markets will buy their bonds at all. Taking this logic to a disturbing extreme, Tomz (2008) and Sinclair (2003) cite the hoax in the early 1800s of Poyas, a country fabricated by a Scottish explorer, which managed to borrow at around the same rates as other legitimate Central American countries. Even though the country did not exist, investors ascribed to it essentially the same risk as other nations in their neighborhood. This means that markets are responsive to using information that they know about some countries to guide their assessments of other nations. Policy makers are aware of this process as well: "Investors don't have enough resources to monitor everything; there are not enough analysts who are up to date on everything, so they just take shortcuts and put countries into baskets," says one.[21] "We all want to be rational as people, but unfortunately we're emotional beings as well. Particularly for less informed market participants – they don't have time to follow these things closely. They just rely on the research of third parties. There's no onset of due diligence," says another.[22]

How can these insights be applied to emerging markets specifically? Both IPOs and the new ventures in those studies have no history on markets whatsoever, but in a way this is not so different from the structure of emerging market debt. Even if emerging markets have a long history of issuing their debt, leaders are constantly changing, and often those changes are accompanied by radical policy reversals.[23] In fact, countries' type can change in different contexts, either through elections bringing a new leader or through the exogenous shocks that countries face.[24] These nations are especially vulnerable not only to shocks such as drought or natural disasters, which may affect their ability to uphold regular debt servicing. They are also prone to changes in government that bring substantial ideological shifts. Or the leaders themselves might undergo significant changes in their policy making. Brazil's Enrique Cardoso was initially a leading proponent of anti-market "dependency theory," but later in life turned to embrace free trade, and in fact was a founding member of Mercosur, a prominent South American free-trade agreement. Some years later in that same country, markets panicked over the election of the socialist-leaning Ignacio Lula di Silva, who then turned out to be a proponent of free-market policies

---

[21] Author interview, Magdalena Lewandowska, European Commission Directorate General for Economic and Financial Affairs, 9 May 2010.

[22] Author interview, Karlis Bauze, Latvian Central Bank, 1 June 2010.

[23] See McGillivray and Smith (2000, 2004) on electoral turnover and reputations.

[24] Following on Bulow and Rogoff (1989), Eaton (1996), and Cole and Kehoe (1998), who distinguished between "honest" and "normal" governments, Tomz (2008) characterizes countries as "fairweathers" who pay when times are good, in contrast to "lemons," who never pay.

(Campello, 2006). Additionally, information in emerging markets is especially poor and uncertain.[25] In short, the reputations of emerging markets can swing on political as well as economic shocks, making them almost like perpetual new ventures with reputations that are constantly being renewed – not so different, then, from the new business ventures in the studies cited previously.

Developed countries, of course, also experience changes of government and economic shocks, but traders tend not to react too strongly to those events. The reason is that most developed countries have a reputation for making good on their debt obligations in any context, thanks to long histories of repayment (Eaton, 1996; Tomz, 2008). Electoral turnover is not a bad thing, as long as other political and legal institutions on the ground uphold contracts and guarantee debt service regardless of who is in power, such as constitutional provisions (Milgrom, North, and Weingast, 1990). Similarly, developed countries are less likely to be significantly derailed in the medium term by economic, electoral, or environmental shocks, because the structure of their economies is usually fairly diversified, and well-developed political institutions insulate the country as a whole from the agendas of any one particular leader (Campello, 2008).

From this discussion, a few features of what investors look for in emerging markets can be extracted. They are looking for relatively durable signals of a government's intentions – that is, commitments that will likely extend beyond any given leader's time in office. Keeping the potential dangers of herd behavior in mind, it is also important for them to be aware of signals that are plainly visible to other investors as well. Additionally, these signals or events must be easily and uniformly interpreted by other investors. The next section elucidates how exactly international organizations, and specifically the members within them, can reduce investor uncertainty.

2.4 A THEORY OF THE COMPANY STATES KEEP

It stands to reason, then, that visible international allegiances are easier for investors to observe, and lead to a greater commonality of interpretation, than the enacting of domestic reforms. In other words, joining international institutions where members have good reputations can be well-understood signals to investors. These affiliations serve as shortcuts that investors take to determine the trajectory of countries about whom there may be conflicting information. For example, Podolny (1994) empirically demonstrates that where uncertainty is high, investment banks engage in exchange relations with those with whom they have transacted in the past, particularly those of similar status.

---

[25] For example, as a Serbian former central banker noted, data from his country in the 1990s are problematic because they are at too low a level of granularity to capture the often-hourly distortions of hyperinflation, and in any event the data are "doctored before publication and do not reflect real movements in the given period. . . . We wish all econometricians good luck!" (Dinkić, 1995).

Of course, as centuries' worth of burst bubbles attest, these shortcuts can be a poor substitute for evaluating actual performance.[26] But these are shortcuts that investors take nonetheless. Just as a seminal work in sociology claims that states are made through a voluntary commitment to a joint identity (Anderson, 1991), so to are organizations formed as a way of shaping regional identity, and investors are responsive to those identities.

International organizations work not as a signal but as pieces of public, visible information within a set of noisy or imperfect information.[27] The perceived quality and shared nature of this information allows investors to make more informed choices. In an environment where bond traders have equal access to a wide variety of information, membership in certain types of international organizations can serve as a credible and public piece of information that facilitates information processing by individual economic agents. The uncertainty here is not strategic; it is environmental, owing to noise and differing individual perceptions. Within a Bayesian framework, rational actors who have equal access to the same set of private, noisy information could still reach different conclusions. But if the organization is public and if perceptions of its meaning are reasonably shared by many, international organizations can coordinate those expectations.

This process is understood by policy makers as well as investors the world over. In Peru, one trade minister says that "trade agreements are part of our brand.... The right kind of trade agreement can send a signal that policies will continue as expected."[28] In Botswana, according to one representative in the stock market, "when national events are unclear, international events can sometimes be more helpful in terms of communicating our direction."[29] Investors also recognize this phenomenon, in both directions: "A chain is only as strong as its weakest link," one comments. "Getting in bed with a bunch of weaker trading partners could widen spreads for the group."[30] Similarly, when asked about Mercosur, Milton Friedman was said to have commented that, although he did not know much about the group, it seemed to him that if "you have four sick people in the same bed, it won't be very useful."[31]

International organizations with strong linkages among certain types of countries can move a country from one category of association to another. For example, when the EU formally announced the future opening of negotiations

---

[26] Rao (1994) shows how, in the early days of the U.S. automobile industry, the absence of rating agencies meant that cars had to build credibility through performance tests.

[27] The concept of noisy information is widespread in finance but has only recently begun to make inroads in political science; see Kurizaki (2007).

[28] Author interview, Benjamin Chávez, Mincetur Peru, 6 July 2009.

[29] Author interview, Geoffrey Bakwena, 21 November 2008. This recalls Oppenheimer (2004) on how supranational language helped Germans advocate peace post–World War II.

[30] Author interview, Carlos Sharpless, Stern Agee, 7 June 2007.

[31] Quoted in *Brazzil Magazine*, "For Brazilian Expert New Members Only Delay Mercosur's Integration Process" 26 December 2006.

with Croatia, credit ratings agencies moved that country from a peer group that included Serbia and Montenegro, Macedonia, Brazil, Ukraine, and Turkey to one that comprised fellow EU negotiators Bulgaria and Romania.[32]

Indeed, a 1997 World Bank study argued that regional trade agreements could provide "nontraditional" – meaning, not related to economic or technology-type – gains, especially when information asymmetries are significant (Fernandez, 1997). The study describes one possibility as follows:

> Consider a country which could have two types of government: liberal or protectionist. In fact, it has a liberal one, but this is not immediately apparent to outside observers. Potential investors are not particularly interested in the exact provisions of any international organization, but they do care about the type of government. In that case, entering the RTA may be a way for the government to signal to investors.

These sentiments align to some extent with the constructivist literature on the effects of international institutions, yet it differs in a key way. Much of that literature focuses on how members of an organization can take on the identities of their peers.[33] Usually, however, the focus is on the methods of transmission of those identities. It looks at the shaping of identities as an internal process, and takes the logic further to map the levels of convergence in member states.[34] The literature on socialization focuses on mechanisms through which actors actually change their behavior as a result of repeated interactions with others (Axelrod, 1997; Ikenberry and Kupchan, 1990; Beck and Jennings, 1991). However, the theory proposed in this book is less concerned with actual changes in state behavior, but rather with changes in how those states are perceived as a function of their membership in international organizations. Indeed, at times these changes in investor perception are independent of changes in state behavior. Additionally, as is demonstrated in the later chapters, investor perceptions of members of institutions can shift very rapidly, whereas the socialization processes described in the constructivist literature takes place over long periods of time.

Although they both emerge from situations of information asymmetry, the argument here is not a signaling argument per se. Much of the classical work on realism, as well as studies on signaling in diplomacy (Fearon, 1994; Schultz, 2001), argues that states act in a way to convey information about their "type" to international audiences and thus increase their credibility in diplomacy.

---

[32] Author interview, Lidija Marić, Croatian National Bank, 5 July 2006.

[33] This vast literature includes insights on how norms are diffused, through socialization or coercion (Finnemore (1996b,a); Beyers and Dierickx (1998); Checkel (1999); Johnston (2001); Kelley (2004); Beyers (2005); Checkel (2005); Lewis (2005)), as well as what types of institutions make interests converge (Bondanella, 2009).

[34] Much of the literature on the European Union focuses on the convergence angle; see, for example, Kelley (2004); Beyers (2005); Gheciu (2005); Hooghe and Marks (2005); Lewis (2005); Schimmelfennig and Sedelmeier (2005).

Indeed, the idea that international agreements can act as signals is not novel (Martin, 2005; Fang, 2009). In those cases, however, the signaling is strategic, an attempt of one actor either to mislead or to convince another actor of their intentions.[35] Here the uncertainty is environmental, not strategic. With some exceptions – the initial idea behind the formation of Mercosur as a counterpart to NAFTA;[36] the proposed creation of the Bolivarian Alternative for the Americas as a way of providing financing to South America that did not come with the so-called Washington consensus of neoliberalism and market openness – countries enter international organizations for more complex reasons than information processing alone. Thus, the changes in risk levels are to some extent an unintended consequence of entry into trade agreements. Heads of state may at times try to send a message to the world by announcing their affiliations with certain types of countries. But just as often, countries may enter agreements for a variety of political and economic reasons. Investors react to these cues irrespective of countries' intentions.

How do investors process the many features of international agreements; that is, what aspects of international institutions might make them well understood by portfolio investors? The literature cited earlier points to two main attributes that affiliations – be they board members, underwriters, or sponsors – had to share in order for them to have an impact on investors. The section that follows goes into greater detail with respect to the mechanisms underlying this effect. In general, however, I argue that investors evaluate trade agreements along two main dimensions: the proposed depth of integration and the reputation of countries in the agreement.

2.4.1 Proposed Depth of Integration

When countries announce *deep* ties with other states, this information is likely to be both more widely heard and taken more seriously, even if agreements ultimately fall short of their goals. Intended close integration with particular countries indicates a state's intentions in terms of the nations to whom it desires to link in the world economy. Similarly, in order for investor expectations to converge in any substantial way, the affiliation must be sufficiently *public*. Not advertising or publicizing one's affiliations make them too obscure to be widely interpreted by investors. Depth is therefore in part a proxy for the public nature of the agreement. Even if there is a shared interpretation of the meaning of a particular type of institution, membership in that organization will not generate any overall changes in perceptions if they are unobserved and private

---

[35] Of course, signaling is not always misleading; in many cases there are separating equilibria.

[36] "We are the victims of of the gross inequality in bargaining power; crumbs of aid are not enough, and self-help, in a self-perpetuating cycle that excludes us, does not provide cure," one champion wrote at the time of the agreement's founding. "Latin America is and remains at the periphery of the world economy to the main poles in Europe and the United States. As a consequence, it has limited bargaining power to trade and is essentially trapped" (Guira, 2005).

(Johnston, 2001; Kuklinski and Hurley, 1996; Halpern, 1997; Valley, Moag, and Bazerman, 1998).

The level of integration proposed in the agreement also measures the seriousness of intent of the union, even if those intentions are not met. Hundreds of agreements exist in the world, but the seriousness and depth of those agreements vary widely. Investors would surely not be expected to have the same reaction to a country's membership in international organizations centered on migratory bird paths or aviation coordination as to agreements that proposed a high degree of economic unification. Thus, agreements that propose deeper levels of integration imply more of a commitment to both the countries that sign onto them as well as the members that accept them, and thus should be more of a coordinating force among investor perceptions.

The proposed economic links influence the perceptions of investors as expressions of a country's intent – but, crucially, the effect is independent of the policy reform that countries are supposed to undertake as part of their membership in the agreement. In practice, the vast majority of agreements do not actually accomplish what they set out to do. Countries often proclaim to establish customs unions or single markets at some date in the future, but they very rarely meet their targets, and indeed are often criticized for not even being functioning free-trade areas.[37] This gap between actual versus proposed integration – that is, de jure versus de facto integration – has long been acknowledged on both a theoretical (Higgot, 1998) as well as an empirical level (Bearce and Omori, 2005; Haftel, 2012; Kim, 2011; Gray, 2014). A recent study (Haftel, 2012) coded about forty economic agreements in terms of their formal as well as their actual integration, finding that 70 percent of those organization fall into the low coding category for implementation of their agreements. This study found that on a comparative basis, the EU was the only agreement that had a good record of implementation. Even within the EU, there has been a significant gap between its written rules and countries' adherence to those rules (Boerzel, 2005; Bearce, 2007; Jensen, 2007). Similarly, when surveyed experts have coded regional economic agreements (Gray and Slapin, 2012), they only code six out of thirty-one agreements as having a significant ability to achieve the goals that they set out paper. Those agreements that have better records of implementation tend to be NAFTA, CEFTA, EFTA, and the EU, with developing-country agreements usually falling far short of their announced goals.

Why would proposed integration with the company a country keeps, then, be a determinant of risk levels? I argue that the depth of integration serves as a proxy for the public nature of the commitment and the *intended* closeness of the ties. Announcing an eventual economic union with a country that is widely

---

[37] See Ravenhill (2008) and Baldwin (2007) for specifics on Asian agreements that have not met their targets; Söderbaum (2005) and Bourename (2002) on Africa, and Vaillant (2007) on Latin America.

known to be in disrepute is not only likely to make the headlines in a way that simply a trade agreement would not. It is also a clearer signal of a country's intent. Take, for example, the respective announcements of closer integration among Russia, Kazakhstan, and Belarus. Those three countries announced the establishment of a customs union in January 1, 2010. That announcement earned 292 news articles from news outlets in the two months surrounding the event, and most of those were media based in the region. Subsequently, however, on 18 November 2011, those same countries announced the formation of a Eurasian Union to serve as a counterpoint to the EU, and with broader-reaching political goals. That mention garnered 723 news articles in the same time period.[38]

Given that few of these arrangements come close to achieving their stated goal of integration, why are they not viewed as cheap talk? If the poor performance of trade agreements is widely known, in expectation, all parties would know that signing a given agreement was not a costly declaration. Even the agreements that are viewed as more costly to enter have fallen short of their goals, as is evidenced by the inability of EU members to adhere to the organization's targets in terms of budget deficits. And if countries begin to announce deep ties with a limitless number of other states, the signal would certainly become degraded. But at present, the number of visible, meaningful agreements is limited enough that they still have an impact on investor perceptions, and agreements that propose deep ties still center on relatively small groups with a few important anchor members (Fratianni and Pattison, 2001). The duration and limits of this effect are explored in subsequent chapters.

2.4.2 Reputation of Countries in the Agreement

Secondly, a key component of investor reaction to organization membership is that the affiliation must be with states about whom there is some degree of shared knowledge. In order for there to be a commonality of interpretation of the significance of a particular group of countries, there must be some consensus as to the meaning of that group. Otherwise, membership in a particular organization would be just another item in a set of noisy information, and investors would draw their own conclusions as to the meaning of membership. Johnston (2001, p. 491) summarized this problem:

> Contractualists often assume that the credibility of information rests on costliness to the provider of the information. In practice they see costliness mostly in terms of some loss of material welfare or political power. No doubt costs often take this form, but ... the social origins of common definitions of costliness, essential for information to be credible, are unexamined. Yet empirically the same information, even economic information, will be interpreted differently depending on

---

[38] Based on LexisNexis searches.

whether it comes from "people like us" (the information is more authoritative and persuasive), or from a devalued "other."

But where would this consensus on quality come from? The theories cited earlier indicate that in most cases, they would come less from the design of the arrangements than from the actors in those arrangements. Indeed, it is *states* that have the most easily observable reputations; those reputations trump the reputation of most international organizations as structures.[39] Much of the formal game-theoretic literature about the convergence of behavior among actors who interact repeatedly has to do with the establishment of a reputation for a certain kind of behavior (Keohane, 1984; Morrow, 2002, 1994; Axelrod, 1984). Thus, the quality of members in a public, meaningful organization could have important reputational effects for less reputable member-states. This effect can go both ways: good members could pull up the reputations of other countries in an organization, or less reputable countries could make other members look worse off.

These conditions are nicely summed up in the opinion of one stockbroker:

> [Hugo] Chávez is going around now making a lot of noise, talking about this Bolivarian Alternative for the Americas. If Venezuela were a big economy, and if [Peru] were to join a free-trade area that included Venezuela, Cuba, and Bolivia, all these leftist economies – if those economies were actually big and there were serious linkage, this would not be very good news to investors.[40]

I propose that the level of formal integration interacts with the quality of the members, such that proposed deep levels of integration with either extremely good- or extremely poor-quality members will have the strongest effects. If the general picture of the economic agreement is mixed in terms of the quality of its membership, however, high levels of proposed integration will not have much of an effect. Weak ties with countries who have especially good or poor reputations will not matter to investors, and nor will proposed strong ties with countries who have middling reputations. But proposed strong ties with countries who have distinct reputations will impact risk positively or negatively, depending on whether the reputations are good or bad.

Figure 2.1 illustrates the theoretical expectations for how risk levels interact with both the level of integration as well as for the quality of members. High levels of proposed integration with high-quality members should be associated with the biggest drops in risk, as represented by the lower righthand corner of the cube. Similarly, high levels of proposed integration with low-quality members should be associated with the biggest increases in risk, as depicted in the upper lefthand corner of the cube. The effects are mitigated by movements

---

[39] See Sartori (2004); Tomz (2008); Wolford (2008); Mercer (1996); Gaubatz (1996); Milliken (2996); van Ham (2001); Potter (2008) on the importance of reputations in international relations.

[40] Author interview, Alberto Araspe, Kallpa Securities-Lima, 7 July 2009.

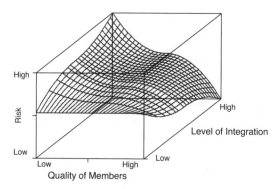

FIGURE 2.1. How Risk Varies as a Function of Integration and Member Quality (Theoretical Graph).

either along the proposed integration axis or the quality axis; less integration with good-quality members (as in the case of NAFTA) dampens the improvement of risk levels, as does high integration with medium-quality members (as is the case for Mercosur). In the middle areas – where political risk as well as integration are mid-level – there should be no observable impact on risk. This could possibly stem from divergent opinions about the benefits of a particular organization, which might then cancel one another out. In this case there would be no change in point estimates of risk, even though the variance surrounding those estimates would increase.

But when "good" countries join agreements with "bad" members, or when a "bad" country joins an agreement with "good" members, which effect dominates? The dynamics can fluctuate given the uncertainty surrounding the new entrants and the perceived credibility of existing members. For example, the postcommunist countries got a considerable boost in reputation once they progressed in their negotiations with the EU. By the same token, the most economically stable member of the union, Germany, saw the risk levels associated with its debt increase slightly. However, current EU negotiators see much less of a drop in risk – perhaps because of the dimmed credibility of Germany, the dilution of the EU brand as a function of having so many new members who are very visibly struggling with meeting EU targets, and the uncertainty of whether EU negotiation means that membership is an eventual guarantee. To borrow an analogy from thermodynamics: imagine the effects of REO membership working in a similar way as ice in water. The speed and extent to which the ice is absorbed or remains intact depends on the size of the glass and the temperature of the water within it. Just as dropping ice into already cold water has little effect, when countries join groups of the same uncertainty or risk levels as theirs, little impact would be observed in either direction. However, when a very high-uncertainty country joins a group of less risky members, the uncertainty for that country would decrease

TABLE 2.1. *Expectations for Effects on Risk*

	Proposed Weak Ties	Proposed Strong Ties
Bad Company	MRU, AU, SCO SPARTECA	COMESA, ALBA, Eurasian Union (+)
Good Company	CAFTA, European Neighborhood Policy, APEC	European Union, NAFTA (−)

(melt), while at the same time observing a slight *increase* of uncertainty on the others.

On the other hand, when a member of notably poor or good quality enters an agreement of relatively few members about whom uncertainty is high, their entry can have a marked effect on risk perceptions of those other members. Take, for example, the entry of Myanmar and Cambodia into the Association of Southeast Asian Nations in 1997. This was an example of countries with clearly repressive political systems and stagnant, closed economies entering a loose confederation of member-states whose profiles varied from relatively successful state-led growth (Singapore) to partially open (Malaysia) to integrated and booming (South Korea). At the time, the inclusion of those states led to serious questions about Southeast Asia's economic and political trajectory – questions that were only further aggrieved by the financial crisis that struck the region. Thus, the membership of Myanmar and Cambodia might cast further doubt on the credibility of the other states in ASEAN.

To further illustrate these dimensions and the organizations that fall along those lines, I present a simple 2 x 2 (Table 2.1).

The table demonstrates how a few of the better-known organizations in the world fall into this rubric. The most noticeable changes in risk perceptions would be observed on the righthand column, where high integration exists among countries. High integration with low-quality countries (such as what is afforded by UEMOA and ALBA) would be expected to increase risk (+), where high integration with better-quality countries (such as in the EU and NAFTA) would be expected to decrease risk (−).[41]

This is the argument advanced in this book – that the reputations of influential countries with whom an emerging market forms close links are paramount to investors. This can be stated succinctly in a central hypothesis:

- H_1: Proposed close ties with reputable countries can decrease investor risk and narrow the uncertainty surrounding a country; conversely, proposed close ties with countries whose reputation is of poor quality can increase perceptions of risk and increase uncertainty around a country.

[41] For example, membership in APEC, which with its dramatically large and diverse membership has failed to institutionalize coordination on various issues and policies (Aggarwal and Espach, 2004), should not have any impact on risk.

The mechanism behind this relationship is that public pronouncements of economic links with countries with strong reputations – for better or for worse – allow investors to make inferences about how other investors will perceive an emerging market, and thus those perceptions coordinate around an overall higher or lower risk level. The depth of the commitment matters to the extent that it indicates the intended seriousness of the ties – but because most agreements do not actually meet their integration goals, proposed integration only serves as a shorthand for a country's intended trajectory.

The changes in perceptions of risk that occur as a function of the company a country keeps may be unwarranted, but that does not mean that they do not have real impacts. In finance particularly, there are strong individual incentives for what Keynes 1936 called "following the herd." Even if a desk trader believes that market enthusiasm in a country in times of boom is ultimately misguided, she has little motivation to depart from conventional market wisdom about that country. If she sells off her securities and no crisis occurs, she may well be fired for missing the boat. If, however, those same securities go bust en masse, the blame is shared by all, with no one in particular being singled out for punishment (Scharfstein and Stein, 1990). This goes against traditional economic theory, which would argue that prices are set at the margins, and that there will not be distortions as long as investors are willing to bet against the average – but personal disincentives to be bold distort the bond market. Thus, the aspects of institutions that would most strongly influence portfolio investors are the things that are most easily interpretable by the widest number of people.

The following section will explore some alternative explanations for how affiliations within the context of international organizations might impact investor risk.

2.5 ALTERNATE HYPOTHESES

As mentioned, much of the literature in political science focuses on several different aspects of international organizations that are linked to various positive outcomes. This section describes, in turn, several of the more prominent arguments, as well as potential problems in evaluating the central hypothesis described earlier, and their applicability to the situation under analysis here. I lay out these rival explanations as alternative hypotheses (H_{a1}, H_{a2}, H_{a3}) to be tested in subsequent chapters.

The observable implications of the alternate hypotheses have to do primarily with a country's *ability* to honor its debt obligations. They would impact a country's economy: for example, through real changes in a country's welfare as a result of trade integration; through changes in a country's policies or operating procedures as a result of IO membership; or through emergency funding provided by other members of the organization. Thus, these hypotheses are theoretically distinct in terms of their proposed impact on spreads in sovereign debt; if they were valid, their contributions would be toward investor perception of a country's ability, not its willingness, to service its debt.

2.5.1 H_{a1}: Changes in Member-State Behavior

One might argue that changes in investor perceptions as a function of emerging markets' membership in economic organizations result not from the company they keep but from policy changes. That is, these countries do not simply feed off one another's reputations, but actual changes occur among members, and investors react in anticipation of this change. Potential members can enact reforms as part of the requirements for entry into an international organization, or change their behavior once they enter an organization. Some research suggests that policy reform in the context of an international organization may be particularly important for developing countries, who need a third party to help them push through important reforms (Mansfield and Pevehouse, 2006; Putnam, 1988). Others have argued that an international institution can help consolidate policy reform, either because of the costly commitment involved in joining the institution or because a government can use the institution as a scapegoat and thereby assuage domestic opposition to reform (Pevehouse, 2002).[42] This literature would argue that anticipating or observing policy reform would drive down uncertainty about future outcomes in emerging markets (Rodrik, 1991). If this hypothesis were correct, investors would be reacting not to the sheer fact of membership in international organizations but to positive changes that occurred in members as a result of their affiliations.

If trade agreements increase welfare, and if welfare makes a country more able to service its debt, bond traders ought to look favorably on any type of international trading arrangement. Trade openness creates new markets for a country's goods, while allowing consumers greater access to a wider variety of products. Classical trade theory as well as numerous empirical studies have demonstrated the welfare-enhancing effects of trade openness, through the diffusion of technology and economies of scale.[43] Thus, classical economic theory would predict that membership in any agreement that boosts a country's trade levels should bring in revenue and make it more likely that countries will be able to service their debt, thereby decreasing uncertainty.[44]

---

[42] This has more to do with the effectiveness and durability of reforms on the ground, and those reforms' credibility to *domestic* audiences, not international audiences such as bond traders.

[43] See, for example, Solow (1956); Lucas (1998); Young (1991); Grossman and Helpmann (1991); Sachs and Warner (1995); Ventura (1997); Dollar and Kraay (2001); Alesina, Spoloare, and Wacziarg (2003).

[44] However, empirical evidence is mixed on the benefits and drawbacks of regional trade agreements, both in terms of the gains they offer participating countries and the degree to which they contribute to multilateral free trade. In the former category, the asymmetric benefits of many regional trading arrangements have been well documented. Although some argue that increased

That one country's actions can spill over onto another's has been well documented in theory and empirical work alike. When countries increase their economic ties through trade and monetary cooperation, for example, a currency crisis in one country will have powerful effects in its closest affiliates, owing to changing prices. But many have argued that a more subtle process is occurring: that behavior can and does change as a function of one's affiliates. One of the bedrocks of constructivist thought is the idea that members will converge through processes of socialization and imitation.[45] Empirically, picking up on the behavior of others in close proximity is a phenomenon long observed in the social sciences.[46] Scholars in the field of education show criminal activity and drug abuse patterns tend to be replicated within neighborhoods as a result of "the company you keep" (Case and Katz, 1991). They chalk this up to "collective socialization" and "contagion."

Similarly, in many social sciences as well as in finance, social network analysis has long posited the influence of networks of actors in those networks; this method began to make significant inroads into political science in the 1990s primarily through the study of policy networks (Marin and Mayntz, 1992; Marsh and Rhodes, 1992), though there are earlier, pioneering examples (Eulau and Siegel, 1981; Tichy, Tushman, and Fombrun, 1979).[47] One of the central ideas of network theory is the notion that ideas, norms, and, subsequently, behaviors pass among groups of actors, depending on how closely those networks are linked.

liberalization ought to increase aggregate welfare among all countries by allowing them to reap the gains of comparative advantage (Summers, 1990), in practice, free-trade arrangements tend not to benefit both parties equally. Debate also rages as to whether RTAs divert instead of create trade, with partial liberalization within a few countries inhibiting broader trade among more countries – particularly if barriers are lessened in the participating countries but raised toward other countries (Bhagwati, 1996). More recent studies have tried to disentangle whether countries that are members of international economic agreements trade more than they would have otherwise, with results in both directions (Rose, 2002; Subramanian and Wei, 2007; Tomz, Goldstein, and Rivers, 2007).

[45] On institutions as social environments, see Johnston (2001); Duina (2008); Zürn and Checkel (2005); Beyers (2005); Bearce and Bondanella (2007).

[46] For just a few examples, see Rogers (1962) on the spread of innovations; Gleditsch (2007) on civil wars; Brune and Guisinger (2007) on capital-account openness; Finnemore and Sikkink (2001) and Cortell and Davis (2000) on the diffusion of international norms; Rogers (1962) on the spread of innovations; (Gleditsch and Ward, 2006) on democratic diffusion; Orenstein (2003) on the spread of pension reforms; Berry and Berry (1990) and Volden and Shipan (2007) on the spread of lotteries and anti-smoking policies in U.S. states, respectively; Simmons and Elkins (2004) on the international spread of liberalization; Lutz and Sikkink (2001), Sikkink and Walling (2005), and Kim (2005) on "cascades" in justice, particularly in terms of holding heads of state accountable for past abuses; Baturo and Gray (2009) on the spread of the flat tax; and Meseguer (2002, 2006), who discusses two types of learning processes and uses a Bayesian model to test whether politicians show evidence of updating their beliefs.

[47] In political science, researchers have applied network theory in such disparate areas as the study of public opinion (Huckfeldt et al., 1995), innovation diffusion (Mintrom and Vergari, 1998), political theory (Robin, 2002), and the study of legislatures and the judiciary (Fowler, 2006).

But a problem plagues much of the literature on collective socialization, diffusion, and the importance of network ties. The causal mechanisms behind these processes are difficult to distinguish among one another. How can one tell, for example, if countries whose behavior seems similar are learning from one another or are simply copying one another – or whether those changes are adopted spontaneously or imposed from above?[48] Additionally, the same selection problem described earlier is inherent here – would these changes actually come about as a result of being in the institution, rather than simply being changes that a country would have made anyway?

Furthermore, as is demonstrated in the subsequent chapter on the European Union, in many cases investors are not responsive to indication of divergence from positive group norms. Research has already demonstrated that even within the EU, prior to the 2004 accession, member states experienced far less monetary convergence than economic theory would predict – and the current financial crisis bears this out.[49] Even when countries show signs of breaking the rules of an organization, markets do not show much of a reaction; similarly, investors seem to punish indiscriminately members of an organization once one member starts behaving badly. This indicates that investors are less concerned about actual behavior than with sticking to categories once their perceptions have already been formed.

This rival explanation can be framed as a testable hypothesis:

- H_{a1}: Changes in risk levels that occur as a function of membership in international organizations are not the result of "the company you keep" but of changes in member state behavior either before or during their membership in international organizations.

2.5.2 H_{a2}: Selection and Endogeneity

It could also be the case that countries simply select into the agreements that reflect their previously unobserved preferences. Estimating the effect of regional economic organizations on sovereign debt does bring up concerns about reverse causation. The problem of endogeneity centers on the difficulty of disentangling the effects of international organizations from the determinants of entry – for example, the possibility that a common economic shock could both increase sovereign risk and increase fears of protectionism, thereby prompting the formation of regional economic agreements.[50] Along those same lines, do certain institutions promote economic growth and prosperity, if rich countries tend to be the ones that join those institutions? Do institutions encourage cooperation,

---

[48] On heuristic adoption of policies within neighborhoods, see Weyland (2005); on adoption via learning, see Baturo and Gray (2009) and Jensen and Lindstaedt (2009); on imposition by powerful actors, see Stallings (1992), Simmons (2001), or Henisz, Zellner, and Guillen (2005).

[49] See Bearce (2007).

[50] See Mansfield and Reinhardt (2008), who argue that PTAs hedge against risk and volatility.

or do states seeking to cooperate simply form or join institutions that reflect those preferences? These issues make it difficult to determine the independent effects of institutions on a whole variety of outcomes.

Many of the claims about *international* institutions overlap with those about institutions in general, including property rights, the rule of law, and well-functioning courts. The world's various international institutions, of course, may or may not possess these attributes. Yet many of the arguments about how organizations work and the benefits they bring in terms of cooperation share many features with research in economics and political science about the merits of institutions in promoting, for example, sustained economic growth. Scholars have struggled to disentangle the consequences from the causes in this area: that is, rich nations have sound institutions, but how is it possible to tell whether those institutions are themselves causing growth? Similar problems beset the literature on international organizations: does cooperation occur because of attributes of a particular organization, or are states inclined to cooperate simply the types that form these organizations?

Modeling the effect of institutions requires theoretical precision behind one's operationalization of these different concepts. It is true that much of the alleged benefits surrounding institutions is not directly observable. But there is a distinction between a variable being unobservable because it exists but simply does not happen to be available to the researcher, and being unobservable because its qualities are impossible to measure. For example, some studies have focused on measuring and predicting institutional quality by using surveys that measure foreign and domestic investors' perceptions of corruption in a country (Treisman, 2002). Those measure not the mechanics of the institutions themselves, but how well those norms appear to work. Rodrik (2003) points out that this causes two problems. One is that those perceptions are shaped by many aspects of a country's economic and political situation, not just institutions. This points to the issue of endogeneity, a recurrent plague in the literature linking economic growth and institutions. Because economic growth is both a cause and a consequence of institutional quality, disentangling the true nature of the relationship between the two presents researchers with a problem. This has prompted a number of empirical studies that explore the best way of estimating this relationship, often through instrumental variables used to proxy for institutional quality (Acemoglu, Johnson, and Robinson, 2002; Gallup, Sachs, and Mellinger, 1998).

Thus, specifying both the nature and the effects of institutions has proven difficult. How can norms of behavior be measured? How can the determinants of strong institutions be distinguished from the outcomes? Institutional design is a feature of the literature on exchange-rate arrangements, which seeks to balance a country's political and economic constraints (such as openness to trade and sensitivity to exogenous shocks) with the need to send a strong signal to financial markets. But until recently, few other studies of international institutions have engaged that level of detail.

Still, even if countries uphold their commitments in international treaties, it becomes more complicated if we try to measure the unobserved factors that might compel them toward good behavior regardless of the treaty. The problem of selection bias, addressed more thoroughly in Chapter 4, means that it is often difficult to tell if countries act any differently under international agreements than they would have otherwise.

Some argue that countries simply select institutions whose regulations they would have followed regardless (Vreeland, 2001; von Stein, 2005). Thus, although it is important to measure and control for the enforceability of an organization's rules, there are already theoretical as well as practical reasons to believe that this condition is not of paramount importance to investors. Indeed, the current financial crisis indicates how willing investors were to overlook the security of their investments. For example, once the propensity of countries to select into the WTO is taken account, membership in that organization itself has little effect on trade (Tomz, Goldstein, and Rivers, 2007). In the case examined in this book, this rival explanation would claim that investors would be reacting to countries simply joining organizations that reflected their preferences.

This supposition can also be modeled and tested:

- H_{a2}: Changes in risk levels that occur as a function of membership in international organizations are not the result of "the company you keep" but reflect propensities of good or bad countries to sort into good or bad agreements.

2.5.3 H_{a3}: Enforcement of Rules or Constraints on Behavior

A third alternate hypothesis is the possibility that investors are reacting to the probability that good codes of conduct will be enforced once countries enter into international organizations (Kindleberger, 1986; Keohane, 1984). Much of the IR literature has focused on the rational design of international organizations – that is, the features in an organization's charter or composition that the founding member states give it at inception. This literature places a good deal of emphasis on the structure and language of international organizations in terms of their efficiency, their ability to meet their goals, and their ultimate effectiveness.[51] If these agreements lower the probability of defection, investors would be right to adjust their perceptions accordingly, even if the agreements did not prevent all defections.

International institutions' ability to impose enforceable constraints has received much attention in political science and economics.[52] If members must uphold well-defined rules, and if reneging elicits punishment, an institution

---

[51] A rich literature exists on coding the attributes of international agreements, such as Koremenos (2001); Leeds et al. (2002).

[52] On sanctions effectiveness see, for example, Morrow (1987, 1994); Snidal (1985); Cowhey and Aronson (1993); Fearon (1994); Gaubatz (1996); McGillivray and Smith (1998, 2000);

becomes more credible (Drezner, 1999). A 2000 special issue of *International Organization* looked explicitly at the issue of legalization in international organizations – particularly the concepts of precision of language, the delegation of authority to that organization, and the obligation of those treaties – as primary drivers of the effectiveness of organizations (Simmons, 2000b). By making it costly to renege, international institutions can encourage good behavior from even those states that would not otherwise abide by international law. Some argue that enforcement originates from home, either through audience costs or domestic pressure (Slaughter, 1995). Others cite the power of sanctions (Lebovic and Voeten, 2006). Much of this attention has focused on the presence of dispute settlement mechanisms in organizations. The possibility of adjudication in agreements has been theorized to lead to more cooperative behavior.[53] Even in finance, the enforceability of contracts have been shown to be associated with higher values of stock markets as well as more firms listed on stock markets (LaPorta et al., 1997); higher valuation of listed firms relative to their assets (Claessens and Djankov, 2002; LaPorta et al., 2002); greater use of external finance (LaPorta et al., 1998, 2000); and a greater volume of investments from external funds (Rajan and Zingales, 1998; Demirgüç-Kunt and Maksimovic, 1998). This set of theories would argue that any effect that institutions have on the decrease of risk comes from the threat or actuality of sanctions that are imposed for bad behavior.

Many scholars have discussed the attributes that make international agreements more or less effective. Until recently, much of the existing literature that seeks to measure the effects of institutions focuses on design-driven aspects of international organizations.[54] However, even the most legally binding of commitments do not guarantee good behavior. Take the case of various stages of monetary commitment. Despite currency boards' strict intractability, countries have dismantled them with devastating financial results, most recently in Argentina's collapse of 2001. Even in the case of the gold standard, countries could suspend convertibility under extreme circumstances, such as war, revolution, or a decline in the terms of trade (Knafo, 2005). In other words, even the strictest of commitments are often not followed. Thus, these measures of the qualities of institutions do not necessarily translate into the overall effectiveness

Nooruddin (2002); Marinov (2005); Hafner-Burton and Montgomery (2008); Miers and Morgan (2002); Allen (2005); Hurd (2005). On institutions as constraints on behavior in domestic macroeconomic policy, see Clark (1998). For arguments that the threat of sanctioning is sufficient for cooperation, see Axelrod (1984); Hardin (1982); Shubik (1970); Doxey (1980, 1987); Gilpin (1987); Mayall (1984). Ang and Peksen (2007) argue that the effectiveness of sanctions hinges on the asymmetry in the perceived issue salience between the sanctioner and the sanctionee.

[53] See Rosendorff (2005); Johns, Gilligan, and Rosendorff (2009); Johns and Rosendorff (2009); Rosendorff and Milner (2005); Dai (2005, 2006); Busch and Reinhardt (2003); Busch, Reinhardt, and Shaffer (2009); Busch and Pelc (2010).

[54] See Crawford and Fiorentino (2005); Stinnett (2007); Kim and Hicks (2012); Mansfield and Reinhardt (2008); Haftel (2007).

of the agreement (Gray and Slapin, 2013), even though dispute settlement has met with many successes in the international stage, particularly with respect to the WTO, the ICJ, and the ECJ (Simmons, 2000a; Alter, 2008; Alter and Meunier, 2009; Busch and Reinhardt, 2003). What is important here, however, is not what these agreements do in practice or how well they meet their own goals, but what they announce their intentions to be.

Even the more constraining of the international organizations does not enforce its own rules. The European Union's efforts to constrain its members economically have been resoundingly unsuccessful. The Stability and Growth Pact – an attempt to set limits on eurozone countries' fiscal and monetary policies – was ultimately scrapped after nearly every signatory found itself in breach of the rules. The eurozone economic crisis demonstrates that many of the southern European states in particular have long been in violation of the Maastricht criteria's rules, a discrepancy that had long been noted but only recently acted upon by investors (Bearce, 2007). This indicates that even strong IOs have little real ability or willingness to sanction their members.[55]

However, even if policies are not enforced, the presence of powerful members with a stake in the health of their associates could actually make default cheaper for emerging markets, because they would be virtually guaranteed a bailout.[56] In fact, the U.S.-backed rescue of Mexico in 1994 was driven in large part by then-President Bill Clinton's interest in preserving NAFTA's credibility. Similarly, the European countries whose finances ran aground in the wake of the 2008 financial crisis did so in part because there was a widespread perception that those errant countries would be bailed out by stronger ones, rather than to risk the financial health of the system as a whole.

The case of EU accession serves as a good illustration of the market view of this situation. When economic concerns delayed EU entry for some of the new members, markets remained relatively sanguine. One report maintained, three years before accession, that Romanian sovereign spreads were "likely to tighten to 40–50 basis points [hundredths of a percentage point] over [German] Bunds by the end of 2005, or 2006 if EU entry is delayed to 2008, and that these yields offer the best value in the second wave convergence trade."[57] Similarly, even in the face of exogenous shocks, investors remained calm, as long as those countries still maintained a credible line of entry into the EU. One brokerage noted that potentially tumultuous parliamentary elections that were slated to take place in Hungary, the Czech Republic, and Slovakia two years before accession were "unlikely to pose problems for the convergence process toward

---

55 Indeed, some argue that the only time that the EU has been able to exercise leverage on states is in the run-up to accession. See Vachudová (2002, 2005); Schimmelfennig and Sedelmeier (2005).

56 This is the argument of the "moral hazard" literature, particularly in addressing IMF rescue packages.

57 *ING Financial News*, Romania Quarterly Analysis, June 2004.

the EU.... We continue to think that the risks to EU enlargement are more to its timing than to whether it will ultimately happen."[58]

The enforcement hypothesis can be put as follows:

- H_{a3}: Changes in risk levels that occur as a function of membership in international organizations are not the result of "the company you keep" but of enforcement of rules and prevention of backsliding in those institutions.

These rival explanations will be examined alongside the central hypothesis in subsequent chapters.

2.6 CONCLUSION

For emerging markets, where uncertainty is high, determining a government's willingness to service their foreign debt obligations is paramount. To do so, investors rely on easily interpretable signals, and membership in international institutions can help investors' expectations about that country's behavior converge. Even if bond yields take into account all available information, as the much-debated efficient markets hypothesis supposes, there may be gross inefficiencies in the way that their information is processed. The reputation of other members in an agreement, combined with the public announcement of proposed deep ties, may be a common denominator in international agreements that help investors sort countries into "peer groups" of similarly inclined nations.

The following chapters show that for emerging markets, international economic agreements can help investors coordinate their expectations about a country's levels of political risk. This could be attributable to a halo effect; that is, if everyone believes that a state is creditworthy, it becomes something of a self-fulfilling prophecy. That state will be able to tap funds relatively easily, and it will also be cushioned from exogenous shocks. Because markets operate on principles of uncertainty, investors look for an unambiguous sign from a credible institution that a country has moved from one "peer group" to another; that is, countries that joined certain groups would have made a clear shift from a developing country to a developed country.

This argument hinges on a convincing disentanglement of the different factors that drive reputations. That is, do those reputations come from actual changes in policies or in behavior, or are they founded on something more ephemeral? The subsequent chapters provide closer examinations of what drives reputations in good international institutions.

---

[58] Morgan Stanley Global Economic Forum, 18 February 2002.

3

The Company You Keep in Comparative Perspective

How important is "the company you keep" for emerging markets? This chapter sets out to establish empirically the effect of membership in international organizations on investor risk. The central proposition is that investor perceptions of countries' willingness to repay their debt depends on the quality of other countries with whom they establish ties. When emerging markets align themselves with other countries, in the eyes of investors they absorb those countries' risk levels – associations with good company make a country look less risky, while bad company makes a country look more risky. Specifically, however, the risk that is absorbed comes from investors' perceptions of their partner countries' *willingness* to repay their debt. The proposed closeness of ties often does not translate into policy reform explicitly, but it serves as a proxy for both the public nature of the commitment and the seriousness of the country's intended allegiances with other countries.

This chapter offers a broad view of the relationship between international economic organization and risk, and shows how that relationship holds up across countries and across time. To test the central hypothesis, I examine the comparable effects of membership in many different types of international organizations, across many regions of the world. I show that the quality of other members in an organization has a distinct relationship with risk perceptions in emerging markets. All else equal, a country that seeks close ties with nations of low political risk will itself look less risky to investors, and the converse is true as well. This chapter shows that even taking into account a country's existing economic and political conditions, markets evaluate what types of international organizations a country joins, and with whom.

Explicitly, this chapter gives evidence for the core theory of the book – that visibly close ties with reputable countries can decrease investor risk for an emerging market. Regression analysis on data from 129 emerging markets over the past 30 years shows that, all else being equal, proposed integration with countries whose political quality is high on average decreases risk for emerging market. This relationship is robust to several different specifications. The magnitude of this effect is considerable. International ties cannot substitute for low inflation or for strong economic growth. But the effects of the company a country keeps ranks just below those variables in terms of the magnitude, and surpasses magnitude even for domestic political quality.

I also examine the alternate hypotheses that investors react to changes in a country's behavior, that the relationship between risk and REO membership is endogenous, or that investors anticipate possible enforcement of an organization's rules. I take into account the possibility that investors react not to REO membership per se, but to changes in countries' behavior as a result of entering that organization (H_{a1}). Lagging of independent variables helps take into account the possibility that the same processes drive both risk and REO entry (H_{a2}). Further estimations examine whether risk changes as a function of the organization's dispute settlement processes or with the presence of a hegemon within the group, which would make enforcement of rules more likely (H_{a3}). The explanatory power of "the company you keep" is robust to all these rival explanations.

This chapter starts by describing the way in which we will operationalize our main variable of interest – the default risk associated with emerging markets. I then describe the dataset, including key explanatory variables as well as control variables. I demonstrate that the general patterns of this variable conform with the theory: organizations whose members have good political quality also have lower levels of risk associated with those members. The subsequent sections consider various factors, both at the country level and at the level of the organization itself, to pin down precisely what matters to investors. Economic indicators control not only for changes that a country might undergo as a result of membership in an organization, but also for fundamentals that determine a country's ability to make its debt payments. I show that the average political risk associated with an organization members – that is, an indicator of its *willingness* to service its debt – influences emerging market risk independently. That is, if a country keeps good international company closely, its risk level decreases.

This pattern holds under many different circumstances. I demonstrate the resilience of this finding in more than 100 developing countries across a nearly 30-year sample at an annual level. This time coverage is consistent with the scope of the theory; trade in emerging market assets grew in the 1990s in particular, and the risk climate has substantially changed following the onset of the 2008 financial crisis. At a more fine-grained level of detail, the dynamic also persists in 129 countries in quarterly data from 1993 to 2007. In both levels of analysis, high political quality of a country's international associates, and the depth of those associations, decrease risk even when held against changes in member-state behavior and the possibility of enforcement of rules. This shows that for emerging markets, the broad effect of the company a country keeps robust across time and place.

3.1 OPERATIONALIZING RISK THROUGH SOVEREIGN DEBT

The first task of this chapter is to describe the universe of cases and the operationalization of our outcome of interest. The theory applies primarily to countries where information is relatively poor and expectations of future trajectories vary. In those circumstances of uncertainty, international economic organizations can serve to coordinate investor expectations about a country's intended direction. That is, the theory is most appropriate in describing dynamics within emerging-market countries. Even though the financial crisis of 2008 demonstrated that investors also use heuristic shortcuts when evaluating assets from developed countries – hence the boom in asset-backed securities, whose lack of worth was only revealed too late – there tends to be more consistent information available from richer countries. Developed-country markets are deeper and more liquid, and investors have less of a need to rely on information-processing signals than they do in high-uncertainty emerging markets. The gap between the interest rates of commonly traded securities, such as U.S. Treasuries or German bunds, and those of government paper in emerging markets is termed the spread – essentially, the extra premium that investors demand as a compensation for holding riskier investments, taking into account the general levels of market sentiment as expressed through the interest rates on OECD securities.

In order to measure default risk across countries – the dependent variable – it is necessary to find an indicator that is relatively common across countries. However, there is some variation in sovereign paper across and even within countries. Governments can issue dozens of publicly traded debt instruments, and very few governments use identical instruments. In developed countries, these different debt instruments can exhibit significant divergence, both in terms of their levels and their elasticity to particular kinds of events. However, in emerging markets these different debt instruments are highly correlated with one another, and thus it is reasonable to believe that some degree of substitution is appropriate. I compiled data from Global Financial Data, JP Morgan's Emerging Market database, and the Economist Intelligence Unit on publicly traded debt instruments for these countries. Though the maturities varied, the most common note was a three-year maturity. The majority, but not all, of these debt instruments were denominated in foreign currency. Interest rates on those instruments are expressed in basis points, or hundredths of a percentage point.

This sample represents countries from all regions of the developing world, albeit slightly better off countries – the poorest or war-torn developing countries tend not to issue their debt publicly, as there is not much of a market for it. There remains, however, substantial variation even within this sample, across

TABLE 3.1. *Summary Statistics for Key Variables*

Variable	N	Mean	Std. Dev.	Minimum	Maximum
Logged spread on sovereign debt	6496	1.66	1.53	−15.25	9.36
Current-account balance	5046	−0.48	13.93	−210.91	58.22
Budget expenditure (as % of GDP)	1678	219.48	1371.45	3.59	11699.70
External bond issues	2832	10341.89	68211.24	−840.00	522160.00
Real GDP (USD at 1996 prices)	2965	452.27	1646.59	0.02	13225.00
Inflation (%)	8374	118.56	8560.66	−100.00	782799.00
Growth (% change in GDP)	3797	3.96	4.20	−26.65	39.70
Change in value of stock market index	4466	6.33	30.47	−98.29	1003.16
Exchange rate LCU:USD	9559	480.10	1760.82	0.00	30000.00
International reserves	9052	23.18	69.97	0.00	1688.35
Net portfolio investment flows	2630	41576.94	632663.30	−10600000.00	10300000.00
Domestic political quality	6218	66.80	13.43	20.33	97.00
Political representation	3273	4.25	2.05	1.00	7.00
Civil liberties	3272	4.25	1.69	1.00	7.00
Economic reform index	401	5.45	1.10	2.30	8.70
Dispute settlement	8256	2.41	1.98	0	5
Proposed integration	8256	3.83	1.44	0	6
Company	8256	16.02	19.38	0	127.01

both time and place (thus, selection on the dependent variable is not a concern here). To parse out the performance of any given asset from overall market trends, I take the difference of the yields on each asset (that is, the interest or dividends received from a security) from yields on U.S. treasury bills of three-year maturity. The *spreads* on these sovereign debt instruments (here, the difference between the quoted rates of return on an emerging-market debt instrument and a U.S. treasury bill of comparable maturity) captures the risk premium on sovereign paper from emerging markets, holding overall market sentiment constant.

The average spread on sovereign debt across the sample is around 13 percentage points, and the standard deviation for the whole sample of countries is around 176 percentage points. Times of financial crisis are responsible for the highest spreads; Argentina, Brazil, Angola, Zimbabwe, Serbia, and Russia – all countries beset by hyperinflation or financial crisis in the past twenty years – have among the highest-recorded risk levels in this sample. Table 3.1 presents summary statistics for each variable in the analysis, while Table 3.10 in the appendix shows statistics on sovereign debt for each country in the dataset.

TABLE 3.2. *Investor Risk in Key Economic Agreements*

	Proposed Weak Ties	Proposed Strong Ties
Bad Company	African Union (7.99) BSEC (26.79)	Andean Community (60.29) CIS (29.74) Mercosur (140.92) COMESA (17.55)
Good Company	OECD (5.75) APEC (4.73)	NAFTA (1.87) EU (.86) SPARTECA (4.06)

Thus, the spreads on sovereign debt will serve throughout this book as our indicator of the risk associated with default in any given country at any given time. As noted before, this risk usually consists of market perceptions of a country's ability as well as its willingness to repay its debt. There is no real way to disaggregate those two components from the overall risk premium prior to any further analysis. The control variables help identify the various factors that have an impact on those risk perceptions.

3.1.1 Sovereign Risk of Members of Regional Agreements

How do countries of different risk profiles tend to sort themselves out on the international stage? At the most basic level, the expectations in the 2 x 2 table described in Chapter 2 would be borne out simply by examining the overall levels of risk associated with membership in an international organization. That is, organizations that comprise members of high political quality and with high levels of proposed integration should be associated with lower levels of risk, whereas groups that entail high integration with poor-quality members should be associated with higher risk over all. Indeed, if we did not observe higher levels of risk in closely integrated organizations whose members are of poor political quality and lower levels of risk with organizations whose members are of good political quality, the foundations of the theory would be called into question (Achen and Shively, 1995). Thus, I first provide a basic depiction of the relationship between risk and international organizations before focusing on finer-grained units of analysis.

Table 3.2 replicates the 2 x 2 laid out earlier in the chapter with the actual observed levels of sovereign risk among member states in organizations. To keep the values consistent with the typology provided earlier (where there are expectations that risk should increase or decrease), I put all values at a baseline of the spreads among the emerging markets in the dataset, from 1980 to 2008.

The organizations in question exhibit the overall pattern that the central theory describes. Organizations whose members are associated with good political quality (such as NAFTA and the EU) generally have lower levels of risk (that is, lower values of sovereign spreads) than organizations that comprise members with worse political quality (COMESA and Mercosur), where there are higher levels of risk. Similarly, those organizations whose members are of variable political quality or offer low levels of de jure integration – such as APEC, which includes Australia, the United States, and New Zealand as well as China, Russia, and Indonesia – have somewhat middling levels of risk. Again, it is important to keep in mind that the announced level of integration more often than not does not translate into actual policy changes on the ground, as most economic organizations do not meet the targets they set out for themselves. Rather, the depth of integration serves as a proxy for both the public nature of the commitment and the intended closeness of ties.

Of course, this table leaves much unsaid; any number of characteristics could be driving that pattern. Most of the organizations whose members have low risk levels are also relatively wealthy as well as politically stable. Additionally, because these values are averages over a nearly thirty-year period, many important temporal dynamics are left out. But it is important to establish first that the logic of the theory holds true for reality, at a basic level. The subsequent section examines the dynamics behind this pattern.

3.2 KEY EXPLANATORY VARIABLES

The theory proposes that investors should make inferences about emerging markets based on the political quality of countries with whom they integrate closely. The political quality of their close associates gives investors an indication of countries' *willingness* to service their debt; information about their ability to honor their debt obligations is deduced separately. In other words, any material gains that a country reaped as part of being a member of an international organization would express themselves through that country's economic indicators; those are observable on a direct level, and it is easy to control for those factors. Economic gains represent increases in a country's *ability* to repay its debt. I argue, however, that investors make inferences about a country's *willingness* to repay its debt as a function of the political quality of other members of an organization. Thus, the central hypothesis is that proposed high integration with countries of high political quality should decrease sovereign risk, but proposed high integration with low-quality members should increase risk.

Political quality is easy to recognize but difficult to pin down; it is usually considered to be a function of some combination of the rule of law, political stability, low levels of corruption, and accountability, to name just a few of the characteristics that usually are lumped under this description. In terms of operationalization, consistent cross-country measures with adequate time coverage, unfortunately, are rare. For example, the World Bank offers governance indicators that only run from 1996 to 2008 and only has observations every three years. Transparency International codes nations on their perceived level of corruption, but these data only go back to 1996.

The most comprehensive coverage, in terms of granularity of detail, comes from the International Crisis and Risk Group (ICRG), which has extensive data originating in 1980 that exist at a monthly level for 150 countries. The ICRG's rating system is the sum of twelve weighted variables and fifteen subcomponents covering both political and social attributes of a given country, including government stability, corruption, democratic accountability, and the quality of bureaucracy.[1] Higher values indicate high political quality and lower potential risk, whereas the lowest number (o) indicates worse political quality and the highest potential risk. This variable constitutes the *Domestic Political Quality* variable.[2]

When capturing the over-time dynamics, it makes sense to average the political quality of all member states of a given organization. This captures the dilution effect of the political quality of members of a given organization. For example, the effects of joining the European Union differed over the given rounds of its enlargement; when Greece joined the nine-member EU in 1981, for example, the effects were very different than those of Bulgaria and Romania joining the twenty-five-member union in 2007, even though the political quality of the largest members were more or less the same.[3] The number of countries in an organization can dilute the reputational signal that investors see. Thus, to represent how the political quality of organizations is perceived by investors, averages are the most appropriate metric. This is not to say that individual countries have no impact on how investors perceive members of a given organization in the short run. As Chapter 6 demonstrates, economically small countries that have gained a degree of political notoriety can cause shockwaves in an organization's image and the image of its members; Venezuela's accession to Mercosur demonstrates this. But in order to best capture, across time and space, the dominant dynamics at work in how emerging markets are perceived as a function of their IO membership, this more general operationalization is appropriate.[4]

As the theory describes, investors should react not only to the political quality of members of a given organization but also the proposed depth of

---

[1] Government Stability; Socioeconomic Conditions; Investment Profile; Internal Conflict; External Conflict (twelve each); Corruption; Military in Politics; Religious Tensions; Law and Order; Ethnic Tensions; Democratic Accountability (six each) and Bureaucracy Quality (four).

[2] Other measures of political quality exist, but these are usually only available at the yearly level. Regardless, as a robustness check, I replicated the estimations for the yearly analyses with these alternate measures of political quality, including data on political rights and civil liberties from Freedom House, a USAID-funded nongovernmental organization. Those specifications produced similar results.

[3] The subsequent chapters explore this phenomenon in greater detail.

[4] I did run alternate specifications of the "company" variable as described earlier, including political quality of the lowest and highest member. Those variables were for the most part not statistically significant.

ties. Proposed integration also tends to mean a more visible agreement, which should make investors take notice, as discussed in Chapter 2. It should also be an indicator of the seriousness of a state's intention; an agreement that proposes close integration is one where the relationships are taken seriously, even if the actual integration does not come to fruition.

To operationalize the depth of ties between countries, I draw from the coding of economic unions in Bearce and Omori (2005); I supplemented their coding where gaps existed. *Level of Proposed Integration* is coded as 1 if a country is a member of an international organization but no economic integration is proposed; 2 if a free-trade area, where countries agree to eliminate tariffs, import quotas, and preferences on most goods and services; 3 if a customs union, in which members of a free-trade area agree to impose a common tariff on countries that are not in the agreement; 4 if a common market, where countries agree to have common policies on product regulation as well as freedom of movement for capital and labor; 5 if an economic union, which combines a common market with a common external tariff; and 6 if a monetary union, in which members share a currency.[5] These come from the Balassa (1961) ordinal scale for the depth of economic integration. The coding matches the proposed level of integration, even if the organizations fail to meet those proposed targets, as most of them do.[6]

The perceived quality of members, if high, should have a negative effect on risk. This approximates reputational effects of a trade agreement, where inclusion in organizations whose members have a high institutional caliber might send a signal to investors of the country's "type." Here, the quality of the known members would have positive or negative effects on the new members, depending on whether the quality was poor or strong. This variable, however, should also be mitigated by the proposed depth of ties of the agreement. Thus, I interact the average political quality across members of a given organization with the proposed depth of ties, as described earlier. This variable – *Company*Proposed Integration* – ranges from 0 to 123. The European Monetary Union – which promoted deep ties among countries of high political quality, particularly prior to the 2008 sovereign debt crisis in the eurozone – receives

---

[5] Other codings of the depth of ties among organizations exist – see, for example, Haftel (2012) – but these correlate highly with the Bearce and Omori data.

[6] The agreements included are APEC, ASEAN, ASEAN AFTA, African Union, Bangkok Agreement, BSEC, CACM, CAEU, CAFTA, CARICOM, CBSS, CEAO, CEFTA, CEMAC, CEPGL, CES, CIS, CMEA, COE, COMESA, COMESA-PTA, EAC, EACM, EAEC, EC-Albania FTA, EC-Algeria FTA, EC-Andorra FTA, EC-Bosnia FTA, ECCAS, EC-Chile FTA, EC-Croatia FTA, EC-Egypt FTA, EC FYROM FTA, EC-Israel FTA, EC-Jordan FTA, EC-Lebanon FTA, EC-Mexico FTA, EC-Morocco FTA, EC-Norway FTA, ECO, ECOWAS, EC-Romania FTA, EC-South Africa FTA, EC-Syria FTA, EC-Tunisia FTA, EC-Turkey FTA, EFTA-Chile FTA, EFTA-Egypt FTA, EFTA-FYROM FTA, EFTA-SACU FTA, ENP, EU, EMU, GAFTA, GCC, IOC, LAIA, Mercosur, MRU, MSG, NAFTA, OAS, OCAM, OECS, PATCRA, PICTA, PTA, SAARC, SACU, SADC, SAFTA, SPARTECA, UDEAC, UEMOA, UMA, US-Bahrain FTA, US-Israel FTA, US-Jordan FTA, US-Morocco FTA, US-Oman FTA, US-Peru FTA, and US-Singapore FTA.

the highest scores overall; free-trade agreements, with looser ties, by the EU and the United States score in the middle of the range (scores in the seventies and eighties, depending on the partner). For larger organizations that promote some economic integration but among several members, such as APEC, the average political quality is mediated by both the low levels of integration and the number of members, and those scores also range in the thirties. Similarly, organizations such as COMESA, which promote high levels of integration with members of relatively low political quality, rank lower.

Simply including an indicator variable for whether a country is a member of a trade agreement is not very illuminating; the only country that is not is Mongolia. Thus, I use indicator variables only in the first baseline specification, to see whether being in an international organization has any effect on sovereign risk. Subsequently, I used the aforementioned dimensions in place of indicator variables for those agreements, although the structure is the same: countries receive a 0 for each year that they were not a member of a trade agreement, and the combined measure of political risk for every year that they were in an organization, including countries both within and outside of the data. Thus, variation on the scoring of trade agreements comes from the addition of new countries to the agreement (for example, if a country with low institutional quality joins in, say, 1998, the overall score on institutions decreases from the value in 1997), as well as in whether a country is a member of the agreement in a given year (if not, I coded the observation as a 0).

Establishing the predictors for sovereign risk is important not only for model specification purposes, but also as a means of testing one of the alternate hypotheses. If REO membership promotes change in member state behavior that is attractive (or, for that matter, unattractive) to markets, then investor response to those changes (as manifested by the control variables) should overwhelm any independent effect of international organizations. Furthermore, if there are some real effects of integration with other states that take the form of economic contagion – through changes in a country's direction of exports or imports, and subsequent vulnerabilities in its terms of trade based on potential economic downturns in their new trading partner – those will be captured in the control variables, and any additional effect of the *company* variable would be separate from those contagion effects. The control variables will also account for technical reasons why portfolio investors might or might not look kindly on an emerging sovereign issuer forming trade alliances. For example, there is wide variation in the level of sophistication of the issuers. Initially, sovereign debt is denominated in local currencies. As debt market size increases with the growth of a particular economy, countries try to attract sovereign debt denominated in hard currencies. Investors are primarily interested in debt that is backed by hard currency, because there are generally limited capital markets in emerging economies. Hard currency exposure is riskier unless it is hedged with hard currency exports like oil. Trade agreements could therefore have the effect of increasing current account deficits and drive up spreads.

However, controlling for current-account deficits should take this explanation into consideration.

Thus, other variables are necessary to capture the determinants of investor risk in emerging markets. Most of these signify a country's ability, not willingness, to repay its debt because they indicate economic health. A country's *current-account balance* (measured in units of 100,000) is an indicator of its exposure to trade; while that might increase volatility and exposure to shocks, it can also indicate hard currency coming into an economy, which would make it more likely for a country to be able to service debt payments, and thus decrease risk. *Budget expenditure* as a share of GDP indicates a government's spending commitments; higher values would make debt service potentially less likely, and would increase risk. High levels of *inflation* indicate not only rising prices but also a degraded value of local currency with respect to hard currency; this would be linked to increased difficulty of debt servicing and therefore risk for portfolio investors. Real GDP (measured in USD at 1996 prices) is a sign of a country's wealth and should decrease risk. The level of hard-currency *reserves* indicates a pool of currency to draw from in case of an economic shock and should decrease risk. I also include variables to proxy the depth of the country's portfolio investment market, including net *portfolio investment* flows, the *exchange rate* index, and external *bond issues*, which show a country's exposure to foreign investors. Changes in a country's *stock-market index* capture overall market sentiment in that country. A deeper market for bonds indicates more liquidity and lower risk for investors, who will have a greater opportunity to trade those assets on secondary markets. These are all standard inclusions in estimations of the determinants of emerging-market spreads.[7]

The next section describes in greater detail the dataset and the methods chosen.

3.3 TESTING OF CENTRAL HYPOTHESIS (H$_1$): THE COMPANY YOU KEEP

To test the central hypothesis as well as the rival explanations, I gathered data for 129 emerging markets, all of which issued foreign-currency-denominated debt on international markets from 1980 to 2008. I used the Economist Intelligence Unit's database of cross-country indicators for many of the control variables. These data exist at different degrees of granularity; quarterly data for these countries are available from 1993 onward. Because of the time sensitivity of the dependent variable – market data fluctuates on a minute-by-minute basis in many cases – it is important to use as fine a level of detail as possible. A higher level of time detail would be desirable, because portfolio investment fluctuates even on a daily basis. However, similarly fine-grained data on the majority of the control variables are not available for most of those countries,

---

[7] For a good summary, see Rowland and Torres (2004).

and across the sample not all emerging markets release sovereign debt data on more than a monthly basis.[8] Therefore, I do the majority of testing on quarterly data, but I show that the models also hold for annual data over a broader period of time – in fact, the effects of "the company you keep" are even stronger in the yearly sample, although twenty-nine countries were dropped from the annual sample as a result missing values. This might indicate that in the 1980s, a period of less-active trading in emerging market debt, investors relied even more heavily on the information provided by international organization.

The time period is appropriate for theoretical as well as practical reasons. Not much of a market existed for developing-country debt prior to the 1980s. The trade in emerging-market debt picked up particularly in the 1990s, where more and more countries began issuing their debt on international markets, and emerging-market debt became a standard feature of many investment portfolios. The end-date of this analysis coincides with the advent of the global financial crisis that kicked off with the bursting of the mortgage-backed securities bubble, and the contraction in economies the world over. Risk appetites have subsequently changed, as even assets that were previously thought secure have proven worthless, and OECD countries such as Iceland, Ireland, Spain, and Greece have had their ability to service their debt called into serious question. The type of heuristic that this theory describes is one that best holds in a period of relative market exuberance, when investors are more willing to take inferential shortcuts.[9]

Testing hypotheses on cross-national historical datasets presents specific econometric problems. Time-series cross-section datasets violate the standard Gauss-Markov assumptions of OLS; namely, that observations are independent and identically distributed. Where data trend over time, the observations in one year will be related to the observations of the previous year; similarly, errors tend to cluster spatially where panel dynamics are present. Though there are many fixes, no one method will work for all types of data (Wilson and Butler, 2002). For this dataset of emerging markets, the problem would most likely be related not to trends over time, since emerging markets are volatile, but rather for particular patterns associated with a given year or country (for example, the East Asian financial crisis and its contagion to other emerging markets in 1997 or the Russian default in 2001). Thus, I control for panel heteroskedasticity by including region indicator variables, and for shocks in a particular year by including year indicator variables. I use region rather than country indicators, because it is important to distinguish the effects of international organization – which often clusters on the regional level – separate from the effects of simply being in a given region (that is, distinguishing the effects

---

[8] Chapter 5 uses daily data to examine investor response to specific announcements pertaining to regional integration with "bad company."

[9] However, this logic does hold up even in more recent data, as shown in investor reactions to integration movements in Latin America in 2009 and 2010.

of a country's membership in SADC from the effects of being geographically located in sub-Saharan Africa).

The fixed-effects approach assumes that the intercept of a regression varies across the t (time period) units. Those indicator variables account for shocks or characteristics associated with certain countries and years. Controlling for those time-specific occurrences affords empirical findings that may hold true after accounting for local factors, such as the Argentine default of 2000 and the Mexican "tequila crisis" of 1994.[10] Because n > t (129 countries and 20 years, or 60 quarters), following Beck and Katz (1995), I did not compute panel-corrected standard errors.

Another complication is the presence of a high degree of missingness across variables (around 35 percent), as failing to account for missing observations can lead to biased and inefficient estimations. Unlike in the matching data described earlier, I used Amelia II (Honaker, King, and Blackwell, 2007), which uses a bootstrapping-based algorithm to impute guesses of the missing observations. Those guesses map the patterns in the observed data; in the event that weak relationships exist among the covariates and missing observations, the algorithm will simply impute noise observations. Reported coefficients and standard errors are averaged across five imputed datasets. The standard errors are a function not only of the within-dataset variation, but also the between-dataset variation; thus, in the event of variable imputed guesses, the coefficients will remain the same as they would have for unimputed data, but the standard errors will be large. This means that incorrect betas are not a risk if no patterns in the data exist; the only effect of imputation in that instance will be larger standard errors than would have otherwise been observed. This approach affords as much leverage as possible from the observations in the dataset while avoiding the bias caused by listwise deletion when observations are not missing completely at random (Honaker et al., 2001).

Estimations include the control variables described previously as well as the ICRG political risk score for each country at the domestic level. Except for the latter, all those control variables, both at the quarterly (1993–2008) and the yearly (1980–2008) levels, are from the EIU database.

3.3.1 Empirical Results for the Company You Keep (H_1)

The results presented in this section demonstrate the basic applicability of the central hypothesis: the independent effect of international organization on investor risk. Models A and B show the baseline results, putting membership in economic organizations simply as a indicator variable (that is, coded 1 if an organization is a member of any economic agreement and 0 if not), using fixed effects for region as well as fixed effects for quarter and a lagged dependent

---

[10] To preserve the constant, I used n-1 region and time indicator variables. I omit the coefficients on those variables for the sake of space.

variable, alternately. Models C and D look at the political quality on average of the members of those organizations to which a country is a member in a given year. The variables average the political quality of the members of the organizations, interacted with the level of proposed integration, with fixed effects and a lag alternately.

The theory predicts *opposing* effects for organizations with different membership content: positive effects (reductions in risk) for organizations with good-quality members, and negative effects (increases in risk) for organizations with poor-quality members. In terms of our estimation, what this might produce would be a coefficient that was not statistically different from zero, because equivalent positive and negative forces would cancel each other out.

Table 3.3 shows these results. It bears repeating that all of the control variables should pick up any actual changes in countries that result from IO memberships. Thus, any magnitude or statistical significance associated with the REO variables that remains once both are included in the model are the *independent* effects of REO membership on risk – that is, the effects that are distinct from those of actual economic or other changes that might result from membership in those organizations. Thus, these results serve as a test of H_{a1}, which states that changes in investor perceptions of countries that enter certain REO are only a result of attendant changes in those countries' behavior. If the REO variables have no effect when controlling for economic and political conditions, this would confirm that hypothesis; an effect, however, would mean that investors evaluate REOs independently of their economic effects. Additionally, the economic indicators point to a country's *ability* to repay its debt.

The control variables, for the most part, have the expected signs and are for the most part statistically significant; strong economic growth, high levels of income, large holdings of hard currency in reserve, and a liquid secondary market through external bond issues all decrease risk. The variables for the stock market index, portfolio investment flows, and budget expenditures are exceptions to this; they are not statistically significant. Current-account balance is only just above the conventional .10 threshhold for significance, and its effects are positive, perhaps indicating that when emerging markets open themselves up to trade, the volatility offsets any potential gains of commerce. Furthermore, the variable on inflation has the opposite sign as expected; positive inflation seems to be associated with a drop in risk. However, many of these variables are highly collinear, so it is perhaps not surprising that including all of them in the models cancels out some of their effects.

The most important thing to notice is that, when controlling for economic and political conditions on the ground, there is still an added effect of various types of economic agreements on risk. The consituent terms for the average political quality and the level of proposed integration in the first two models are significant and negative, indicating that investors react to both phenomena. But the interaction between those two variables – that is, averaging the political

TABLE 3.3. *Evidence for Central Hypothesis (H_1): The Company You Keep (Quarterly Data)*

Variables	(A)	(B)	(C)	(D)
Constant	1.811***	3.905***	1.587***	3.203***
	(0.226)	(0.310)	(0.222)	(0.327)
Current-account balance	0.009**	0.011*	0.009**	0.011*
	(0.005)	(0.006)	(0.005)	(0.006)
Budget expenditure	−0.000	−0.000	−0.000	−0.000
	(0.000)	(0.000)	(0.000)	(0.000)
External debt issue	−0.000***	−0.000***	−0.000***	−0.000***
	(0.000)	(0.000)	(0.000)	(0.000)
GDP	−0.000***	−0.000***	−0.000***	−0.000***
	(0.000)	(0.000)	(0.000)	(0.000)
Growth	−0.031***	−0.057***	−0.031***	−0.056***
	(0.005)	(0.008)	(0.005)	(0.008)
Inflation	−0.000	−0.000	−0.000*	−0.000*
	(0.000)	(0.000)	(0.000)	(0.000)
Stock market index	−0.001	−0.000	−0.001	−0.000
	(0.002)	(0.004)	(0.002)	(0.004)
Exchange rate	0.000	0.000***	0.000	0.000***
	(0.000)	(0.000)	(0.000)	(0.000)
Reserves	−0.001***	−0.001**	−0.001***	−0.001***
	(0.000)	(0.001)	(0.000)	(0.001)
Portfolio investment	0.000	0.000	0.000	0.000
	(0.000)	(0.000)	(0.000)	(0.000)
Domestic political quality	−0.016***	−0.029***	−0.016***	−0.030***
	(0.003)	(0.005)	(0.003)	(0.005)
Proposed integration	−0.041***	−0.100***	0.033**	0.115***
	(0.011)	(0.016)	(0.014)	(0.022)
Company	−0.021***	−0.039***	0.128***	0.402***
	(0.006)	(0.010)	(0.023)	(0.035)
Company *Integration			−0.026***	−0.076***
			(0.004)	(0.007)
N	8,127	8,256	8,127	8,256

Dependent variable is logged spreads on sovereign debt (three-year or shortest maturity available). Standard errors in parentheses. OLS regressions across five imputed datasets. Models B and D include fixed effects for year and region; Models A and C include fixed effect for region and a lagged dependent variable. Quarterly observations from 1993 to 2008, for 129 countries.
***p < 0.01, **p < 0.05, *p < 0.10.

quality of members and interacting it with the level of proposed integration – has a negative and statistically significant effect on risk, indicating that the higher the values of political quality in an IO, the lower the risk associated with a given country.

Coefficients on interaction terms are difficult to interpret substantively. To aid in understanding the impact of this change, Figure 3.1 shows the marginal

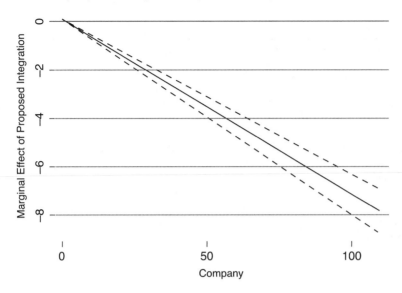

FIGURE 3.1. Marginal Effect of Proposed Integration on Risk as Company Changes.

effects of increasing average political quality in an agreement on investor risk (Brambor, Clark, and Golder, 2006).

The confidence interval is tighter where the values of average political quality in an REO are closer to zero; in general, confidence intervals tightest around the largest distribution of cases and widest where there are the fewest cases. Here most of the observations have values of company near 0 and fewer cases near 100. The curve of the graph also is consistent with the results that the proposed integration constituent term is insignificant and very close to zero, and that the interaction term was negative and highly significant. But proposed integration does matter when a country is with the right company.

What do these effects mean in practice? Specifically, how do we compare in substantive terms investors' reactions to all these forces? Table 3.4 shows the magnitude of these effects, when set against the mean values of the other control variables.[11] Because these variables are denominated in different units, it is difficult to get a sense of their effects simply through looking at the coefficients; how does one compare an additional dollar of GDP to a point in political risk? Therefore, the table that follows estimates the change in the expected value of the dependent variable, holding all variables at their mean values, and sequentially moving each independent variable from its mean value to the mean plus one standard deviation. This allows us to compare these variables' effects in standardized units. Column 1 depicts those differences in the expected values.[12] I ordered the variables in terms of the magnitude and direction of their effect.

---

[11] I present here the results of first differences of Model C from Table 3.3, with region and time fixed effects.

[12] First differences calculated using Clarify (Tomz, Wittenberg, and King, 2003).

TABLE 3.4. *First Differences: Quarterly Data*

	First Difference	SE
Inflation	−14.217	6.582
Growth	−9.950	1.208
Company*Integration	−8.357	0.673
Political Quality	−2.251	0.308
Reserves	−2.239	0.754
Bond Issue	−1.073	0.271
GDP	−0.844	0.180
Stockmarket Index	−0.403	3.010
Public Debt	−0.259	0.191
Portfolio Investment	0.170	0.251
Proposed Integration	0.247	0.045
Current Account Balance	0.917	0.409
Exchange Rate	1.710	0.322
Company	6.973	0.566

Inflation and economic growth, in standardized units, have the strongest effect (in standardized units) on a country's domestic political quality. This reinforces the notion that investors are particularly sensitive to indicators of willingness to pay in emerging markets. Economic growth is also strongly associated with drops in risk. The variable with the third-strongest effect, however, is the company a country keeps, which is associated with a around an 8 percentage point drop in risk. In substantive terms, relating these values back to actual countries, joining an organization with an average level of integration with members of average political quality to one that is one standard deviation above the means gives countries a drop in risk that is roughly equivalent to moving from the average risk level of Uganda to that of Tanzania.

Another interesting thing to note is that the effect of the company a country keeps is actually substantively greater than domestic political risk, by over 4 percentage points. That indicates that in this sample, the political risk associated with a country's economic ties can trump the political risk that a country itself experiences on the ground. This is only an aggregate affect, but it is striking nonetheless.

I then establish the effect on a different sample. Quarterly data are only available from 1993, but annual data on sovereign risk go back to 1980. For the subsequent robustness checks, I extend the time coverage of the analysis, albeit at the cost of losing a level of detail. I run essentially the same models on annual data for the same countries, extending back to 1980. Although this eliminates the granularity of the quarterly data, it does provide us with a broader temporal sense of how this variable works over the decades. Some of the control variables were not available for that expanded time period,

TABLE 3.5. *Evidence for Central Hypothesis (H₁): The Company You Keep (Annual Data)*

	(A)	(B)
Constant	2.156***	1.168***
	(0.255)	(0.212)
Current-Account Balance	−0.000	−0.000
	(0.000)	(0.000)
Public debt	0.001	0.001
	(0.001)	(0.000)
GDP	−0.000***	−0.000***
	(0.000)	(0.000)
Growth	−0.015***	−0.013**
	(0.004)	(0.006)
Inflation	0.000	0.000
	(0.000)	(0.000)
Exchange Rate	0.000***	0.000**
	(0.000)	(0.000)
Reserves	−0.000	−0.000
	(0.000)	(0.000)
Portfolio	−0.000	−0.000
Investment	(0.000)	(0.000)
Domestic Political	−0.006**	−0.003
Quality	(0.003)	(0.002)
Company	0.157***	0.101**
	(0.049)	(0.041)
Proposed	−0.030	−0.002
Integration	(0.023)	(0.019)
Company*	−0.040***	−0.025***
Integration	(0.009)	(0.007)
N	3,016	2,912

Dependent variable is logged spreads on sovereign debt (three-year or shortest maturity available). Standard errors in parentheses. OLS regressions across five imputed datasets. Fixed effects for region and year in Model A; fixed effects for region and lagged dependent variable in Model B. Yearly observations from 1980 to 2007, for 104 countries.
***$p < 0.01$, **$p < 0.05$, *$p < 0.10$.

however, and so the following models are slightly simplified ones, including the main control variables without the controls for the size and depth of capital markets in those countries (a reflection of the relatively small trade in emerging-market debt prior to 1990).

Table 3.5 establishes these effects on this broader sample and Table 3.6 shows first differences.

Interestingly, the effects of the *company* variable are even stronger for the annual data as for the quarterly data – it ranks second, after the exchange

TABLE 3.6. *First Differences: Yearly Data*

	First Difference	SE
Company*Integration	−2.651	1.215
Growth	−2.429	0.595
GDP	−0.892	0.210
Reserves	−0.871	1.442
Current-account balance	−0.627	1.323
Political quality	−0.248	0.097
Portfolio investment	−0.120	0.249
Reforms	−0.067	0.100
Proposed integration	−.0769	0.0591
Dispute settlement	−0.017	0.064
Public debt	0.399	0.301
Hegemon	0.427	0.243
Inflation	1.739	1.254
Company	2.40	0.743
Exchange rate	4.359	0.913

rate index, in terms of the magnitude of its effect. The variable is still negative and statistically significant. Furthermore, when the sample is extended back to 1980, the constituent term for proposed integration is not statistically significant, and the term for average political quality is actually positive. This perhaps implies that prior to 1990, investors had even less information to go on, and so their inferences about international organization gained particular weight. Furthermore, there were relatively fewer organizations in the 1980s, which might mean that their dynamics were especially informative to investors. The table of first differences – using the same method as described earlier – shows the magnitude of these results even further.

In the annual data stretching back to 1980, the substantive magnitude of "the company you keep" is even stronger. The effects of international organization, in these models, are even stronger than the effects of domestic-level economic variables. This indicates that for this sample, the things countries did at home actually mattered less to investors than the international groups that they joined.

The subsequent sections examine the robustness of this finding and explore rival explanations for this effect.

3.4 ROBUSTNESS AND RIVAL EXPLANATIONS

Even though there is a strong relationship between the company a country keeps and its perceived risk of default, there are various mechanisms that could underlie this link. What other attributes of these organizations and countries might be driving this relationship? The subsequent sections test the alternate hypotheses, modeling other features of international organization that might be affecting sovereign risk.

3.4.1 Test of Changes in Behavior (H_{a1})

One rival explanation is that investors react not to international organization explicitly, but to the changes in member state behavior that may occur in the process of signing up to the organization or once those states became members. Market-friendly policy reform undertaken and locked in as part of an international agreement might also signal that a country is retreating from government intervention in economic policy, and that an economy can stand on its own in the global marketplace.[13] Thus, investors could also be reacting to changes in the member states' behavior that come alongside their membership in international organizations.

To some extent, the existing economic control variables already take this argument into account. For example, take the demonstrated investor aversion to agreements with poor-quality members. There is wide variation in the level of sophistication of sovereign issuers. Initially, sovereign debt is denominated in local currencies. As debt market size increases with the growth of a particular economy, countries try to attract sovereign debt denominated in hard currencies. That is what investors want to buy, because there are generally limited capital markets in emerging economies. Hard currency exposure is riskier unless it is hedged with hard currency exports like oil. Trade agreements could therefore have the effect of increasing current-account deficits and driving up spreads. However, because the model already accounts for current-account balances, that variable would control for this phenomenon; that the "company" variable remains significant even accounting for changes in trade shows that economic factors alone do not explain this phenomenon.

Given that international organization still had effects beyond what was captured by those variables, it is possible to conclude that the effects of international organization hold even while looking at economic conditions that may or may not have come about as a result of joining an international economic organization. It is worth pointing out, however, even if countries undergo policy reforms while being in an international organization, it is difficult to know what to attribute to the organization and what they would have done regardless (von Stein, 2005). Additionally, it is not clear that investors are interested in *how* effective policy reform comes about (that is, if it is attributable

---

[13] It should be noted, however, that particularly in emerging markets, the actual changes in trade policy that come about as a result of RTAs are often minimal. Non-tariff barriers are usually more of an obstacle to trade than tariffs, but those are difficult to measure. Trade levels can also remained unchanged because countries have similar export structures and are more competitive outside their region (commodity producers, for example, have no reason to export to one another).

TABLE 3.7. *Test of H_{a1}: Changes in Behavior*

	(A)	(B)
Constant	1.955***	0.997***
	(0.648)	(0.149)
δ Current-account balance	−0.000	−0.000
	(0.000)	(0.000)
δ Budget expenditure	−0.000	0.000
	(0.000)	(0.000)
δ External bond issues	−0.000	0.000
	(0.000)	(0.000)
δ Growth	−0.041***	−0.017***
	(0.007)	(0.005)
δ Inflation	0.000	0.000
	(0.000)	(0.000)
δ Stock market index	0.002	0.000
	(0.003)	(0.001)
δ Exchange rate	0.000	0.000
	(0.000)	(0.000)
δ Reserves	−0.000	−0.000
	(0.000)	(0.000)
δ Portfolio investment	−0.000	0.000
	(0.000)	(0.000)
δ Domestic political quality	−0.000	−0.000
	(0.000)	(0.000)
δ Proposed integration	−0.095**	−0.063***
	(0.038)	(0.024)
δ Company	0.090	−0.035
	(0.067)	(0.038)
δ Company	−0.025**	0.006***
*Proposed integration	(0.012)	(0.002)
N	5,297	5,297

Dependent variable is logged spreads on sovereign debt (three-year or shortest maturity available). Standard errors in parentheses. OLS regressions across five imputed datasets. Model A includes fixed effects for region and year; model B has fixed effects for region and a lagged dependent variable. Quarterly observations from 1993 to 2008, for 129 countries.
***p < 0.01, **p < 0.05, *p < 0.10.

to an IO or not), as long as it has real effects. Therefore, the controls are a nontrivial test of that hypothesis.

However, this notion can be proxied by looking at the changes in economic indicators that do take place while in an economic agreement. The previous estimations only looked at levels of the economic and political indicators. Table 3.7 shows the same models on the quarterly data from 1993, where the control variables are modeled as quarter-on-quarter changes rather than levels. If investors are responsive to changes in a country's domestic conditions that may come about as a result of international organization, these variables should overwhelm that of the company a country keeps.

The change variables have no impact on the original finding – the coefficient for international organization still has the same magnitude as well as statistical significance. This is an indication that investors are still responsive to the company a country keeps, even when taking into account changes that might occur in a country's behavior or in its economic conditions.

3.4.2 Test of Endogeneity (H_{a2})

It is important to address the possibility of endogeneity in the relationship between risk and the company a country keeps. As Alternate Hypothesis 2 discusses, this situation emerges when explanatory variables (in this case, the company a country keeps) correlate with the error term in a regression – that is, when unmodeled and unobserved factors drive both the variation in the outcome (investor risk) as well as with the key regressor (company*proposed integration). There is also the possibility of reverse causation: that risk levels are driving membership in international organizations, and not the reverse. Furthermore, if these variables are correlated through some omitted factor, both risk and company could also be correlated with any shock to the system. If endogeneity is a problem, OLS methods will yield inconsistent estimates of any regression including both price and quantity.

The difficulty in addressing these problems empirically for all regional economic organizations across time is that the determinants of membership vary widely across organizations. The subsequent chapters examine in better detail the requirements to entry and driving factors for entering various organizations, such as the EU and ALBA. But many of the techniques that account for endogeneity assume a common process that would determine the main regressor. The degree of policy reform required to gain entry into, for example, the EU is very stringent. By contrast, NAFTA had initially been designed to consider more members and would have required a similar degree of reform, but it effectively closed its doors for political reasons soon after its inception. Many other organizations change their admissions requirements over time; Mercosur initially started out with a pro-markets focus but veered away from this commitment when Venezuela applied for membership. In still other organizations, such as the many overlapping regional agreements in Africa, countries come and go at will. Thus, it would be difficult to establish an equation that effectively predicted membership in various organizations across time and place. Indeed, very few studies of IOs specifically addresse the systematic determinants of IO accession, across countries and across time.[14]

---

[14] For exceptions, see Schneider and Urpelainen (2012); Stone, Slantchev, and London (2008).

TABLE 3.8. *Test of Reverse Causation (H_{a2})*

	(A)	(B)
Constant	2.441***	1.100***
	(0.282)	(0.349)
Current-account balance (lag)	−0.000	−0.000
	(0.000)	(0.000)
Budget expenditure (lag)	0.001	0.001
	(0.001)	(0.001)
GDP (lag)	−0.000***	−0.000*
	(0.000)	(0.000)
Growth (lag)	−0.012***	−0.005
	(0.004)	(0.004)
Inflation (lag)	0.000	−0.000
	(0.000)	(0.000)
Exchange rate (lag)	0.000***	0.000
	(0.000)	(0.000)
Reserves (lag)	−0.000	−0.000
	(0.000)	(0.000)
Portfolio investment (lag)	−0.000	−0.000
	(0.000)	(0.000)
Domestic political	−0.005**	−0.003
quality (lag)	(0.003)	(0.003)
Proposed integration (lag)	0.179***	0.114***
	(0.054)	(0.041)
Company (lag)	−0.031	0.015
	(0.022)	(0.020)
Company	−0.043***	−0.033***
*Integration (lag)	(0.010)	(0.008)
N	3,015	2,912

Dependent variable is logged spreads on sovereign debt (three-year or shortest maturity available). Standard errors in parentheses. OLS regressions across five imputed datasets, fixed effects for region and year in model A; fixed effects for region and lagged DV in model B. Yearly observations from 1980 to 2007, for 104 countries.
***$p < 0.01$, **$p < 0.05$, *$p < 0.10$.

However, reverse causality can be addressed in part by estimating the same models with lagged control variables. If the fear is that perceived investor risk might motivate countries to sign onto individual agreements, this can be accounted for in part by modeling the relationship as the effect of REO membership in the previous year with investor risk in the present year. If the variable for the company a country keeps were no longer statistically significant – that is, if REO membership yesterday no longer was associated with investor risk today – this might indicate that reverse causation was at work in the relationship. Table 3.8 displays the results of these models.

However, even when the main independent variable is lagged, it still remains negative and statistically significant, with much the same magnitude as in previous specifications. Results are similar when the independent variable is lagged for two years as well. This should serve as some evidence that reverse causality is not an immediate concern. However, countries' membership in international organizations is relatively static, fluctuating only when a country joins or leaves a group, or when political quality in member states changes, or in the rare occasions when organizations change their level of integration. Thus, simply lagging the variable does not produce much variation. Nonetheless, there is at least some indication that these processes are not tightly linked.

Another way of addressing a situation where variables are jointly determined in a given model is through methods using instrumental variables. This method – explored further in Chapter 4 with respect to the EU – involves running a first-stage estimation predicting values for a key independent variable and then including that prediction into a second-stage equation with the primary outcome of interest. These methods work best if there is an instrument that is sufficiently correlated with the outcome in the first stage (here, the company a country keeps) while still being orthogonal to the outcome in the second stage (investor risk). That is, instrumental variables regressions depend on the specification of factors that are strongly linked to one of the endogenous variables but not the other. If the instrument is weak (that is, if does not predict the company a country keeps, even if it is not a factor in investor risk), then there is a severe loss of precision of those estimates, such that IV estimates are not an improvement over OLS. Both theoretically and empirically, there are no obvious instruments that are valid in predicting membership in all economic agreements while being orthogonal to investor risk – indeed, very few variables systematically predict membership in different regional organizations around the world.[15] Table 3.11 in the appendix uses a two-stage model to account for selection; though results are similar, the lack of sound instruments make this a preliminary test only. Subsequent chapters examine endogeneity and selection into specific organizations.

3.4.3 Test of Enforcement (H_{a3})

Another rival explanation is that investors react to constraints placed on members' behavior as a function of the rules and regulations enshrined in IO membership. As mentioned, however, one of the assumptions behind that

---

[15] Some attempted instruments included political and regional factors, exposure to trade, and membership with other international organizations – but those tended to produce very low first-stage model fits and poor underidentification statistics. Specification for the best-performing model included in the appendix in Table 3.11. In this model, the central variable still has a negative and statistically significant effect even once the first-stage selection process is modeled, albeit weakly.

hypothesis is that the language of the charters of these treaties is actually effective in changing member state behavior – and this assumption is hotly contested in the literature on international organizations. Many studies have shown that even the most highly legalized agreements are often ineffective.[16] These concerns relate to the central hypothesis only tangentially; if the legal language and provisions of organizations do not produce cooperative outcomes, then investors may ignore those attributes. Ultimately, it is not the purpose of this book to test the effectiveness of organizations, but rather those organizations' impact on perceptions of risk. Nonetheless, if these features affect investor perceptions, it would be a sign of support for the alternate hypotheses, and thus I explore this argument in more detail below.

The provisions of an organization for enforcement can be examined by measuring the level of *legalization* of the treaty. Efforts to parse out the differing aspects of international organizations have tended to focus primarily on the language and content of the treaty itself.[17] Much of the literature in political science focuses on the presence of a dispute settlement mechanism (DSM) as a representation of a high level of legalization.[18] In addition to making rulings, researchers have shown that a well-functioning DSM can play an important informational role to members of the organization.[19] Having a permanent means of redress for member states can provide security for investors that members can be taken to task by others for noncompliance. A strong dispute settlement mechanism would indicate a process by which member states could sue for breach of the agreement, representing not only the degree of commitment within the agreement but also the reliability of enforcement.[20] Thus, a strong enforcement mechanism in the agreement should decrease levels of risk.[21]

I operationalize this concept through the variable *Legalization,* which is taken from McCall Smith (2000).[22] This variable is coded 1 if a treaty provides

---

[16] For developing countries' use of the WTO's dispute settlement mechanism, see Lacarte-Muro and Gappah (2000); on the lack of correlation between legalization and an organization's ability to meet its own goals, see Gray and Slapin (2012); on the ineffectiveness of Asian PTAs despite their high levels of legal provisions, see Ravenhill (2008).

[17] See Koremenos, Lipson, and Snidal (2001); Koremenos (2001, 2005).

[18] See Keohane, Moravsik, and Slaughter (2000); Alter (2000, 2008); McCall Smith (2000); Rosenthal and Voeten (2007); Simmons (2000a); Johns (2009); Johns, Gilligan, and Rosendorff (2009); Busch and Pelc (2010).

[19] Dai (2005); Chapman (2009); Fang (2009).

[20] But see Gray and Slapin (2012).

[21] Dreher and Voight (2008) hypothesize that ratified conventions that promise to protect private property rights should increase credibility for countries; however, they only create data for four organizations.

[22] It would be ideal to have an indicator of the actual effectiveness of those courts rather than what is written down on paper, and indeed empirical studies exist of whether disputes resolved through the WTO, the European Court of Justice, and the International Court of Justice have

no independent third-party review of disputes; 2 if it does provide such a review but is beholden to decisions by political bodies such as a council of ministers; 3 if some version of standard international arbitration exists; and 4 if the agreement establishes a standing tribunal that issues binding rulings. If the hypothesis of enforcement is correct, the expectation here would be that higher levels of legalization would translate into a greater ability for an organization to enforce its own rules, and therefore should decrease risk.

Another way to take into account the possibility of enforcement in a given agreement is by examining whether the agreement has a hegemon. A large body of literature in political science argues that cooperation is more likely when one powerful influential actor undertakes an agreement; that actor is more likely to have both the ability and the willingness to absorb the costs of cooperation, including enforcement of the agreement's rules (Keohane, 1984; Kindleberger, 1986; Simmons, 1996; Milner, 1998; Ikenberry, 2001). Thus, the larger the market relative to others in the reasons, the more likely enforcement would be according to this theory, and risk should decrease.

Controlling for a large market in the agreement speaks to both Alternate Hypotheses 1 and 3. A large market could affect the economic prospects of the agreement, because such a market would act as a target for smaller members' exports. Thus, this variable could be risk-reducing both because of the greater probabilities of agreement enforcement in a large market as well as the welfare benefits that it would potentially bring to all concerned if the agreement involved economic cooperation.

I also include a specification that further tests Alternate Hypothesis 1, that policy reform is driving the result. One might argue that governments can also undertake policy reforms that might not manifest themselves immediately in economic indicators. But investors are still able to see these reform efforts even before their effects kick in – in the passing of legislation, for example, or the announcement of certain measures. So, it is necessary to look at measures of reform that might exist separately from the actual conditions on the ground in a given country.

Reform indices offer a broader look at policies passed despite their levels of implementation. Some researchers have constructed indices for reform that are specific to particular regions, including Eastern Europe (Campos and Horvath, 2006; Kostadinova, 2007) and Latin America (Loayza and Soto, 2003). But detailed and uniform historical indicators for cross-national policy reform are hard to come by. For this next test, I use the Fraser Institute's

---

any subsequent impact on parties' behavior; see, for example, Alter (2008); Boerzel et al. (2010); Busch and Pelc (2010). However, this is only a small subset; many agreements that include these courts do not publish easily accessible records of their cases. Additionally, if these theories are to be believed, there is no gap between the *de jure* and the *de facto* workings of organizations; the legal language of the treaties is equivalent to their effectiveness.

"economic freedom" index (Gwartney and Lawson, 2004). This index groups policy indicators into five categories – size of government; legal structure and security of property rights; access to sound money; exchange with foreigners; and regulation of credit, labor, and business – and weights then to create an overall index value. These data are collected on five-year intervals from 1975 to 2000, and annually thereafter. I use these data for estimation at the annual level and impute missing values using Amelia, through the same procedure described previously.[23]

Table 3.9 demonstrates the performance of the two variables relating to enforcement on the central hypothesis. Model A is the baseline model, repeated again for comparison's sake. Model B includes McCall Smith's (2000) legalization variable, coded high for more levels of legalization. Model C shows the effects of the presence of a *hegemon* – that is, the size of the largest market – in the group, a variable that captures both the degree of enforcement as well as the economic gains that might be reaped from an agreement. Model D includes the reform index for economic liberalization. Models E and F run the full specification, with both region and year fixed effects and a lagged dependent variable, respectively. All of these codings are such that high is positive; thus, if it were the case that investors were reacting to the potential observance of *future* good behavior from countries who belong to organization with a strong potential for enforcement, then the effects of these variables should be negative (risk-reducing) and should wash out the effects of the *company* variable.

It is important to observe that throughout the models, the basic effect of the company a country keeps remains essentially unchanged. The magnitude of the coefficient, its direction (negative), and its statistical significance remain basically unchanged. This indicates that this variable's effects are orthogonal to those proposed by the enforcement hypothesis, and thus I can be confident of investors' distinct assessment of the political quality of members of close organizations.

However, the enforcement variables have effects in the opposite direction of what were expected. The possibilities for dispute settlement in an organization have positive, not negative, impacts on sovereign risk (even though they are not statistically significant). This indicates, again, the bidirectionality of risk that can occur from joining an international organization. Many of the most legalized organizations of the world are also filled with members of low political quality, such as COMESA, SADC, and the Andean Community. Thus, without taking into account the political quality of members, simply estimating the effect of legalization gives us only a partial understanding of the dynamics of international organization.

---

[23] An imputation to extract for quarterly data would have had nearly 85 percent of these data, which is too extreme of a condition for multiple imputation to be feasible.

TABLE 3.9. *Test of Policy Change (H_{a1}), Enforcement (H_{a3}) on Yearly Data*

	(A)	(B)	(C)	(D)	(E)	(F)
Constant	2.156***	2.157***	2.058***	2.243***	2.147***	1.145***
	(0.255)	(0.255)	(0.252)	(0.305)	(0.298)	(0.270)
Current-Account	−0.000	−0.000	−0.000	−0.000	−0.000	−0.000
Balance	(0.000)	(0.000)	(0.000)	(0.000)	(0.000)	(0.000)
Public Debt	0.001	0.001	0.001	0.001	0.001	0.001
	(0.001)	(0.001)	(0.001)	(0.001)	(0.001)	(0.000)
GDP	−0.000***	−0.000***	−0.000***	−0.000***	−0.000***	−0.000***
	(0.000)	(0.000)	(0.000)	(0.000)	(0.000)	(0.000)
Growth	−0.015***	−0.015***	−0.015***	−0.015***	−0.015***	−0.012**
	(0.004)	(0.004)	(0.004)	(0.004)	(0.004)	(0.005)
Inflation	0.000	0.000	0.000	0.000	0.000	0.000
	(0.000)	(0.000)	(0.000)	(0.000)	(0.000)	(0.000)
Exchange Rate	0.000***	0.000***	0.000***	0.000***	0.000***	0.000***
	(0.000)	(0.000)	(0.000)	(0.000)	(0.000)	(0.000)
Reserves	−0.000	−0.000	−0.000	−0.000	−0.000	−0.000
	(0.000)	(0.000)	(0.000)	(0.000)	(0.000)	(0.000)
Portfolio Investment	−0.000	−0.000	−0.000	−0.000	−0.000	−0.000
	(0.000)	(0.000)	(0.000)	(0.000)	(0.000)	(0.000)
Political Risk	−0.006**	−0.006**	−0.006**	−0.006**	−0.006**	−0.003
	(0.003)	(0.003)	(0.002)	(0.003)	(0.002)	(0.002)
Company	0.157***	0.160***	0.078	0.156***	0.081	0.163***
	(0.049)	(0.049)	(0.068)	(0.049)	(0.072)	(0.048)
Proposed Integration	−0.030	−0.027	−0.078**	−0.030	−0.076*	0.028
	(0.023)	(0.024)	(0.037)	(0.024)	(0.040)	(0.026)
Integration*Company	−0.040***	−0.040***	−0.027**	−0.040***	−0.027**	−0.034***
	(0.009)	(0.009)	(0.012)	(0.009)	(0.013)	(0.008)
Dispute Settlement		−0.011			−0.005	−0.002
		(0.020)			(0.021)	(0.019)
Hegemon			0.000*		0.000*	−0.000**
			(0.000)		(0.000)	(0.000)
Reforms				−0.017	−0.017	0.005
				(0.025)	(0.025)	(0.023)
N	3,016	3,016	3,016	3,016	3,016	2912

Dependent variable is logged spreads on sovereign debt (three-year or shortest maturity available). Standard errors in parentheses. OLS regressions across five imputed datasets, fixed effects for region and year. Yearly observations from 1980 to 2007, for 104 countries.
***p < 0.01, **p < 0.05, *p < 0.10.

The variable for hegemony – the size of the largest market – is statistically significant only slightly above the .10 level (p > .102). Its effects, however, are also positive (risk-increasing); when GDP is denominated in tens of thousands of dollars, the coefficient is .024. This also indicates that for emerging markets, simply integrating with other large markets does not give a complete picture on investors' calculation of risk; if that large market is itself of poor political quality, or if others in the group share that distinction, integration can actually increase risk regardless of the economic benefits such integration might bring.

Interestingly, the effect of the Fraser reform index is not statistically different from zero. As before, the main variable of interest, on international organization, retains its negative effect on risk as well as its statistical power. Thus, the alternate hypothesis of changed behavior as a result of IO membership does not seem to be valid. Additionally, the variables for enforcement also do not change the central finding when the sample is broadened to include the 1980s.

As before, I also calculate first differences on the fully specified model (Column D) for the annual data. The magnitudes of change associated with moving each variable from its mean to maxiumum value are equivalent to the earlier finding. The effect on risk of the company of a country keeps, in standardized units, is -3.307 (statistically significant, with a standard error of .803). Contrast this with the effect of a similar change in the Fraser scores (a change of .022, standard error .090). The effect of a strong dispute settlement in the agreement is $-.006$ – a value that is not statistically different from zero (standard error .059). Although the presence of a large market in an agreement is statistically significant, its magnitude in standardized units is far smaller ($-.189$, standard error .08). Substantively, the effects of the company a country keeps remains quite large in comparison to the effects proposed by rival explanations. Here, the variable for the company you keep is second in magnitude of its effect on risk, after a country's exchange rate.

3.5 CONCLUSION

This chapter has demonstrated that, consistent with the core theory, investors in government securities view as less risky those countries that join organizations that promote high levels of closeness among members who score high in terms of political quality. Those investors do not, however, look kindly on countries that propose deep integration among countries where perceived political and economic quality is weak. This result was shown to hold true for 105 emerging markets over the past nearly 30 years.

This finding stands against many rival explanations. Whether an agreement is likely to be enforced – as captured through the level of legalization of an agreement, the presence of a formal court for dispute settlement, or the presence of a large market in an agreement relative to other members – has no impact on the magnitude and the statistical significance of the company a country keeps. Those changes in risk are not the result of changes in member state behavior either before or during their membership in international organizations. Furthermore, the effects of enforcement itself on investor risk are mixed. The effects of close international organization with good-quality members is not simply the result of changes that occur in a country, either as they can be observed in economic indicators or simply in reform efforts.

The substantive impacts of this finding suggest that countries should look closely at the supranational organizations that they enter. In the quarterly sample from 1993 to 2008, the effects of the company a country keeps outweighed many other types of economic indicators; in the annual sample from 1980, those effects trumped equivalent changes in eight other economic and political variables. This indicates that in some circumstances, international organization is a more important consideration for investors than domestic policy or economic conditions.

This chapter shows that markets respond most strongly to agreements that bind countries to states that have a relative degree of political and economic stability. That is, where the level of proposed integration is high, markets pay particular attention to the types of members in an organization. It is telling that markets seem to care less about the contents of an organization's legal language or the level of proposed integration in and of themselves. Rather, markets are most responsive to the political and economic quality of the countries that claim to be closely bound in terms of their economic ties. Interestingly, markets seem indifferent to whether the proposed levels of trade actually materialize. What matters is the membership content behind the proposed grand unions.

The issue of the effectiveness of these agreements – in terms of their ability to meet their goals, whether those goals are economic or political – is relevant here. If investors are rational and perfectly informed, we might expect them to evaluate organizations on the basis of their competencies and the changes they promote in member states. However, the heuristic at work here is a bit more complicated. Because investors are aware of other investors' perceptions of these organizations, they actually have little incentive to evaluate these organizations in detail in terms of their effectiveness. What they look for instead are easily identifiable clues about the associations that countries are making on the international stage. The depth of proposed integration and the type of other members are two such clues; details about their effectiveness are secondary concerns, and can be picked up in more easily identifiable indicators about the country themselves (such as increases in economic product as a result of trade, or fewer external conflicts). Thus, the issue of the effectiveness of the agreements should manifest itself to investors in country-level statistics, not in details on the organization itself.

It is possible that changes in the level of perceived risk could be a reaction not to any actual new information about a country, but rather to the information available to other investors. The pricing of an investment has much to do with its attractiveness to other potential investors. Thus, membership in international organizations could simply send a signal, in one direction or another, about the mainstreaming of a country into or out of the developed world. As discussed earlier, it is not strictly rational for markets to evaluate countries on this basis, in the sense that international organizations – particularly those whose proposed levels of integration do not match the actual levels of integration – do not consistently transmit political or economic instability to their members. Instead, investors seem to be taking their cues not from the reality of the economic and political situation on the ground in emerging markets, but rather from the more visible configurations of countries. As in the Keynesian beauty contest described in Chapter 2, investors perhaps anticipate the reactions of other investors by taking stock of the company a country keeps.

This chapter has focused on the generalizability of the core theory. There is a tradeoff between establishing that the effect of IO membership on risk cuts across countries and over time and examining the dynamics of that effect in close view. This chapter errs on the side of the former, leveraging large-N statistical evidence to demonstrate the external validity and generalizability of the central hypothesis. Thus, it is limited in terms of its ability to test many of the observable implications of that hypothesis. The methods used in this chapter cannot tell us much about the dynamics of membership in a given organization. Because organizations differ so profoundly in their missions, design, and scope, these broader tests can provide only basic ways of distinguishing among the characteristics of international organizations. As such, these tests are merely the first piece of empirical evidence that demonstrates an aggregate effect of certain types of IO membership across countries and across time. I leave more detailed mechanism testing to subsequent chapters, with examinations of the duration of market reactions to specific events that indicated risk-prone behavior on the part of members, as well as a more careful modeling of the selection process that countries undergo in order to gain entry into some organizations. As such, the testing of precise mechanisms was sacrificed for the sake of establishing the overall applicability, across different regions of the world. The following chapter employs statistical as well as qualitative evidence to establish some of the micro-level processes that underlie this finding.

3.6 APPENDIX

TABLE 3.10. *Summary Statistics for (Unlogged) Spread on Sovereign Debt*

Country	Mean	SD	Min	Max
Albania	10.63	7.26	1.53	29.50
Algeria	3.83	4.20	−2.00	11.74
Angola	60.78	65.17	−5.20	306.30
Argentina	6.52	12.09	−0.30	64.82
Armenia	19.43	17.95	2.88	92.40
Azerbaijan	30.50	87.20	5.53	536.03
Bahrain	0.72	0.43	−0.67	1.35
Belarus	42.77	53.62	2.95	243.88
Belize	6.35	0.93	4.55	8.09
Benin	−0.76	1.36	−2.42	2.21
Bolivia	9.00	2.27	4.19	14.21
Bosnia and Hercegovina	17.57	20.31	−0.58	79.64
Botswana	7.74	1.99	4.99	11.43
Brazil	568.41	1966.38	15.45	11602.72
Bulgaria	27.61	63.46	−1.12	348.48
Burkina Faso	−1.05	1.47	−2.94	1.71
Burundi	8.63	3.49	3.36	14.87
Cambodia	5.99	1.38	3.11	7.76
Cameroon	5.67	1.93	3.69	8.75
Cape Verde	2.88	1.66	0.63	6.00
Chad	5.29	1.70	2.23	9.24
Chile	5.15	5.48	−0.16	24.71
China	0.84	2.65	−3.08	6.50
Colombia	15.09	10.23	2.41	33.16
Congo (Brazzaville)	7.11	1.55	3.58	9.24
Costa Rica	17.88	4.62	5.54	28.28
Croatia	72.89	303.03	−1.37	1612.41
Cyprus	−0.66	1.27	−3.30	1.32
Czech Republic	1.65	3.07	−2.89	8.28
Dominican Republic	14.83	5.24	4.93	25.99
Ecuador	4.04	2.44	−0.30	9.06
Egypt	5.82	2.16	1.76	10.95
El Salvador	5.23	4.07	−0.02	13.63
Equatorial Guinea	5.29	1.70	2.23	9.24
Estonia	2.60	5.09	−2.13	23.14
Ethiopia	1.82	3.04	−2.39	8.02
Georgia	19.03	11.64	6.34	61.19
Ghana	20.40	9.24	2.96	34.40
Greece	4.54	6.22	−2.28	19.16
Guatemala	6.50	3.17	2.55	14.88
Guinea	10.37	3.14	3.86	17.43

(continued)

TABLE 3.10 *(continued)*

Country	Mean	SD	Min	Max
Guyana	5.64	2.99	1.07	14.99
Haiti	12.67	4.35	5.37	21.92
Hong Kong	−0.51	0.89	−2.10	3.02
Hungary	9.20	6.43	0.85	22.64
India	5.69	2.97	1.42	13.01
Indonesia	11.48	9.05	3.12	45.18
Iran	8.78	2.02	5.71	11.78
Israel	2.50	2.24	−1.49	7.23
Ivory Coast	−0.73	1.37	−2.42	2.21
Jamaica	19.91	9.63	8.20	44.42
Jordan	2.67	1.27	0.46	4.91
Kazakhstan	3.53	3.74	−1.32	13.74
Kenya	11.60	9.39	2.28	43.81
Kuwait	0.87	0.68	−0.01	3.51
Kyrgyz Republic	20.86	15.22	3.72	55.28
Laos	15.00	2.88	9.38	20.95
Latvia	6.76	12.45	−1.49	49.59
Lebanon	9.74	4.90	3.13	22.85
Lesotho	6.13	2.39	1.85	11.46
Libya	−0.27	1.45	−2.46	2.13
Lithuania	11.70	24.90	−2.28	97.06
Macedonia	17.74	47.16	0.79	352.07
Madagascar	15.31	3.35	4.50	23.70
Malawi	26.00	10.58	8.23	42.51
Malaysia	0.38	1.61	−2.08	4.40
Malta	−0.09	1.13	−1.85	1.90
Mauritius	7.30	1.27	4.86	9.73
Mexico	11.10	11.28	0.47	54.61
Moldova	16.39	6.96	6.48	28.95
Morocco	1.91	2.08	−2.60	5.18
Mozambique	14.29	8.41	6.10	36.13
Myanmar	6.83	1.38	3.75	8.89
Namibia	6.83	2.62	2.04	13.05
Nicaragua	12.18	3.18	3.59	16.64
Nigeria	10.59	4.60	5.30	23.46
Oman	1.69	1.16	−0.47	3.62
Pakistan	3.19	2.38	−0.74	8.99
Panama	2.53	1.25	0.14	4.89
Papua New Guinea	4.89	3.77	−0.33	11.94
Paraguay	3.00	70.53	0.11	112.91
Peru	12.90	9.46	4.36	53.36
Philippines	5.30	2.78	−1.05	12.19
Poland	10.95	9.82	−1.63	31.23
Portugal	−0.06	1.84	−2.28	5.77

Country	Mean	SD	Min	Max
Qatar	−0.72	0.88	−1.62	3.15
Romania	32.23	23.60	0.69	100.24
Russia	26.94	30.46	0.83	125.42
Rwanda	3.73	2.22	0.34	7.45
Sao Tome and Principe	24.70	9.10	12.86	45.73
Senegal	−0.76	1.36	−2.42	2.21
Seychelles	3.35	2.63	−0.66	8.34
Singapore	−1.71	1.01	−3.48	−0.06
Slovakia	4.87	4.08	−1.13	14.16
Slovenia	7.50	9.68	−1.66	43.11
South Africa	7.24	2.75	2.16	14.44
South Korea	2.57	2.68	−0.91	12.90
Sri Lanka	9.11	4.60	4.17	30.55
Swaziland	4.79	2.47	0.43	9.82
Syria	3.62	1.52	1.83	6.48
Taiwan	−0.60	1.48	−3.61	2.59
Tajikistan	13.76	10.17	4.91	49.20
Tanzania	10.66	8.21	3.92	30.72
Thailand	1.57	3.21	−2.93	9.69
The Gambia	13.37	5.01	8.37	26.65
Togo	−1.05	1.47	−2.94	1.71
Tunisia	1.41	1.82	−1.25	6.33
Turkey	51.33	31.22	10.86	154.34
Uganda	9.95	2.36	6.40	17.36
Ukraine	44.96	68.85	1.96	315.59
Uruguay	3.98	86.35	0.11	146.87
Uzbekistan	19.99	8.45	8.06	30.39
Venezuela	18.81	14.26	4.01	59.35
Vietnam	4.24	3.33	−0.68	13.75
Yugoslavia	12.20	9.76	1.20	42.12
Zambia	31.48	25.03	7.11	126.15
Zimbabwe	83.39	105.12	15.46	467.82

TABLE 3.11. *Test of Endogeneity (H_{a2}): Instrumental Variables Regression*

	First Stage	Second Stage
Constant	−4.038	0.928
	(0.257)	(0.691)
Current-account	0.000	−0.000**
balance	(0.000)	(0.000)
Public debt	−0.005	−0.001
	(0.001)	(0.001)
GDP	0.000	0.000
	(0.000)	(0.000)
Growth	0.016	−0.012**
	(0.007)	(0.005)
Inflation	0.000	0.000
	(0.000)	(0.000)
Exchange	0.000	0.000***
rate	(0.000)	(0.000)
Reserves	0.000	0.000
	(0.000)	(0.000)
Portfolio	0.000	−0.000
investment	(0.000)	(0.000)
Domestic	−0.010	−0.008**
political quality	(0.005	(0.003)
Company	5.324	1.504*
	(0.071	(0.807)
Proposed integration	1.427	0.335
	(0.058	(0.215)
Company*Integration	−.544**	−0.294*
	(0.567)	(0.151)
Exports	0.001	
	(0.000)	
Corruption	−0.153	
	(0.056)	
Bureaucracy	0.008	
	(0.064)	

Dependent variable is logged spreads on sovereign debt (three-year or short-est maturity available). Two-stage instrumental variables regression. Standard errors in parentheses. Yearly observations from 1980 to 2007, for 104 countries. ***p < 0.01, **p < 0.05, *p < 0.10 Partial R-squared of excluded instruments: 0.002. Test of excluded instruments $F(3, 2960) = 2.35$, Prob > F = 0.07. Anderson likelihood ratio statistic for underidentification 6.49, p-value 0.09. Hansen J statistic for overidentification 0.621, p-value 0.733. N = 3016.

4

The Effects of Good Company[*]

How do investors react when emerging markets sign onto groups with good members? And is it possible to be reasonably sure that it is indeed the members themselves, and not other aspects of the group, that are driving the changes in investor perception? This chapter focuses on the bright side of the central theory – those occasions when the company a country keeps instills confidence in investors. The tests here reestablish, and subsequently unpack, evidence in favor of the central hypothesis: that economic association with good-quality members makes emerging markets look less risky.

The EU makes for a good test case because it has, throughout its history, varied on both of the dimensions described in the central hypothesis. First, it has seen different strengths of the "good company" it has offered in terms of the asymmetry of those members joining – think of the accession of Portugal, Spain, and Greece to a politically stable EU in the 1980s, versus the possible membership of Turkey or Macedonia today to a twenty-seven-member EU with much greater diversity in terms of members' political quality. Second, the intensity of those associations have also varied, from full-on integration into the EU, to weaker association agreements through the European Neighborhood Policy, to proposed free-trade areas (the Economic Partnership Arrangements).[1] Examining the impacts on investor risk of these naturally occurring variations will afford a better understanding of the dynamics of the company a country keeps. Additionally, detailed information about its accession processes makes it possible to take a closer look at the alternate mechanisms through which IOs could potentially impact risk.

[*] This chapter draws from Gray, Julia. "International Organization as a Seal of Approval: European Union Accession and Investor Risk." *American Journal of Political Science* 53(4), 931–949.
[1] These agreements are examined in Chapter 6.

This chapter proceeds as follows. In a further test of the central hypothesis, I first establish empirically that EU integration is associated with drops in risk for all rounds of EU expansion, although the strongest effects were seen in the postcommunist countries. This fits with the theory, in that the postcommunist countries were less of a known quantity than the Western European countries – that is, the uncertainty surrounding their trajectories was higher than for any other group of countries negotiating with the EU. The subsequent sections take on the possible mechanisms underlying this effect, using the postcommunist countries as a sample. The impact comes when Brussels sends public signals that policy reform in accession countries meets EU standards – even if that reform had already taken place well in advance. Once the EU endorses a country's policies, market expectations for that country's performance converge. Interestingly, this suggests that markets pay less attention to the actual path of reform than to the EU pronouncements on it. Thus, the things that countries have to do to join the EU matter less than the signal from the institution.

This chapter also tests each of the alternate hypotheses. Controlling for preexisting policy reform (H_{a1}) does not detract substantially from the previously observed drops in risk associated with EU negotiations. The problem of selection (H_{a2}) is addressed by using instrumental variables to model first the probability that a country will be asked to open negotiations with the EU. The number of UNESCO World Heritage sites, the level of domestic-language movie production, its distance from the West, and civil liberties proxy for a nation's proclivity to join the EU. Instead, markets react primarily when it becomes public that the EU has validated country's reform efforts. Investors take countries' policy reforms seriously once they are endorsed by the EU. Controlling for the percentage of economic chapters of the *acquis communautaire* of which the EU has approved swamps the previous effects of advancing through stages of EU negotiation. This indicates that policy endorsements from the EU allow investors' expectations to converge – a finding that elucidates some of the psychology behind the heuristic of the company a country keeps.

The drops in risk, however, have proven not to be entirely warranted. I further examine the possibility that markets are anticipating the enforcement of rules once countries enter the EU (H_{a3}). Looking at the case of the EU holds the level of proposed integration constant; the EU has one of the highest levels of de jure integration of all other international organizations. However, the crisis in the eurozone shows that member governments had long ducked EU rules. But interestingly, even in the face of clear information that countries were not abiding by EU rules – including the economic targets laid out in the Stability and Growth Pact as well as Hungary's budget crisis in 2006 – market assessment of risk in the backsliding countries remained more or less unchanged. This is an indication of the circumstances leading up to the 2007 financial crisis, where markets proved to be overly reliant on shortcuts in their calculations of country risk. Taken together, these tests demonstrate in a more detailed manner the findings from the previous chapter: that institutions reassure markets not necessarily because of changes that occur in countries, but simply as a seal of approval from better-quality members.

I also examine what happens when the EU offers the prospect of looser integration with countries in Eastern Europe and North Africa, through the European Neighborhood Policy (ENP). First promoted in 2002, the ENP was supposed to offer nonmembers "everything but institutions"[2] – meaning that participants would receive the same treatment and economic advantages of EU members, but they could not participation in EU institutions (Kelley, 2006b). Essentially, this is a case where the "company" is the same, but the level of proposed integration varies – though, crucially, along a political more than an economic dimension. In this circumstance, markets do not react in a uniform manner – another indication that the economics of these agreements matters less than the politics.

4.1 INVESTOR RISK AND EU ENLARGEMENT

The EU has expanded its borders drastically since its inception. Belgium, France, Germany, Italy, Luxembourg, and the Netherlands formed the original European Economic Community in 1958, with Denmark, Ireland, and the United Kingdom joining in 1973. Greece joined in 1981, and Portugal and Spain in 1986. What was by 1995 known as the European Union then admitted Austria, Finland, and Sweden. The year 2004 saw the most sizeable enlargement, with ten countries, most from the former communist bloc – the Czech Republic, Cyprus, Estonia, Hungary, Latvia, Lithuania, Malta, Poland, Slovakia, and Slovenia – becoming new members. Romania and Bulgaria were originally slated to be part of that enlargement round but ultimately joined in 2007. Official talks have been opened with Croatia (which is slated to join in 2013), Macedonia, and Turkey, with discussion underway on including Albania, Bosnia and Herzegovina, Iceland, Serbia, and Montenegro.

Initially set up as a facilitator of free trade, the EU has evolved into an institution of joint governance, setting common policies not only in economic areas including agriculture, fisheries, and trade policies, but also in spheres such as cultural programs, social standards, foreign policy, and human rights. Joining the organization brings the expectation of not only policy harmonization but – at least for relatively poorer countries – future levels of growth and development delivered by the common market (Schimmelfennig and Sedelmeier, 2005; Vachudová, 2005). Many have written about the benefits of EU accession, though there is disagreement as to the extent to which member states reliably implement EU policies – a matter that the recent eurozone crisis has amplified. Some researchers (Brada and Kutan, 2001; Cappelen et al., 2003) have

---

[2] This was a promise made by then-Commission President Romano Prodi, in a speech to the Sixth ECSA-World Conference in Brussels, 5–6 December 2002.

demonstrated convergence of various economic as well as sociopolitical indicators for EU entrants.[3] However, others argue that economic convergence has not occurred at either the monetary or the fiscal policy levels (Garrett, 2004; Bearce, 2007), and the 2007 financial crisis and the subsequent vulnerabilities in government finances as well as fiscal policies more generally put the notion of convergence in serious doubt.

However, for most of the postcommunist countries that began official negotiation with the European Union, the impact was immediate in at least one respect: investor risk premiums and yields on government bonds dropped almost as soon as Brussels announced their official candidacy, and the fluctuation of yields on those instruments dropped as well – meaning that more and more investors converged onto similar estimates of that country's default risk. For example, from the time that Croatia signed the EU's Stabilization and Association Agreement in October 2001 to the time that it officially opened negotiations in October 2005, spreads on its Eurobonds against German notes dropped from 170 to 28 basis points apart. Croatian National Bank officials credit the drop solely to credible entry into the EU; one claims that "yields were very much elastic toward positive signals from Brussels. . . . Croatian bonds were almost junk bonds until the EU started taking us seriously."[4]

To illustrate this point more vividly, take the case of Slovakia. After the dissolution of Czechoslovakia in 1992, the country was ruled by the autocratic Vladimir Mečiar, notorious for corruption, especially with respect to privatization of the country's formerly state-owned industries. As soon as a pro-reform coalition ousted Mečiar in November 1998, yields on Slovak sovereign debt fell by nearly 7 percentage points. But risk perceptions continued to fluctuate until a year and a half later, when Brussels opened negotiations for membership in October 1999. From that time forward, yields dropped and the variance around those yields tightened – from standard deviations of 2.21 after negotiations began compared with 5.77 in the pre-negotiation period. Not only were investors inclined to regard Slovakia as being less risky, but their assessments did not change dramatically in the period thereafter, particularly when compared with the pre-EU period for those countries, where yields would fluctuate within a 15-percentage-point band. All told, Slovakia's default risk dropped by 11 percentage points from the first formal move by Brussels to the time of full membership, and the difference in means between those two time periods (pre- and post-EU accession) was 9.65 percentage points (standard error 3.55).

---

[3] See Boerzel (2001), who argues that on the whole, compliance within the EU is strong, and that instances of noncompliance are statistical artefacts, and similarly, Levitz and Pop-Eleches (2010a,b); Cortell and Jr. (1996); Checkel (2001); Risse, Ropp, and Sikkink (1999); Underdal (1998).

[4] Interviews, Ivan Hulják and Lidija Popović, both of the Croatian National Bank, 5 and 6 July, 2006.

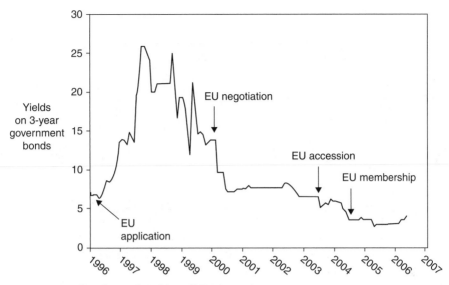

FIGURE 4.1. Slovak Bond Yields and EU Accession.

Figure 4.1 illustrates the change in spreads of sovereign debt for Slovakia during that time period. Note that the pattern described in the preceding paragraph, where risk drops in accordance with progress along the road to EU membership, is visible even in this single series. For Slovakia, the biggest drop seems to have occurred between the stages of negotiation – when the EU formally opens discussion on chapters of the *acquis* – and accession, when countries ratify EU treaties into domestic law, and where EU members approve a country's accession in their own assemblies.

Of course, many things happen to countries such as Slovakia in the run-up to EU negotiations. As described in the hypotheses in Chapter 2, they are also taking concrete steps to reform their economies, which would have an impact on their ability to service their debt. Furthermore, certain types of countries may be more likely to be picked for entry by the EU in the first place. But if there was still an impact of EU negotiations that went beyond those two possibilities, it would indicate what sort of signal international organizations actually send to investors. The sections that follow explore these possible mechanisms in more depth.

4.2 DATA ANALYSIS: AGGREGATE EFFECTS OF THE EU AS GOOD COMPANY

The central hypothesis suggests that the debt instruments of EU candidate countries began performing differently once they began talks with the EU. This section sets out to establish this proposition empirically. First I test whether

TABLE 4.1. *Test for Structural Breaks at Time of EU Accession*

EU Entry	Test Statistic	Coefficient on Break
1980s (n = 120)	−1.99*	−8.04*** (2.28)
1990s (n = 120)	1.38	−.47 (.29)
2004 (n = 72)	−5.78***	−14.38*** (3.15)

the bond instruments for countries that have recently signed onto the EU experience a structural break, using a commonly used procedure outlined by Perron (1989). This test helps establish that a character of an asset changes fundamentally after a given moment (here, EU negotiation). In this test, the null hypothesis is that no structural break exists; instead, the series can be described by a unit root and a constant rate of drift. The alternate hypothesis proposes a trend-stationary series structural break at time t_b. The Perron test allows researchers to exogenously specify t_b – in this case, set to be the date of opening accession negotiations with the EU. The test statistic on the coefficient serves to establish the validity of the unit-root hypothesis.

Table 4.1 indicates the presence or absence of a structural break for quarterly spreads on three-year sovereign debt for countries that negotiated for EU accession in the 1980s (Greece, Portugal, and Spain), the 1990s (Sweden, Austria, and Finland), and then the "big bang" of 2004, with eight postcommunist countries plus Cyprus and Malta. For ease of interpretation, I collapse these series into averages, setting each country's year of opening negotiations as the proposed year of the structural break. Standard errors are in parentheses.

The strongest evidence by far of a structural break in the series is seen in the postcommunist countries that fully acceded to the EU in 2004. Greece, Spain, and Portugal also experienced a structural break, after which the series shifted to lower levels of risk, but there is little evidence of such a break in the Scandinavian countries and Austria. This confirms the justification of the research design stated in the earlier chapters: that the effects of integrating with international institutions are felt more strongly in developing countries, where information is noisier. Because the postcommunist countries were less of a known quantity, markets were more sensitive to information from the EU regarding their candidacy.

I next use a more elaborate specification to examine these effects in detail. The dependent variable here is *logged spreads on three-year sovereign debt*, differentiated against German sovereigns of the same maturity. Using spreads takes into account not only overall market fluctuations and euro-dollar exchange rate risk, but also Europe-level shocks, such as the ERM crisis of the early 1990s and the Russian rouble crisis of 1998, both of which impacted German yields. The variable is logged to better approximate a normal distribution.

The estimations also include variables for the stage at which countries are invited to apply for EU membership. Formal EU accession is a four-stage process. First, the EU must invite a country to apply for membership; no country can apply without being invited to do so. Then the EU approves an applicant to enter the negotiation stage, which I describe in further detail later. After a country and the EU successfully close negotiations over all the relevant policy areas, the country enters the accession period, in which a country ratifies EU treaties into its own domestic legal system, and the EU in turn formally approves a country's membership. The applicant subsequently becomes a full member at a formal date after this process is completed.

The EU makes its clearest pronouncement on the state of a country's economy during the negotiation of chapters of the *acquis communautaire*. After a "screening" period in which the Commission explains the details of the *acquis* to a candidate, that country's ministers or deputies justify their degree of preparedness in the chapter in question. Negotiating to close chapters centers on the harmonization of domestic legislation with the EU's body of law. After the EU and the candidate country have agreed on the terms of the individual chapter of the negotiations, including any exceptions and a timetable for implementaiton, that chapter is considered closed. The process can take anywhere from a few months to two years; countries that are better prepared in a given area can move more quickly through some chapters than others. Glenn (2004) argues that despite applicants' divergent levels of preparedness and varying speeds of negotiations, negotiations on the adoption of the *acquis* have been "unexpectedly uniform."

Closing chapters of the *acquis* is ostensibly a technical, rather than a political, process that is carried out by experts in the Commission, whose mandate is enlargement, and any political delays or obstructions have usually been the result of objections from member states, not from the Commission itself.[5] Because the order in which specific chapters are negotiated is not fixed, any politicking tends to be reserved for the opening of chapters that are the subject of political sensitivities between applicants and member states, and economic chapters (with the possible exception of free movement of people) have tended not to fall in this category (Schneider, 2009).

Recent studies have shown that a country's level of democracy as well as its progress in market reforms help determine whether it will apply for EU

---

[5] Although some have argued that the EU chapters are too general to be suitable for objective assessment (Grabbe, 2002), little quantitative work has fully analyzed this proposition. An exception is Hille and Knill (2006), who find that bureaucratic efficiency on the part of candidate countries is a better predictor of advancement in the *acquis* than politics (veto points). Admittedly, the suspension of Turkey's negotiations in 2007 was certainly a political decision, reflecting widespread anxiety amid EU public opinion about the pace of enlargement, even though the ostensible reason was a ports dispute with Cyprus. But for the postcommunist countries, political will for enlargement was stronger, and the chapter negotiations are generally believed to have been more technocratic.

accession, while the EU's decision to accept those countries only takes place after the EU evaluates the reform process in applicant countries imposed by the *acquis* (Plümper and Mattli, 2002; Plümper, Schneider, and Troeger, 2005). This points to the extent of reform that countries undertake *prior* to opening negotiations with Brussels. Even though countries enact significant policy reforms in the run-up to formal EU negotiations, the EU's acceptance of those reforms is a far clearer signal for investors. Thus, there is already a theoretical reason to believe that the negotiations stage might carry more weight with investors than the other stages of the EU accession process.

4.3 EVIDENCE FOR THE COMPANY YOU KEEP (H₁)

This section establishes systematically that risk perceptions lower – and variance of those perceptions tighten – when countries initially sign on to the European Union. I code the EU variables as indicator variables at the beginning of each of the four stages of accession. These variables are: *EU apply*, when a country is first invited to apply for membership; the start of official negotiations, during which chapters of the *acquis communautaire* are closed (*EU negotiate*); the accession stage, where countries ratify EU legislation into their own domestic legal systems (*EU accession*); and full membership (*EU membership*). All of these variables receive a value of 1 for each country and quarter when a particular stage is initiated, as well as for years thereafter, such that coefficients on each variable represent the added effect of each new stage of membership, given advancement from a previous stage. Variables change their codes at the beginning of each step in the process.

Because different stages of EU accession can be expected to reduce not just the levels of risk but also the variance, I show an ARCH-in-means model, as described by Engle, Lilien, and Robins (1987). In this model, a variant of the autoregressive conditional heteroskedasticity (ARCH) model, the determinants of both the mean and the variance of an asset can be specified, and the point estimates of the mean are a function of the conditional variance σ_ε, or the standard deviation of the error term, as well as other covariates.[6] This is in accord with the literature in international finance on sovereign debt yields; investors often demand higher yields as a function of an asset's past volatility.[7]

---

[6] See Leblang and Bernard (2006); Stasavage (2007) for political-science applications of ARCH and GARCH models.

[7] Specifically, ARCH-in-means models assume serial correlation in the variance of the series, which is addressed by the inclusion of a term for past squared realizations of the error (the ARCH(1) term, ε_{t-1}^2) as well as of the variance (the GARCH(1) term, or σ_{t-1}^2). Thus, the equation for the point estimate of the mean is $\mu_t = \beta_0 + \beta\sqrt{\mathrm{Var}[\varepsilon_t|\varepsilon_{t-1}]}$, where $\mathrm{Var}[\varepsilon_t|\varepsilon_{t-1}] = \gamma_0 + \gamma_1\varepsilon_{t-1}^2$. Notation taken from Stasavage (2007).

Table 4.2 shows the effects of each stage of EU membership for subsamples of the data.[8] The results are broken down into four groups in an attempt to investigate whether EU candidacy might have had different effects in different times, regions, or types of countries. First is the full sample. Second are Greece, Portugal, and Spain, which joined in the mid-1980s. Third are Austria, Norway, Finland, and Sweden, which opened EU talks in the early 1990s.[9] Third are the countries that were part of the "big bang" of expansion in 2004, including the Czech Republic, Cyprus, Estonia, Latvia, Lithuania, Malta, Hungary, Poland, Slovakia, and Slovenia.

When reading the coefficients, recall that positive values indicate higher levels of investor risk (higher yields), whereas negative values indicate factors that decrease risk (lower yields). As predicted in most of the literature on emerging-market assets, the debt yields of the economy to which that country is most linked – in this case, Germany – has a strong and significant effect on yields for the subsidiary economy; higher German yields are associated with higher yields in EU entrants. Inflation also has a strong and statistically significant effect on candidate country yields; more inflation makes a country look less risky. The coefficient on reserves varies across the specifications; in the full model, higher levels of reserves are associated with drops in lending risk, a statistically significant effect. However, that effect is lost when considering the individual rounds of selection; in some cases the sign even reverses. Similarly, the coefficients on overall volumes of debt and on current-account balances are not statistically significant in any of the models, with the sign switching in different specifications.

Note, however, the equation for point estimates of the mean of an asset in the variables for each of the stages of EU entry. Unsurprisingly, the variable for EU application is insignificant in all of the models: Turkey, for example, was in the application stage for around 20 years. The statistically significant effects begin at the EU negotiation stage, which until recently had meant the start of an irreversible process of EU entry. Additional effects are seen at the accession stage. EU membership is not associated with the mean equation (which gives point estimate for yields) but rather with the variance of yields. Thus, once countries experience the drops in risk at the accession and negotiation stages, they see little further decrease in their levels of risk, but decreases in variance once they become members in the full sample.

Additionally, note that for the Mediterranean countries, the statistically significant effects are most pronounced in the variance equation. This corresponds

[8] Data are quarterly, from 1970 to 2006, for thirty-nine accession countries in Eastern and Western Europe: Albania, Austria, Belarus, Belgium, Bosnia and Herzegovina, Bulgaria, Croatia, Cyprus, the Czech Republic, Denmark, Estonia, Finland, France, Germany, Greece, Hungary, Iceland, Ireland, Italy, Latvia, Lithuania, Luxembourg, Macedonia, Malta, Moldova, Netherlands, Norway, Poland, Portugal, Romania, Russia, Slovakia, Slovenia, Spain, Sweden, Switzerland, Turkey, Ukraine, and the United Kingdom.

[9] All but Norway became full members; Norway officially opened negotiations but later withdrew.

TABLE 4.2. *Effect of EU Candidacy*

Variable	Base	Full	1980s	1990s	2004
Constant	2.08***	1.86***	1.94***	1.94***	1.41***
	(.17)	(.18)	(.17)	(.32)	(.30)
German debt	.08***	.09***	.07	.06***	.21***
	(.008)	(.008)	(.10)	(.006)	(.04)
Inflation	.003***	.002**	.01	.01	.0009***
	(.001)	(.001)	(.003)	(.003)	(.0004)
Reserves	−.03***	−.04	.42***	−.04	.02
	(.01)	(.01)	(.19)	(.19)	(.14)
Debt liabilities	−.002	−.003	.002	.01	.30***
	(.002)	(.002)	(.008)	(.02)	(.11)
Current account	−.004	−.001	.004	−.03	−.25
	(.008)	(.008)	(.02)	(.02)	(.18)
EU application	−	−.03	.03	.001	−.15
		(.03)	(.03)	(.09)	(.11)
EU negotiation	−	−.09***	−.07	−.02	−.40***
		(.04)	(.06)	(.09)	(.02)
EU accession	−	−.10**	−.05	.06	−.51***
		(.05)	(.08)	(.10)	(.18)
EU membership	−	−.01	−.03***	.01	−.04
		(.01)	(.10)	(.04)	(.05)
σ	−	−.01	−.35	9.69***	−.05
		(.03)	(.29)	(2.46)	(.25)
Variance Equation					
EU negotiation	−	−.28	−3.76***	−2.84	−1.37***
		(.62)	(.60)	(4.13)	(.60)
EU accession	−	.61	−3.73	−17.73***	−2.40***
		(.88)	(2.29)	(1.45)	(1.11)
EU membership	−	−1.77***	−.24	19.85	−.04
		(.71)	(2.25)	(12.14)	(.05)
constant	−	−5.60***	−1.66***	−10.95***	−3.75***
		(.69)	(.59)	(1.40)	(.54)
ARCH(1)	1.31	1.21	.69	.16	.34
	(.26)	(.27)	(.13)	(.04)	(.22)
GARCH(1)	.27	.25	−.02	.86	.44
	(.10)	(.08)	(.02)	(.03)	(.14)
AR	.97	.97	.98	.98	.95
	(.01)	(.01)	(.007)	(.008)	(.02)
MA	.25	.25	.37	.33	.20
	(.04)	(.04)	(.62)	(.06)	(.09)
N	1879	1879	291	413	342
LL	1389.78	1393.77	328.34	537.68	42.78
χ^2	12481.51	21701.48	26768.15	15035.01	4014.97
Prob χ^2	0.0	0.0	0.0	0.0	0.0

Dependent variable is the natural log of yields on government bonds, quarterly from 1970 to 2005. Pooled ARCH-in-means regressions with robust standard errors in parentheses; region fixed effects.

TABLE 4.3. *Effects of One SD Change of Independent Variables on Sovereign Spreads*

Variable	Full Sample	Mid-80s	Early 90s	2004
Debt liabilities	−0.01	0.01	0.02	0.24
Reserves	−0.12	−0.11	0.06	0.07
Current account	0.00	0.02	−0.07	−0.41
Inflation	14.44	−0.34	−0.19	1.47
German yields	−4.32	−3.45	−2.77	−11.29
EU apply	−0.42	−0.81	0.01	−2.41
EU negotiate	−1.47	−1.31	−0.27	−7.40
EU accession	−2.53	−1.62	0.42	−11.49
EU membership	−2.67	−7.78	0.53	−11.72

to what might be expected in the long run for countries that join the EU. Even if there was somewhat less of a drop in the mean levels of risk, there was far less deviation in what investors perceived about these countries after they joined the EU. This lends strong support to the institutional theories laid out in Chapter 2. Not only do those relatively high-risk countries that have been in the EU for several decades look less risky after joining, but there is also marked convergence – specifically, decreased variance – in investors' perceptions of their risk level.

To make comparisons across variables easier, given that all are measured in different units, Table 4.3 shows the expected results of a change in one standard deviation of each of the independent variables. The stages of EU talks, however, are measured as a change from 0 (not active) to 1 (active).

Across time, the rounds of enlargement had strikingly different effects. For the Mediterranean countries, the biggest effect was seen once they became full members, with drops in risk substantively far greater than any of the non-EU independent variables. The effect of joining the EU is about three times the magnitude of changes in the market for German securities. The total effect of joining, from start to finish, is a decrease in yields of 10.70 percentage points.

Additionally, the round of enlargement in the early 1990s, where Austria, Sweden, and Finland joined, sees the smallest effects – in total, the effects added together from the time of negotiation add up only to an *increase* in yields by 0.69. This could be a function of the relatively low yields in those countries even prior to their dealings with the EU. Because they were less risky at the outset, they also had less far to fall in terms of their risk assessment.

The effect is greatest by far in the postcommunist countries. Starting with the negotiation stage, advancing along the road to the EU is accompanied by drops in risk – the whole process after negotiation is associated with decreases in yields by 30.61, a huge drop for investment data. To compare, during the onset of the Russian rouble crisis in 1998, yields went from 16.51 in July to 48.62 in August, a change of almost identical magnitude (though in the opposite direction). Next to changes in German yields, advancing in the stages of negotiation with the EU has a stronger substantive impact on risk than any other economic fundamental. For Bulgaria, a country with around average economic fundamentals as well as average risk, opening negotiations with the EU gives it the same risk rating as Portugal's in 2007. This indicates that signing into the EU did not altogether erase the perceived risk associated with new members, but it brings them to the level of the lower tier of preexisting EU members in terms of risk levels.

4.4 EFFECTS FOR POSTCOMMUNIST COUNTRIES

I now turn to the possible mechanisms behind this effect, through an examination of the former command economies of Eastern Europe. The postcommunist countries are a particularly good test case for examining the engines behind the changes in investor perceptions as a result of EU negotiations. First, even though all of them had varying levels of wealth and economic conditions, they emerged from the command economies with a need to undertake similar policy reforms at around the same time (Basu, Estrin, and Svejnar, 2000). Secondly, the time at which many of them were applying to the EU coincided with a consolidation of opinion in Brussels of the need to exercise stronger conditionality on accessor countries – indeed, this decision was spurred in large part by the number of politically diverse and poorer countries lining up for EU admission (Vachudová, 2006). EU accession in the late 1990s meant something very different than in previous rounds. Brussels very vocally applied *ex ante* conditionality to the accessor states, with constant public pronouncements about candidates' readiness to join at different times. Additionally, the requirements for entry became more stringent, with the number of *acquis communautaire* chapters increasing from thirty-one to thirty-five. Thus, unlike the quieter previous rounds of expansion that included the Mediterranean and Scandinavian countries, all the candidate countries in the late 1990s were subject to a negotiation regime where policy reforms were expected to meet stringent criteria.

I first reexamine the central hypothesis in this subsample. Table 4.4 presents results from quarterly data from the first quarter of 1990 to the fourth quarter of 2006 from seventeen of the postcommunist countries to establish the magnitude of the effect of EU accession, and yearly data to test the mechanisms, based on the granularity of the available controls. Not all countries issued their debt on international markets in the time period under study, which necessitated a limit to the countries included.[10] For subsequent analyses, because many of the control variables were not available on a quarterly basis, the analyses

---

[10] The countries are Albania, Belarus, Bulgaria, Croatia, the Czech Republic, Estonia, Hungary, Latvia, Lithuania, Macedonia, Moldova, Poland, Romania, Russia, Slovakia, Slovenia, and Ukraine.

TABLE 4.4. *EU Effect across Stages of Expansion –*
Postcommunist Countries

Variable	A.	B.
Constant	1.18***	1.60***
	(−0.22)	(−0.13)
Inflation	.001***	001***
	(−0.0003)	(−0.0003)
Current account	0.0004	0.0008
	(−0.002)	(−0.002)
Reserves	−.0002***	−.00002***
	(−0.00007)	(−0.00007)
Portfolio liabilities	−.0004	−0.0008
	(−0.001)	(−0.002)
EU apply	−	−0.14
		(−0.12)
EU negotiation	−	−.49***
		(−0.08)
EU accession	−	−.31***
		(−0.08)
EU membership	−	−.75***
		(−0.13)
Wald χ^2	26.7	159.33
Prob $> \chi^2$	0	0
N	496	496

* Dependent variable is the natural log of spreads on government
  bonds, quarterly from 1991 to 2006, for seventeen postcommunist
  countries. Prais-Winsten regressions with panel-corrected standard
  errors in parentheses.

use annual data from the same time period, even though a finer degree of
granularity would be desirable.

To correct for serial correlation while avoiding the downward bias caused
by including lagged dependent variables (Achen, 2000), I use Prais-Winsten
transformations, which allow for the estimation of time-series regressions in the
presence of autocorrelated errors, with panel-corrected standard errors. Recall
that positive values indicate higher levels of investor risk (higher spreads),
whereas negative values indicate factors that decrease risk (lower spreads). The
results for this estimation largely mirror those in the ARCH-in-means models.
Inflation has a strong and statistically significant effect on candidate country
sovereigns; more inflation makes a country look more risky. Higher levels of
reserves are associated with drops in lending risk, an effect that is statistically
significant at the $p < .01$ level across specifications. Save for in the fixed effects
model excluding EU entry, the coefficients on current-account balances are not

TABLE 4.5. *Effects of One SD Change of Independent Variables on Sovereign Spreads*

Inflation	−5.56
Current account	1.08
Reserves	−1.26
Portfolio liabilities	−1.01
EU apply	−1.06
EU negotiation	−3.44
EU accession	−5.67
EU membership	−3.57

statistically significant, nor are those for overall volumes of portfolio debt. As before, the EU negotiation stage remains significant.[11]

To make comparisons across variables easier, given that all are measured in different units, Table 4.5 shows the expected results of a change in one standard deviation of each of the independent variables. The values are transformed back into their original, antilog units. The stages of EU talks, however, are measured as a change from 0 (not active) to 1 (active).

Put another way, holding all other control variables at their mean values, risk levels drop by 1.06 percentage points at the application stage, then down a total of 4.50 at negotiation, reaching −10.17 at accession, and a drop in risk of 13.74 percentage points all told, by the time the country reaches the membership stage. According to the model, a country such as Bulgaria, which has the closest to mean values of most variables of any country in the dataset, would see the expected values of its risk levels drop by a total of 14.79 percentage points from application to membership: 0.77 at application, 11.62 at negotiation, 1.97 at accession, and 0.43 at membership. To compare, during the onset of the Russian rouble crisis in 1998, spreads for Bulgaria increased by a maximum of about 10 percentage points. Thus, the positive impact EU accession is almost 50 percent more than the contagion impact of a major trade partner defaulting on its debt.

---

[11] To see if these results were robust to the inclusion of different international organizations, I included in separate estimations additional variables for membership in the North Atlantic Treaty Organization (NATO), the Organization for Economic Cooperation and Development (OECD), and the World Trade Organization (WTO). These organizations operate quite differently from the EU in terms of their criteria for admission, their mission statements, and the benefits of membership; thus, an adequate exploration of their effects would require a separate set of hypotheses and different empirical specifications. Nonetheless, the EU effects were larger than those of the other institutions, an interesting finding that deserves further inquiry.

4.4.1 Test of H_{a1} – Policy Reform

A rival explanation for the effect of "the company you keep" deals with the observable changes that states undertake prior to or alongside the prospect of EU accession. Particularly in the run-up to EU accession, many countries underwent stringent periods of policy reform in order to be considered for EU candidacy (Schimmelfennig and Sedelmeier, 2005; Vachudová, 2005).[12] The process of accession can entail substantial policy reform, as countries must comply with the rules and regulations set out in the 80,000-page *acquis communautaire*. Lower levels of risk observed around the time of EU negotiations might be just a function of that preexisting reform. If this were the case, controlling for policy reform, either undertaken prior to EU negotiation or after the time that negotiations begin, would obviate any presumed effects of EU entry.

The economic controls to some extent control for this possibility; high levels of inflation, for example, and unemployment are of course partially the result of government's policy choice or a lack thereof. However, they are also an indicator of the composition of a particular economy, which is a result of factor endowments as well as geography. Particular reform policies may be enacted – say, attempts at privatization or of boosting employment – that may stall or be altogether ineffective. Thus, in addition to those controls, it is worthwhile to disentangle an actual government policy from the way it plays out on the ground.

To test whether markets are simply responding to policy reform enacted by governments, the next group of models includes reform indices compiled by Kostadinova (2004), which measure three areas of reform. The first is institutional reform, which covers banking sector reform, bankruptcy law, company law, competition policy, contract law, pledge law, stock exchange, and taxation. The second is price liberalization, and the third is privatization, or the transfer of large- and small-scale state-controlled property into private hands.[13] These scores do not measure the effectiveness of policy reform (the economic indicators already included in the specifications probably are a better proxy for effectiveness), but rather the degree of reform that a government has

---

[12] For a similar argument about monetary union, see Cote and Graham (2004), who argue that yields are elastic toward the policy reform surrounding euro adoption, and not the currency itself.

[13] Other reform measures exist, but as Kostadinova (2004) points out, they are subjective, cover a shorter time-span, have limited variation, and focus on the end results of economic transformation rather than policy makers' efforts in particular fields. That said, the same model specification, using policy reform measures from the European Bank for Reconstruction and Development, produced similar results, although the sample size ($N = 58$) was quite small. Similarly, the Campello (2006) reform scores, although quite comprehensive in substance, only extend to 2001, well before most countries in the sample completed negotiation or initiated accession.

TABLE 4.6. *Test of Policy Reform (H_{a1})*

Variable	A.	B.
Constant	5.29***	4.15***
	−1.49	(−1.52)
Inflation	0.002***	0.003***
	−0.0007	(−0.0008)
Current account	0.0002**	0.0002**
	−0.00009	(−0.00009)
Reserves	−0.00004**	−0.00005**
	−0.00002	(−0.00002)
Portfolio liabilities	0.0001	0.0002
	−0.0002	(−0.0002)
Privatization	−0.06	−0.05
	−0.05	(−0.05)
Price liberalization	0.001**	0.001**
	(0.0005)	(−0.0005)
Institutional reform	−0.05**	−0.03
	−0.02	(−0.02)
EU apply	—	0.34
		(−0.31)
EU negotiation	—	−0.66**
	(−0.32)	
EU accession	—	−1.73***
	(−0.64)	
EU membership	—	0.56
		(−0.75)
σ_μ	1.79	1.53
σ_ϵ	1.05	0.99
N	113	113

* Dependent variable is the natural log of spreads on government bonds, annually from 1991 to 2006, for seventeen postcommunist countries. Prais-Winsten regressions with panel-corrected standard errors in parentheses.

pursued. If those variables have a stronger impact than EU negotiation itself, this rival explanation would hold more power than the central hypothesis. Table 4.6 includes these variables in the base specifications, along with the EU variables in a second set of specifications.

If EU entry simply sent markets information about the existence of policy reform, these two variables would be collinear – such that the effects of the policy reform variables would be weakened by the introduction of an EU variable to the base model controlling for policies, or vice versa. Notice, however, that negotiating with the EU has effects that operate more or less independently of policy reform. Price liberalization is significant, but the effect does not attenuate when the EU variables are introduced into the reform, indicating that the effects of these two processes are distinct. In those specifications, the significance of institutional reform, as well as the magnitude of the coefficient, decreases when the EU variables are included. If multicollinearity among the policy variables and EU negotiation existed, then the coefficients should have changed. But the variables for EU accession and negotiation are statistically significant in these models, and the magnitude of the coefficient on accession increases from previous specifications.

It is reasonable to suppose that policy reform can have weak or mixed effects – simply enacting legislation on capital adequacy requirements for banks, for example, does not ensure compliance with those standards. But these tests should serve as an indicators of market reaction to attempts at domestic policy reform. When EU negotiation enters the fixed-effects model, there is very little attenuation of the coefficients on policy reform – or on most of the control variables that are themselves manifestations of the implementation of successful policies. This indicates that the two processes (EU talks and policy reform) are not collinear for markets, and that portfolio investors price market reform into their expectations of a country's default risk separately from that country's dealings with Brussels. This again points to an effect of negotiating with the EU that is independent of policy reform.

4.4.2 Test of H_{a2} – Selection

Another rival explanation is that states sign onto organizations to whose rules they would adhere regardless (Downs, Rocke, and Barsoom, 1996; Vreeland, 2003; von Stein, 2005). Though this issue has long been discussed in economics (Heckman, 1976), empirical work in political science has only recently begun to focus explicitly on the bias caused by selection.[14] In the case that this chapter addresses, the problem originates when the same observable or unobservable factors that drive countries to be asked to open EU negotiations also influence countries to look less risky to investors. Thus, a researcher would falsely attribute the effect of one variable to an omitted variable or groups of variables that are driving both that independent as well as the dependent variable. If this were true, we would expect that modeling the selection process would cause any previously observed significance on the EU variables to disappear, once their effect was correctly attributed to selection.

---

[14] See von Stein (2005) on how, once controlling for selection, signatories to IMF agreements look no more likely to comply with the provisions than before, and Vreeland (2003) on how modeling the preexisting factors that make countries more likely to receive international aid attenuates the previously observed effects of lending.

Alternate Hypothesis 2, which focuses on selection bias, would posit that countries that end up negotiating with the EU are inherently more stable and prosperous than those who do not, and that the EU is simply selecting prospective members through the same logic that investors might use (although even if that were true, negotiations could still have an impact on market perceptions). This section takes into account the potential endogeneity of EU negotiations by measuring and controlling for the unobservable factors that drive states to negotiate with the EU and that also affect market perceptions.

In the EU case, selection bias could occur when the same attributes that would lead to lower spreads also lead to EU accession. This conflation is widespread in reports about particular countries. Analysts, for example, speculate as to "whether Albania can curb its reputation for lawlessness and secure a place in the queue for membership of the EU."[15] But if spreads fell in the event that Albania opened EU talks, would they be a result of improved conditions in the country, such as corruption reform and strengthening of the judiciary, or of EU negotiation itself?

One method of addressing this source of potential bias is to model first a country's propensity to take part in a dichotomous treatment (here, the "treatment" is the opening of EU negotiations) and then include that probability in a second stage of analysis. One first specifies a selection, or treatment, equation in which the dependent variable is the absence or presence of the treatment (opening EU negotiations, in this instance). Ideally, these variables should be uncorrelated with the second, outcome, equation. However, it is necessary to address not only the correlation between the two equations but also the fit of the selection equation to the treatment variable. In practice, balancing these two concerns becomes a matter of degree on both dimensions.

One place to look for variables that correlate with opening EU negotiations but not with investor risk is in the chapters of the *acquis communautaire* itself. As mentioned, the *acquis* lays out in exhaustive detail all the issue areas on which potential new members must have EU-compliant legislation. Though many of these areas are of potential interest to portfolio investors, such as economic reform and liberalization, some concern cultural areas that would not be of direct relevance to bond spreads. Although culture might correlate with other factors that are important to portfolio investors, such as overall levels of wealth in a country, it is difficult to imagine how cultural heritage issues would directly affect investor risk. Nonetheless, they are crucial steps in EU integration and thus are theoretically and practically distinct from any outcome equation modeling determinants of bond spreads.

For the selection equation, two new variables proxy for the cultural factors driving countries to join the EU. The first, *movies*, measures the number of native-language movies released in a country in a given year. Local movie

[15] "A bright future around the corner," *Financial Times*, 12 April 2005.

production is explicitly mentioned in chapter 20 of the EU's *acquis communautaire,* on culture and audiovisual policy.[16] A large volume of domestically produced movies indicates government efforts toward promoting at least one form of local culture, which the EU explicitly values, but movie production per se should be of no particular interest to investors. The basic patterns of film production do not, at first glance, map a country's progress in EU talks; it is a necessary but not sufficient condition for accession. Relatively closed Albania produced an average of three domestic films a year, on par with Slovakia, which was at the time the regional leader in foreign investment. Thus, there is little reason to believe that portfolio investors would be concerned with domestic movie production in and of itself. This variable is weighted by population size, to take into account the potential audience, as well as supply factors, for locally produced films.

The second new variable counts the number of UNESCO World Heritage sites in any country in a given year. Chapter 8 of the *acquis* makes specific reference to such sites.[17] Countries must file to have a given site receive this status, and the postcommunist countries had not taken part in this process until after the fall of the Berlin Wall. UNESCO recognizes World Heritage sites on a rolling basis; Croatia went from having three in 1990 to six by 2004, and the Czech Republic started 1990 with no recognized sites at all, but it claimed twelve by the end of 2006. Although a high number of World Heritage sites might promote tourism, which would indicate a greater openness to the world economy that might be associated with lower risk premia, it is not necessarily the case; Belarus has four sites, twice as many as economically open Estonia. Thus, it is reasonable to assume that this variable will do a good job in predicting EU accession and not sovereign spreads. To take country size into account, this variable is weighted by the total land area of each relevant country.

Other variables are necessary to predict the probability of EU accession. To that end, the first-stage equation also uses Freedom House's measure of civil liberties, which serves as a third-party assessment of the strength of civil liberties such as freedom of speech and expression in a country. Again, this should be positively correlated with EU accession, given that human rights and respect for civil liberties appear in several different chapters of the *acquis*.[18] However, civil liberties should at best be of indirect concern to investors.

To make sure that the first-stage equation is not underspecified, the equation includes variables that are not orthogonal to the outcome equation: GDP per

---

[16] The question reads, "What are (if any) the financial support systems in place for the audiovisual sector (including cinema)?"

[17] The relevant portions are under the subheadings: "What, if any, are the support programmes in the field of cultural heritage?" and "What legal regime applies to the preservation of cultural heritage?"

[18] See, for example, the chapter on minorities as well as the chapter on the judiciary.

capita,[19] and distance (measured in number of kilometers) from Bonn, which has commonly been cited as a proxy for cultural and economic closeness to Western Europe (Gallup, Sachs, and Mellinger, 1998). Though these variables are likely to help predict bond spreads, their inclusion ensures that the model predicts the probability of EU accession with reasonable accuracy. Among the postcommunist countries, proximity to Western Europe as well as overall levels of income have been strong predictors of the likelihood to join (Plümper, Schneider, and Troeger, 2005). I include these variables in the first-stage equation as well.[20] Because the treatment must be binary (either a country receives the treatment, or it does not), I use the stage of entering into EU negotiations and time periods thereafter, as that is the stage at which the first impact of lower spreads was initially observed.

The probability of EU accession as predicted by the selection equation is then included in the second-stage equation, in which the dependent variable and the control variables are the same as those employed in previous analyses.[21] The outcome equation also includes a measure (ρ) of the degree of correlation between the unexplained variance in both equations. That is, if the models do a poor job of explaining both EU negotiations and risk perceptions – and if there remains something unexplained in both process that seems to be linked – then the models have not effectively taken into account the things that might be driving both EU negotiations and investor perceptions at the same time. Put technically, the ρ term measures the correlation of μ (the error term of the selection/treatment equation) and ε (the error term of the outcome equation). If ρ is close to -1 or 1, then standard statistical techniques will produce biased estimates of δ. Any part of ε that is correlated with μ will in this case be

---

[19] Although GDP per capita is not statistically significant, I include it as it appears in most specifications in the literature on the determinants of EU accession.

[20] Specifically, the selection equation is as follows: $EU\ Negotiations = \alpha + \beta[movies]_i + \beta[UNESCO]_i + \beta[civil\ liberties]_i + \beta[GDP]_i + \beta[Km\ from\ Bonn]_i + \mu_i + \varepsilon$ where *UNESCO* is the cumulative number of UNESCO World Heritage sites in a country, weighted by the land area; *movies* counts the number of domestically produced, native-language movies in a given country year, weighted by the population of the country; *GDP* is gross domestic product, weighted by purchasing-power parity; *Km from Bonn* measures the distance of each country's capital from Bonn, Germany; and *civil liberties* measures the degree of civil liberties present in a given country and year, as assessed by Freedom House. This measure is coded such that high values indicate a higher degree of civil liberty. To make expectations consistent with the other variables, where more movies and more UNESCO World Heritage sites would be associated with a higher tendency to open negotiations with the EU, I invert the *civil liberties* variable. Similarly, kilometers from Bonn proxies both for previous history with European political frameworks as well as proximity to European markets (Sachs and Warner, 1996; Campos and Coricelli, 2002).

[21] Specifically, the outcome equation is as follows: $Risk = \alpha + \beta[Controls]_i + \delta[EU\ Negotiations]_i + \varepsilon_i + \rho$ where $\varepsilon \sim N(0, \sigma)$, $\mu \sim N(0, 1)$ and $\rho = corr(\varepsilon, \mu)$.

attributed to δ; in other words, standard techniques would attribute to being in EU negotiations the unobservable shocks that affect both market ratings and the propensity to enter into negotiations (von Stein, 2005). If, however, ρ is close to 0, then μ and ε are independently and identically distributed. As a result, δ would be unbiased, and one could be confident that δ represented the independent effect of EU negotiations on investor perceptions of risk.

Table 4.7 displays the results of the selection as well as the outcome equation.

Though the treatment-effects model does not address the problems in TSCS datasets, I include country and year indicators in both stages of the regression. For μ, ρ would be expected to have a negative sign, meaning that the same unobservable factors that led countries to have low bond spreads (a negative effect on the dependent variable for *EU negotiations* in the outcome equation) would also make them more likely to enter into EU negotiations (positive coefficients on the variables in the selection equation). Here, ρ is positive, although the magnitude of the coefficient is small and is not statistically significant. If that parameter were closer to 1 and of high statistical significance, it would indicate the presence of selection bias, which would mean that standard estimation techniques would tend to understate the impact that opening EU negotiations has on market perceptions of risk. Even though selection models are highly sensitive to model specification, the relatively weak magnitude (.16) of any selection effect indicated by the low and insignificant values of ρ should alleviate concern about omitted variable bias, namely the concern that this specification has left out a key explanatory variable that would predict both EU negotiations and sovereign spreads.

Additionally, the coefficient on the *EU negotiations* variable is still strong and significant below the .01 level. This indicates that, even when modeling and controlling for the selection process, opening EU negotiations is still associated with lower risk perceptions. This should give confidence that the effect of EU accession on investor risk is not mistakenly attributed to any underlying process that drives both investor perceptions and EU accession.

For a robustness check, I also ran the same model using a slightly different procedure, namely the Balestra and Varadharajan-Krishnakumar two-stage least squares generalizations of panel-data estimators for exogenous variables. Although this specifies a linear equation for the first stage, this procedure produced similar results as in the Table 4.7. The overall R^2 for the first stage was 0.308, which indicates that the regressors are indeed correlated with the endogenous regressors. As further evidence for that correlation, I evaluated joint significance with an F-test adjusted for country-year clustering. The $F_{(12, 107)}$-statistic is equal to 5.00, which is significant at the 0.000 level. Similarly, the Hansen J statistic, which tests for overidentification of the instruments, is 6.88, with a χ^2 p value of 0.14. The p-value for testing the null hypothesis that the overidentifying restrictions are valid is 0.78, which shows that there is no basis to reject that assumption. Thus, the selected instruments are relevant

TABLE 4.7. *Treatment Effects – Test for Selection Bias H_{a2}*

Variable	Full
Constant	2.54***
	(.17)
Inflation	.004***
	(.0008)
Reserves	−.00006**
	(.00002)
Debt liabilities	.0001
	(.0002)
Current account	.0001
	(.00009)
EU negotiation	−1.02***
	(.36)
Selection	**Equation**
Constant	3.73
	(1.14)
Movies	.02*
	(.01)
UNESCO sites	.11*
	(.06)
Civil liberties	−1.41***
	(.49)
GDP per capita (PPP-weighted)	.0004
	(.0001)
Km from Bonn	.002*
	(.0006)
ρ	.16
	(.26)
σ	1.10***
	(.07)
λ	.18
	(.28)
N	124

* Dependent variable is the natural log of spreads on government bonds, quarterly from 1991 to 2006, for seventeen postcommunist countries. Treatment-effects regression, with country and year indicators suppressed. N = 128. Likelihood ratio test of independent equations ($\rho = 0$): $\chi^2(1) = 0.39$ Prob > $\chi^2 = 0.53$.

in their ability to predict EU negotiations. Additionally, the Anderson-Rubin-Wald test demonstrates the exogeneity of the instruments to the second stage, where bond spreads are the dependent variable (p value of 0.00). Thus, these instruments are robust in terms of both identification and instrument validity.

4.4.3 Test of Mechanism Underlying H₁: The Company You Keep

If neither policy reform nor selection explain the link between risk perceptions and EU accession, what is driving this process? It is possible that even
though countries may enact reforms well in advance of EU negotiation, markets respond to public signals from the EU that its potential members meet EU
standards. Studies on signaling in diplomacy (Fearon, 1994; Schultz, 2001)
argue that states act in a way to convey information about their "type"
to international audiences and thus increase their credibility in diplomacy.
In many economic policies, such as central-bank independence and pegged
exchange rates, publicizing a commitment to fiscal discipline is an important
psychological component of that policy's effectiveness (Posen, 1995; Lohmann,
1992). Other work has argued that international institutions provide public
information to external observers (Mansfield, Milner, and Rosendorf, 2000;
Fang, 2009). Similarly, an international institution's endorsement of candidates
could also regularize expectations of new members in the eyes of financial
markets. In an environment of nonstrategic information aggregation, international institutions can provide public information that unifies investors'
expectations.

Unlike in the selection hypothesis, where the EU "picks winners" (meaning
that the same attributes drive a country both to make strides in EU accession
and simultaneously to have lower risk levels), here the announcements from
Brussels act as judgments that investors can interpret in a similar manner.
But in order for EU accession to give a viable signal, there must be some
commonality of interpretation of the significance of the closing of chapters. For
this group of countries, closing of *acquis* chapters brought them irreversibly
closer to EU membership. As the chapters of the *acquis* are clearly spelled
out, and their closure is widely documented, market reaction to an EU "seal
of approval" would be more widespread than the assessments that individual
investors might make of previously observed policy reform. Even if investors
have private information about that reform, the EU's public signal allows
divergent expectations and interpretations to converge around one focal point
(Garrett and Weingast, 1993).

This final test examines the hypothesis that portfolio investors' expectations about a country's risk levels converge when Brussels officially claims that
candidate countries' policies are up to EU standards. As mentioned earlier,
accession to the EU requires substantial de jure policy harmonization, not least
in economic policy; out of its thirty-five issue areas, the *acquis* includes thirteen
chapters on economic matters. These range from fiscal policy to budget deficits
to exchange-rate stability. Closing these chapters indicates that the Commission
considers not only a country's legislation but also its existing economic reforms
to be compatible with the broader EU. Investors would pay close attention to
such a signal from Brussels, not just in terms of the substantive content of

the message (that countries are up to EU standards) but also the highly public nature of such an announcement. Much of the risk (as well as the potential profit) in investment lies in diverging expectations of country performance, and when such a clear indication of progress is made by a visible third party, investors' expectations could align.[22]

Testing this hypothesis involves an evaluation of the performance of a separate variable (*Economic Chapters Closed*) that indicates the percentage of those thirteen issue areas on which a country had closed negotiations.[23] For an illustration of this process, take the case of *acquis* chapter on taxation, chapter 10. This *acquis* chapter covers both direct and indirect taxation, as well as excise duties on alcohol and cigarettes, and business taxation. Slovakia opened that chapter in June 2001, and it was provisionally closed after fifteen months of negotiations – a few months above the average year that negotiations on that chapter had taken for the other accession countries. Slovakia had bargained for transition periods for taxes on gas, electricity, and distilled spirits – a concession that was particularly important to Slovaks, who wanted to safeguard their home production of plum brandy for personal consumption.[24] "This was a difficult chapter, maybe not the most difficult, but one of them," Ján Figel', Slovakia's chief negotiator, was quoted as saying.[25] The taxation chapter was the twenty-third chapter that Slovakia had successfully negotiated. "It shows the people watching the market that we're on the train and it's moving forward," said Toma Kme, an analyst at the Slovenská sporitel'ňa bank.[26]

It is possible to analyze just how closely markets were watching this bit of news through an event study of market returns around the date in question. Event studies are common in finance as a means of estimating financial markets' reaction to particular occurrences. After identifying the event of interest and defining an "event window" around that event – usually a few days before an event, to take into account market anticipation of an announcement, and a few days after to include the fallout – a researcher uses common indicators of market performance of the asset to predict a "normal" outcome during the event window in the absence of the event. One then subtracts the actual returns from the predicted returns to estimate the cumulative abnormal outcome (returns or

---

[22] This recalls the previously mentioned "beauty contest" paradigm set out by Keynes (1936).

[23] Those chapters include Chapter 1, Free Movement of Goods; Chapter 2, Free Movement of People; Chapter 3, Free Movement of Services; Chapter 4, Free Movement of Capital; Chapter 5, Public Procurement; Chapter 6, Company Law; Chapter 8, Competition Policy; Chapter 9, Financial Services; Chapter 17, Economic and Monetary Policy; Chapter 29, Customs Union; Chapter 32, Financial Control; and Chapter 33, Budgetary Provisions.

[24] The Czech Republic negotiated a similar concession at the time, as did Romania and Bulgaria two years later.

[25] "Slovakia Wins Case on EU Tax Chapter," *Slovak Spectator,* 1 April 2002.

[26] Ibid.

losses) within the event window, then tests whether the cumulative abnormal return is statistically different from zero.[27]

In this case, the "normal" outcome is yields on ten-year German benchmark bonds, a strong predictor of bond market activity in European countries. Defining the event window as two trading days before and after the 21 March 2002 announcement of the provisional closure of the taxation chapter, the logged abnormal returns for Slovak ten-year government bonds are −1.48 – or, in original units, a drop in returns of 4.98. This finding is highly statistically significant, with a test statistic of −6.46, which is more than three times greater than the minimum level needed to achieve statistical significance.[28] Results are similar with an event window of five days surrounding the event. Thus, confidence peaks when markets receive clear, publicized signals from the EU on the state of countries' policy reform, even though Slovakia negotiated a deal that differed from the original standards set up in the *acquis*.

Table 4.8 examines the results of EU's "seal of approval" on countries' legislation in economic policy reform within the time period that countries were negotiating with the EU, indicated by closed economic chapters of the *acquis* (this variable is labeled *Economic Chapters Closed*). The first two specifications compare the results of the "seal of approval" with the indicator variables for different stages of EU integration, as they appeared in previous specifications. The following two compare performance with the policy reform variables, to ensure that the effects of the seal of approval are distinct from those of policy reform. To return to the possible mechanisms delineated earlier, if markets cared more about the actual trajectory of reform than EU signals regarding the state of reform, the coefficients on policy variables would be significant in place of the effects of the "seal of approval." I also include the variable for ICRG political risk, which was the main driver of the effect for the company states keep in Chapter 3.

On its own, the percent of economic chapters closed has a greater magnitude than any one of the stages of EU entry. Similarly, once those other EU variables are introduced in the model, the strength of the *Chapters* coefficient decreases only slightly, indicating a surprisingly small degree of collinearity between those variables. This indicates that the formal channels of EU approval are the part of EU integration that matter most to portfolio investors. Additionally, the significance of the *Chapters* variables against the policy reform variables show that the "seal of approval" is a pure, supply-side signal and not a reflection of

---

[27] For a more in-depth explanation with examples of market responses to environmental performance in developing countries, see Dasgupta, Laplante, and Mamingi (1998).

[28] The test statistic is test = $(1 / n \Sigma AR / AR\_\sigma)$; that is, the inverse of the number of days in the event window, multiplied by the cumulative normal return divided by the standard deviation of the abnormal return. If the absolute value of the test statistic is greater than 1.96 – which comes from the standard normal distribution – it imparts 95 percent confidence that the results are different than zero.

TABLE 4.8. *Test of EU Seal of Approval (H$_1$): The Company You Keep*

Variable	A.	B.	C.
Constant	2.54***	3.66***	5.88***
	(0.17)	(1.19)	(1.66)
Inflation	.003**	.002**	0.001***
	(−0.001)	(−0.0006)	(−0.0007)
Current account	0.00003	0.00009	0.0001
	(−0.0001)	(−0.00009)	(−0.00007)
Reserves	−.00004*	−.00006**	−0.00001
	(−0.00002)	(−0.00002)	(−0.00002)
Portfolio liabilities	0.00008	−0.00005	−0.00018
	(−0.0002)	(−0.0002)	(−0.0002)
EU Seal of Approval	−1.99***	−1.77***	−1.40***
	(−0.31)	(−0.36)	(−0.35)
EU apply	−0.15	−	−
	(−0.34)		
EU negotiation	−0.25	−	−
	(−0.27)		
EU accession	−0.24	−	−
	(−0.27)		
EU membership	(−0.1	−	−
	−0.34)		
Privatization		−0.006	−
		(−0.04)	
Price liberalization	−	0.0009	−
		(−0.0006)	
Institutional reform	−	−0.02	−
		(−0.02)	
ICRG– Political risk	−		0.03
			(−0.03)
Wald χ^2	−	−	62.76
Prob > χ^2	−	−	0
σ_μ	0.85	1.37	−
σ_ϵ	0.98	0.86	−
N	134	134	112

* Dependent variable is the natural log of spreads on government bonds, from 1991 to 2006, for seventeen postcommunist countries. Prais-Winsten regressions with panel-corrected standard errors in parentheses; fixed-effects regressions with robust standard errors in parentheses.

preexisting policy reform, either taken within or outside of the process of EU reform.

Why does the "seal of approval" variable perform better than the policy indices, as well as the ICRG variable, which were significant in the previous chapter? Markets may observe policy reform in developing countries, but are unsure of its strength until it is endorsed by the EU. Information is often noisy in emerging markets, and the EU blessing makes markets more confident in a country's perceived course. The power of the signal at this stage is that the EU has taken a position on the trajectory of a particular policy, and its credibility as a signaler is taken to heart by markets. Whether the country actually sticks to the reform in question is irrelevant at this stage. The EU's very public pronouncement on policy reform trumps private information that investors may have, and aggregate market sentiment on those countries' risk converges to lower levels. This pronouncement acts as a focal point to coordinate investors.

4.4.4 Examination of H_{a3}: Enforcement

In line with Alternate Hypothesis 3, one might still argue that investors are anticipating the enforcement of rules once a country gets into the EU. But interestingly, up until the 2007 financial crisis, there was little indication that, once countries receive that approval, markets wavered in their assessment of new EU members, whether or not that country stuck to the rules. This section takes a closer view of member state violations of EU rules in the late 1990s and early 2000s, starting first with the case of the Hungarian budget crisis and then examining member state infringements of the Stability and Growth Pact. Lack of market reaction to these events indicates that investors had not been considering rule adherence as part of their pricing of country risk (at least prior to 2007). Additionally, investor reaction to announcement of bailout packages for EU and non-EU members alike did not differ as much as would be expected. These tests indicate that expected enforcement of rules is not a primary driver of the reduction in risk that comes with joining good-company organizations.

Markets Did Not Respond to 2005 Hungarian Budget Crisis
Hungary joined the EU in 2004 as part of the "big bang" of enlargement, but this achievement was quickly sullied. In October 2005, Eurostat, in an investigation of public spending in Hungary, publicized the fact that the Hungarian government had left highway construction out of their calculations for government spending. Once that budget line was included, it put the share of government deficit to GDP at 9 percent – flagrantly above the 3 percent cap set by the Stability and Growth Pact. The EU Treaty (Article 104) allows the ECOFIN Council to impose sanctions, possibly as a fine, should a member state exceed the 3 percent limit for its government deficit.

Although the EU called attention to this fact publicly, at the time there was not any serious talk of imposing sanctions on Hungary. The EC could have withheld structural funds from Hungary on account of their overspending. Hungary then would have had recourse to invoke the equal treatment clause, which would require the Commission to invoke similar punishment on Germany and Greece, who also extended their budget cap. There is also a section of the Stability and Growth Pact that cites a fine for breaching the Pact's rules, but no serious mention of this has ever been made with respect to Hungary.[29] Talk of postponing Hungary's date for adopting the euro was always framed in terms of other structural problems, not the breaking of the Stability and Growth Pact per se.

Hungarian officials seemed unbothered about the prospect of EU penalties. Finance minister Tamás Katona was casual about his government's breach, saying that, after all, "the views of the [finance] ministry and the Commission did not differ fundamentally."[30] A Central Bank official dismissed the notion of actual sanctions being imposed, saying that "we'd just bring up the equal-treatment directive, and then neither Greece nor Germany would be safe, and they don't want that to be publicly brought up."[31] A local pundit likened the Hungarian government's stance as "one that doesn't even seem designed to bamboozle the EU – sort of like when a kid fails a class and lamely denies to his parents that he failed, even though he knows that his parents know that he knows that they know he flunked."[32]

What is striking is that there was relatively small market reaction to these events; yields on ten-year maturities, for example, only increased in the month of October by 15 basis points. Finance Ministry officials acknowledged that "markets [were] giving Hungary a break because of the membership in the EU."[33] The National Bank of Hungary attributed the relative lack of market reaction to the fact that "we're part of the EU now, and investors know that the EU governments aren't [like those in] Latin America. We're not going to run away with the money in coffins."[34]

Investor perceptions stayed resilient even in the face of extraordinary events. A leaked tape of a party meeting revealed that Prime Minister Ferenc Gyurcsány admitted that his government had lied "morning, noon, and night" about its financial position in order to retain its standing with EU institutions.[35] The scandal sparked a week of riots – demonstrators set fire to cars and clashed with police – in the Hungarian capital in late September. But markets barely slid.[36] In fact, during the third day of the riots, Hungary brought a new type of government bond to credit markets, with spreads at 25 basis points over

---

[29] There had been some discussion of the German case; the European Commission was pushing for Germany to be fined for exceeding the 3 percent budget deficit, but the European Council refused. The Commission then took the case to the European Court of Justice, which ruled that the Council could refuse to vote fines but could not scrap basic rules of the Stability and Growth Pact without due process.

[30] "Hungary Finance Ministry shrugs off EU budget warning," portfolio.hu, 20 October 2005.

[31] Interview, András Inotai, Hungarian Central Bank, 30 October 2005.

[32] "EU Warns Again on Deficit; Official Mumbles Bullshit Back," pestiside.hu, 20 October 2005.

[33] Interview, Martón Szili, Hungarian Ministry of Finance, 25 July 2005.

[34] Interview, András Inotai, Hungarian Central Bank, 30 October 2005.

[35] "Excerpts: Hungarian 'lies' speech," BBC, 19 September 2006.

[36] The credit agency Fitch downgraded its rating from stable to negative, but other credit agencies, including Standard and Poors and Lehman Brother's, called the move "premature . . . Gyurcsány

European bonds – only slightly more risky than the initial price guidance. Though some investors complained that the bond was too expensive, it sold briskly, with various Western European funds buying up 80 percent of the issue. "It just shows that investors are wearing rose-tinted glasses as long as you are a EU-member country, regardless of the real quality of your credit," said one investor.[37]

Markets did not turn a blind eye indefinitely. After the advent of the global financial crisis in 2007, investors began reevaluating country risk, and in October 2008 the value of the Hungarian forint plummeted. The crisis led the IMF, the EU, and the World Bank to grant the country a rescue package worth $25 billion. Despite the bailout, Hungary's levels of government spending remained unacceptably high, and in 2012, Fitch, Standard and Poor's and Moody's downgraded Hungary's credit rating to junk status.[38] As of 2012, the yields on Hungarian government debt were around 10 percent. This indicates that the credibility boost of the EU seal of approval is not permanent – but it insulates countries from swings in investor risk in the short term, even in the face of evidence that the credibility is not earned.

Markets Did Not Respond to Violation of EU Rules

To further test whether markets are anticipating the enforcements of rules, I next investigate whether markets respond to EU members' violations of the Stability and Growth Pact (SGP) conditions. Put into place in 1997, the SGP was originally designed to ensure that countries in the eurozone maintained a preestablished level of economic soundness, and to prevent any persistent structural economic problems in an individual country that would damage the health of the eurozone as a whole. Among other conditions, the SGP mandated that no country's budget deficit exceed 3 percent of gross domestic product (GDP), and that public debt should stay below 60 percent of GDP. These valiant targets did not last; in 2006, German public debt clocked in at 66.8 percent of GDP, France's at 64.7 percent, and Greece and Italy's were at more than 100 percent of total output. Similarly, Hungary's budget deficit in 2005 was well higher than 13 percent of GDP. Though the SGP contained provisions for a fine to be imposed on members found in breach, and these breaks with EU policy were public and widely reported in the media, the EC confined itself instead to informal expressions of disappointment. In fact, it soon scrapped the SGP altogether, saying that it needed to come up with more realistic expectations for its members.

If the drop in risk associated with EU negotiation reflected investor belief that countries would be constrained by EU rules, it would follow that markets

does not seem to have any intention of resigning or derailing the reform package." "Fitch Cuts Hungary Outlook," Goldman Sachs report, 21 September 2006.

[37] "Hungary Cruises Back To Debt Markets Despite Protests," *Dow Jones*, 20 September 2006.
[38] "Hungary's Third Downgrade to Junk in Two Months Pares Forint Bond Rebound," *Bloomberg*, 6 January 2012.

TABLE 4.9. *Test of Enforcement (H_{a_3}): Market Perceptions of Breaking of EU SGP Rules*

	A.	B.	C.
Constant	2.019***	2.027***	3.456***
	(1.01)	(0.98)	(1.24)
Reserves	−0.040***	−0.041***	−0.003***
	(.003)	(.005)	(.001)
Inflation	0.038***	0.038***	0.001***
	(.002)	(.015)	(.00001)
Exchange rate	0.001	0.001	−0.011
	(.001)	(.002)	(.012)
Budget	0.005	—	0.009
Excess	(0.004)		(.006)
Public debt	−0.01	−0.011	—
Excess	(0.03)	(0.02)	
N	233	237	826
σ_μ	.71	.68	.65
σ_ϵ	.51	.55	.52

* Dependent variable is the natural log of spreads on government bonds, from 1991 to 2006, for seventeen postcommunist countries. Fixed-effects regressions with robust standard errors in parentheses.

should react negatively when it became clear that countries were not abiding by those rules. The SGP was a public and easily visible indicator of whether countries were in violation of EU standards. Thus, news that countries had broken SGP targets should have indicated both that countries had not made credible commitments to reform and also that the EU was not enforcing its own rules. Markets could then be expected to lose confidence in those countries that were in violation of SGP rules.

Table 4.9 takes data from the Western European countries who were members of the EU from 1990 to 2004. I use two different indicators to calculate countries' deviance from SGP guidelines. If budget deficits exceeded 3 percent of GDP, or if public debt exceeded 60 percent of GDP, I created indicator variables that were coded as 1 if those conditions were violated, 0 otherwise. Because these variables were not available for all countries and years – the variable on budget deficits had a particularly high rate of missingness – I analyze three models, two of which include these two variables separately, and the third in combination. The results are presented above.

Although many of the control variables from previous specifications are statistically significant, none of the variables that signify violation of the SGP rules have a statistically significant impact on sovereign risk. If investors were anticipating a convergence of behavior as a result of entering an international institution, or of the enforcement of rules such as those laid out in the SGP, countries that broke EU rules would be treated as more risky once they reneged on those commitments. The lack of investor reaction to demonstrated and even well-publicized breaks from EU economic norms offers yet another demonstration that investors can be relatively unconcerned with actual behavior of countries in an organization. This is further evidence against the alternate hypothesis of enforcement of rules, as well as of changes in countries' behavior once they enter an IO. If investors were really anticipating actual convergence of behavior, they would be quicker to punish deviation from that behavior when it was evidenced. One possibility is that investors' lack of reaction may be linked to the EU's own reluctance to punish its members; if markets are taking their cues from institutions, as was indicated by the results for the "seal of approval" hypothesis, this may be in keeping with their reactive behavior.

EU officials confirm the lack of the organization's ability to enforce its own rules. "There's this huge illusion of risk management, that the EU explicitly takes away the risk, but it doesn't. So there's been huge mispricing – underpricing, that is – of actual risk," says one.[39] "There is no political will from member states to impose surveillance. So far we've been a monetary union with independent fiscal policies. There's all kinds of language about monitoring, but no political will to enforce it. If you yourself have anything under the carpet, you don't want anyone to start looking around." This indicates the open secret that the EU's ability to constrain member state behavior is limited – a fact that the eurozone financial crisis has underscored.

Market Reactions to Financial Crisis Bailouts

Finally, I examine the possibility that investors perceive the drops in risk as a result of EU membership as a guarantor that even if the behavior of member states does not change right away, actions from the core countries or from the institution itself would insulate new members from potential shocks down the road. Investors might believe that the European Central Bank will act as a lender of last resort. In the event of a possible default, the ECB, or Germany, or another interested and able EU member would judge it to be to the benefit of the entire economic area to come to the erring state's rescue. That would indicate that the drops in risk were in fact a rational response to the anticipation that, once they become members of the EU, countries become "too big to fail" and will be protected from collapse by the EU. Indeed, the EU's bailout fund expanded from $15 billion in early 2009 to around $70 billion by June of that year, in anticipation of bailouts of new members. In 2012, the European Financial Stability Facility had nearly $600 billion to deal with financial crises in Greece, Portugal, and Ireland, and a more permanent fund (the European Stability Mechanism) was slated to store $500 billion.[40] Investors might be reacting to the anticipation of emergency funding from EU actors, which would

---

[39] Author interview, Magda Lewandowska, DG-EcFin, 9 May 2010.
[40] "A glance at Europe's bailout funds," *Associated Press*, 30 July 2012.

prevent countries from defaulting on their debt altogether. If so, there would be increases in the risk of core members at the time that higher-risk states are set to join. Additionally, however, if investors anticipated an EU bailout and built that expectation into their previous risk assessments, they should not react when such a bailout occurred. If this were the case, markets would have priced such an institutional response into their assessment of countries earlier down the road, and there would be a minimal reaction to news of subsequent bailouts. I test this extension of the enforcement hypothesis by examining market response to EU assistance to its members as well as to nonmembers in the wake of the 2008 financial crisis.

Since around 2004, most of the Eastern European economies had experienced a credit boom, asset price bubbles, expansionary fiscal policies, and significant increases in external debt. This put them in a vulnerable position once risk tolerance waned. The bailouts orchestrated by both the EU and the IMF in the wake of the financial crisis can serve as an effective test of the importance of this mechanism for members versus nonmembers of the EU. Because the bailouts were directed at a wide variety of nonmembers (Iceland, Belarus, Serbia, and Ukraine), as well as new member countries (Latvia, Romania and Hungary), it is possible to assess whether there was any statistical difference between bailouts orchestrated for EU members and for nonmembers. If markets had been anticipating bailouts for EU member countries, we should see less of a reaction than for nonmember countries.

Starting in the mid-2000s, new EU members and nonmembers alike took advantage of the cheap credit flooding into emerging markets. Banks, businesses, and those seeking home mortgages took out low-interest loans denominated in euro, yen, and the Swiss franc; in Romania, Hungary, and Bulgaria, more than half of all debt is foreign denominated. Private lending soared as much as 64 percent, wages – particularly in the public sector – increased more than 20 percent on the year, and rising foreign investment brought unemployment to its lowest levels since communist times. In the Baltic countries, as well as in the West Balkans, GDP grew at double-digit rates between 2005 and 2007. This trend was not limited to the postcommunist countries; Ireland also experienced a real estate boom and an attendant surge in growth.

Once the global financial crisis hit in the fall of 2008, portfolio investors pulled much of their money out of the Eastern European economies. Throughout Eastern Europe, currencies weakened and growth plummeted, and in 2009, the postcommunist countries were asking for help.[41] As the value of the local currencies has plummeted, financial institutions, companies, and individuals have been left with steeply rising repayments. By the end of 2008, $20 billion had flooded out of emerging-market stock exchanges. Governments in the Czech Republic, Hungary, and Latvia collapsed in subsequent elections. Those countries that had floating currencies experienced swings of up to 30 percent,

---

[41] "EU Rejects a Rescue of Faltering East Europe," *Wall Street Journal*, 2 March 2009.

particularly in Poland, the Czech Republic, Hungary, and Romania; those who had adopted currency boards in anticipation of eventual adoption of the euro (Estonia, Latvia, Lithuania, and Bulgaria) found themselves struggling to defend their pegs.[42]

These economies' troubles put more than $210 billion worth of loans to the region at risk. For instance, loans made to the Baltic states by banks in Sweden left them exposed to the tune of 30 percent of the country's GDP. In the eurozone, Austria and Greece were particularly exposed to these risks, as well as Germany and Italy to a lesser extent. In fact, European banks had lent heavily to, or established subsidiaries in, members and nonmembers alike. The Nordic countries, particularly Sweden, were heavily exposed in the Baltic countries; Austrian, Belgian, Swedish, and Dutch banks had also built up a strong presence in the West Balkans, as well as in Hungary, Russia, and Turkey, with more than $1.6 trillion in loans.[43] The percentage of foreign-owned banks in new member states was around 77 percent, compared with 68 percent in nonmembers – a lesser, but still sizeable, number.

Nonetheless, the EU initially resisted a blanket bailout of the entire region. Instead, it worked with international financial institutions – including the IMF and the European Bank for Reconstruction and Development – to put together bailouts for non-EU countries as well as members, including a $16.5 billion bailout package for Ukraine and a $2 billion standby facility for Iceland. The EU was something of a background presence in these deals, particularly for the nonmember countries; one EU official involved in the program noted that "sometimes [the media] write that it's an IMF program and sometimes they mention the EU, but they never mention the EU on its own. It's always an IMF/EU program at best."[44] Investors also seemed responsive to the IMF presence. "[The IMF money] is a comfort, particularly to countries in eastern Europe who will continue to need that support," said one investor. "It provides some certainty for emerging Europe because the European Union is loath to lend money directly to the east."[45]

Admittedly, the EU contributed more extensively to the bailouts for its member countries, extending $8.1 billion to Hungary, offset by $1.3 billion from the World Bank; $8 billion of Latvia's $10.1 billion rescue, with help from the IMF and the Nordic countries; and $20 billion for Romania, with the IMF putting forward $7 billion. Additionally, although the EU provided a substantial portion of bailout funds to its new members, there is little evidence that nonmembers were lacking in emergency cash. Serbia negotiated a $4.1 billion package with the IMF in March, and Bosnia and Herzegovina began

[42] "Latvia Euro Drive Worsens Slump as IMF Shores Up Eastern Europe," *Bloomberg*, 15 May 2009.

[43] "ECB fears bank crisis in 2010 as recession drags on," *The Telegraph*, 10 June 2009.

[44] Author interview, Zdeněk Čech, DG-EcFin 10 May 2010.

[45] "Emerging-Market Stocks, Bonds Climb on IMF Bailout-Fund Plan," *Bloomberg*, 16 March 2009.

TABLE 4.10. *Test of Enforcement (H_{a3}): Lack of Investor Reaction to Bailout News*

	Abnormal return	T statistic
EU Countries	−7.21***	3.54
EU Nonmembers	−8.01***	2.24
Emerging Market Indices	−7.98***	2.01

talks on a $1.4 billion agreement in April. Although Turkey's previous IMF loan accord expired in 2008, it accepted a deal from the IMF in the summer of 2009. Greece, Ireland and Spain subsequently received even greater bailout packages.

If investors had been anticipating bailout funds for EU members only but *not* for countries that were not members of the EU, the announcement of a bailout for non-EU members would have spurred more of a positive reaction from investors. That would indicate that the bailout of non-EU members was unexpected, whereas the anticipation of a bailout for EU members would have already been priced into investor expectations far in advance, and thus the announced bailout would not have been a surprise.

To test this proposition, Table 4.10 depicts investor reaction to the news of the early bailouts for EU members (Hungary, Latvia, and Romania) and non-member European countries (Bosnia, Iceland, Ukraine, Serbia, and Turkey). To compare this with reactions to emerging markets in general, I use market returns from JP Morgan's emerging-markets bond index (EMBI) as a benchmark.

All of those categories of countries experienced statistically significant drops in risk. But, to emphasize, stocks rose for *all* the countries that received bailouts, whether the money was coming primarily from the IMF or the European Union. For example, spreads on Ukraine's international bonds fell 500 basis points in just a week after the IMF announcements. In fact, risk levels for emerging markets fell on the news of the bailouts; the extra yield investors demanded to own emerging-market notes over treasuries went down 18 basis points to a five-week low of 6.35 percentage points, according to JPMorgan's EMBI+ Index. At the time, commentators noted that the relative jump in emerging-market financial market activity was driven primarily by stocks in Hungary, Peru, and India.[46]

It should be noted, furthermore, that the drops in risk were lowest for the EU countries, and still statistically significant. Those effects do not match the drops in risk observed earlier for the postcommunist countries at the stage where the "seal of approval" started, particularly taking into account the starting

[46] "Emerging-Market Stocks, Bonds Climb on IMF Bailout-Fund Plan," *Bloomberg*, 16 March 2009.

position; emerging-market yields had shot up dramatically at the onset of the financial crisis. Even though the relatively smaller drops in risk compared with non-EU countries indicate that there was some degree of market anticipation that the EU would bail out its members, it is clear that markets had not fully priced the expectation of a bailout into their reactions to those countries' advances in EU negotiations. This indicates that the expectation of corrective action from the institution was not driving the "seal of approval" effect that was observed in earlier models. For a period, markets tended to ignore bad behavior once a country is in the EU, as was shown in the examples of the early days of the Hungarian budget crisis and the SGP violations. Once bailouts actually occurred, market corrections did not put those countries back in the clear.

4.5 CONDITIONS WITHOUT MEMBERSHIP: THE EUROPEAN NEIGHBORHOOD POLICY

This section examines what happens when the policy change "company" offered by the EU stays constant, but the proposed level of integration varies. The European Neighborhood Policy (ENP), an initiative started in 2003, serves as an interesting comparison to the EU itself because it retains many of the structural characteristics of the enlargement process, including action plans, regular reports, and negotiations. However, eventual EU membership is not part of the deal. Thus, the ENP can serve as a further empirical test, holding constant many of the formal elements of the EU accession process but eliminating the ultimate condition of EU accession – even though the ENP offers much the same material benefits to participants as the EU itself, save participation in EU institutions. Examining investor reaction to the ENP shows a reaction to the institution itself, even though the policies and the company are essentially the same.

In addition to economic criteria, the ENP also promotes the strengthening of so-called common values, including democracy and human rights, rule of law, good governance, market economy principles, and sustainable development. Bilateral ENP Action Plans agreed between the EU and each partner establish an agenda of political and economic reforms with short- and medium-term priorities, which are monitored by European Commission subcommittees. ENP members also have access to structural funds as well as to the attendant EU bureaucratic structures, including a Neighborhood Infrastructure Facility, which offers funding to offset transition costs, and a Governance Facility, which awards money to countries that meet the governance objectives (Smith, 2005; Kelley, 2006a). However, ENP officials admit that because the programs are centered on the principle of "joint ownership" of reforms, the EU has no leverage to ensure that reforms are actually undertaken. Furthermore, they admit that the programs are not well publicized. "Elites know about the ENP

TABLE 4.11. *Event Analysis of ENP Action Plans (Same Company, Lower Proposed Integration)*

	Coefficient	Test Statistic
Action Plan with FTA	−1.25	1.11
Action Plan without FTA	.32	1.45
Member without Action Plan	−.38	1.75

Cumulative abnormal returns, pooled into countries with different action plans (Action Plan with FTA includes Lebanon, Israel, Jordan, Morocco, Palestinian Authority, Tunisia, Egypt, and Algeria; Action Plan without FTA includes Armenia, Azerbaijan, Georgia, Moldova, Ukraine, Russia, and Kazakhstan; Member without Action Plan includes Belarus, Libya, Mauritania, and Syria. Test statistics in parentheses; stars indicate statistical significance, where the statistic exceeds the absolute value of 1.96.

programs, but not the public. No one in the streets of Egypt, for example, will know anything about it."[47]

Member countries include Morocco, Algeria, Tunisia, Libya, Egypt, Jordan, Lebanon, Syria, Israel, Palestine, Mauritania, Moldova, Ukraine, Belarus, Georgia, Armenia, Azerbaijan, Russia, and Kazakhstan. Except for Algeria, Belarus, Kazakhstan, Libya, Mauritania, Russia, and Syria, all of these countries presented an action plan between February 2005 and March 2007, which was then implemented about six months later by the partner country. Egypt, Israel, Jordan, Lebanon, Morocco, Palestine, and Tunisia's action plans all have provisions for a free-trade area to be implemented. Armenia, Azerbaijan, Georgia, Moldova, and Ukraine's ENP programs, by contrast, do not include provisions for a free-trade area.

Table 4.11 uses the same event analysis method to investigate the countries that have initiated ENP action plans, both with and without FTA provisions, as well as the countries that simply opened talks to become ENP members. The dates of concluding the varieties of ENP programs all fell between 2004 and 2007. Table 4.11 depicts investor reactions in a thirty-day window around the date that the European Commission approved the ENP action plan. Because many of the countries do not issue debt on international markets, I substituted indices of overall stock market activity in their place. As no stock market or sovereign debt data could be obtained for Mauritania, Syria, and Palestine, those countries are excluded from the analysis.

Note that none of the forms of commitment under the ENP – despite the intensity of the level of commitment – seem to be of much interest to portfolio investors. On the whole, the listed countries did not record statistically significant stock market activity around the time of the approval of their ENP action plans, the level of ambition of those plans notwithstanding. This could be in

---

[47] Interview, Luigiandrea Pratolongo and Fanny Marchal, DG-Relex, 13 June 2008.

anticipation of noncompliance, but ENP officials state that those countries that have initiated ENP programs have thus far been broadly in compliance with the targets of their action plans.[48] However, interviews conducted in one country indicate that even local governments do not take the ENP seriously. According to one think tank head in Georgia – a country whose ENP action plan does not include an FTA – ENP negotiations "have shaped the Georgian reform program not at all...there is a government office but it is hardly of primary importance."[49] Georgia's fulfillment of its ENP action plan goals is more a result of the country's efforts to integrate with NATO and the EU and less to do with meeting the ENP requirements per se. The head of the Georgian National Investment Agency confirmed that foreign investors "are for the most part not even aware of what the neighborhood policy is or what it entails, though they are following the prospects of serious EU negotiations."[50] This is consistent with the view expressed by ENP officials.

Thus, it is more likely that without the lure of membership, markets are indifferent to an as-yet unproven mechanism for European integration. Considering that a quarter of these countries – namely Armenia, Azerbaijan, Georgia, Moldova, and Ukraine – have EU aspirations, markets may have even seen the implementation of the ENP as an indication that those countries are less likely to open formal EU negotiations for membership.[51] In fact, Ukraine's stock market activity dropped slightly on the days surrounding the announcement of the ENP action plan, perhaps because markets were anticipating a better deal than what Ukraine actually received. This would mean that, particularly for countries that seemed potentially likely to open formal negotiations for EU membership, ENP action plans – a decidedly second-best option to full membership – might even leave a country worse off than if it had no action plan at all.

4.6 CONCLUSION

This chapter's primary task has been to delineate on a micro level the three alternate hypotheses identified in Chapter 2 through which markets could view the process of EU integration. Unusually among IOs, the EU actually requires that countries meet certain standards of policy before they can even be considered for admission. This allows an examinination of the explanation put forward by Alternate Hypothesis 1, by looking at preexisting policy reform that the postcommunist countries performed in advance of EU membership. Policy reform, however, is not the main driver of the drop in risk. I also show through

---

[48] Interviews, Fanny Marchal and Luigiandrea Pratolongo, DG-Relex, Brussels, 13 June 2008.

[49] Interview, Alexander Rondeli, Georgian Foundation for Strategic and International Studies, Tbilisi, 5 May 2008.

[50] Interview, Tamuna Liluashvili, Georgia National Investment Agency, 6 May 2008.

[51] Interview, Alexander Rondeli, Georgian Foundation for Strategic and International Studies, Tbilisi, 5 May 2008.

two-stage modeling that the drop in investor risk is not primarily attributable to intrinsic qualities that drive countries both to have lower bond yields as well as to be considered for EU accession. The drops in risk that occur when countries negotiate for EU membership are not a function of selection, as described in Alternate Hypothesis 2, where the EU picks the countries that already have the best policies and the highest level of development. Contrary to Alternate Hypothesis 3, markets are also not reacting to the anticipated enforcement of rules, as demonstrated through the case of the 2005 Hungarian budget crisis. Instead, candidates feel the most forceful drops in sovereign risk when the EU looks favorably on preexisting policy reform. This demonstrates that investors do indeed rely on shortcuts – they pay attention when good-quality members certify the behavior of other members.

Many agreements with good members also promise good things in terms of market access. It is important to isolate an agreement's effects on a country's economic fundamentals – either through policy reform that the countries undertake, or through benefits that a country receives after becoming part of a larger economic entity. This chapter establishes, however, that the benefits of international economic organization go beyond the tangible gains from trade – that is, changes in a country's *ability* to service its debt. I show that further gains are made in terms of investor assessment of a country's willingness to service its debt. Evidence from the eurozone crisis demonstrates that this effect is more a result of herd behavior on the part of investors than of a credible commitment of new EU countries to economic reform.

It is interesting to note that the EU effect is strongest in the stages before countries actually become members. When governments have incentives to reform to be deemed acceptable for membership, the EU leverage may be strongest. Once countries actually become members, Brussels has far less direct influence on countries' behavior. In fact, many have claimed that the EU's only moment of actual leverage is in the accession stage; although Bulgaria has recently been punished with fines for backsliding on corruption, many other breaches of EU regulation have gone unpunished. The trick is that this may not matter to financial markets: the spectacle of clearing an EU-imposed hurdle may be sufficient to categorize a country as being among the EU peer group. That the boost of investor confidence occurs most tangibly at the negotiation stage – not at the moment of membership – implies that markets are most responsive to EU pronouncements on reform rather than the actual path of reform. This challenges our view that markets are efficient. Many have noted that markets seem relatively sanguine toward blatant breaches of EU policy among member states, including Germany, Greece, and Italy's violation of the limit of acceptable levels of government expenditure.

Whether the drop in risk is warranted is a separate point. Membership to the EU does entail access to a rich common market, structural funds, and, for those who adopt the euro as their currency, exchange rate harmonization, which eliminates currency risk across borders, and could doubtless offer stability for members. Membership also provides a framework of regulation through which contracts can be enforced.[52] But some have noted that the spreads between German bonds and those of poorer countries in the unions were unnaturally low and did not reflect the actual differences of risk between the markets (Düllmann and Windfur, 2001; Orlowski and Lommatzsch, 2005; Codogno, Favero, and Missale, 2003). These sections have shown that markets do not react to these attributes per se, but it could be the case that their faith in the EU's seal of approval overwhelms country performance as a result of being in the EU. Of related interest would be a separate empirical investigation of whether the EU seal of approval could be self-fulfilling. In economics, the literature on self-reinforcing behavior is well documented theoretically, although empirical tests are less common.[53]

How might countries that cannot join the EU seek to assure investors? Other visible international signals may not provoke drops in risk of the same magnitude but could offer some benefit. On the one hand, clear signals once entry criteria are fulfilled may be critical in endowing countries with the stamp of credibility; organizations where the requirements for membership are more fungible may not send as strong a signal to markets. On the other hand, as evidence from the SGP and the Hungarian budget crisis shows, under certain circumstances investors pay more attention to these initial signals than they do to subsequent enforcement. Similarly, organizations that do not announce such strong ties with potential members may not confer the same degree of credibility. The following chapter takes a look at the other side of this coin: that is, the impacts of close associations with poor-quality countries.

---

[52] Finance publications mention this phenomenon by name; a January 2003 Deutsche Bank emerging-markets bulletin on Croatia notes that "EU membership will provide a greater degree of legal certainty for both investors at large and corporate direct investment. Therefore, the degree of country risk has decreased."

[53] For formal models, see Corcosa et al. (2002); Vaugirard (2005); for empirical testing through experiments, see Tucker, Matsumura, and Subramanyam (2003).

5

When Emerging Markets Join Up with Bad Company

What types of close ties could signal a country's *unwillingness* to honor its debt obligations? Emerging markets face many potential types of groupings with many different types of countries. Not every country can go along with good company even if it so chooses; one cannot simply proclaim membership in organizations such as the EU and NAFTA. Of the organizations that remain available to emerging markets, some are with less than desirable countries. Practically, then, it is important to examine the many cases where countries sign on to integration arrangements that include members with poor reputations. The task of this chapter is to examine the downside of the company you keep – that is, when joining agreements with countries that have bad reputations tells investors that debt servicing might not be a priority. Following the logic of the theory, when countries form close unions with nations of low political quality, expectations of risk would increase.

Examining the consequences of "bad company" is an important component of the central argument (Hypothesis 1). It shows the mirror image of the drop in risk perceptions that occurs when emerging markets gain credibility by signing on to groups with good members. The flip side of this phenomenon should be an increase in risk when countries join arrangements with poor-quality members. For a country about which investors have mixed expectations, the international signal of closer ties with a known quantity of ill repute should in turn make the joining country seem more risky to investors. That is, when an emerging market country joins forces with a bad apple, it should itself look more risky.

This chapter not only looks at the effects of bad company on risk perceptions. It also demonstrates benefits of staying out of bad company, as is illustrated by El Salvador's refusal to sign onto Chávez's ALBA. The event studies of market reactions to announcements of integration with bad company also show the magnitude and duration of the effect. The change in risk perceptions is far less than that which is incurred by, say, a political coup (as occurred in Honduras) or a default on debt (in the case of Ecuador). But there is still a notable effect.

This chapter also shows – with the example of the proposed Eurasian Union alongside a proposed customs union for Belarus, Kazakhstan, and Russia – variations in the effect based on the level of projected economic integration; I show that the effect is less one of the level of integration itself than of the visibility of the announcement. The case of China's FTAs also demonstrates what happens when countries announce integration with countries whose reputation is somewhat mixed. Finally, this chapter further shows the reach of this effect and the kind of countries that are most susceptible to it. Countries with already established reputations do not gain or lose much when they sign onto bad-company agreements – a finding that also holds true in the case of the countries signing onto the EU, where the postcommunist countries that were relatively new to financial markets had the most to gain. That is, the heuristic of international organization is more influential when uncertainty is high in a country.

It would be necessary to hold constant, however, other attributes in the agreement that might be conflating the finding. Investors might be reacting to anti-market policy reforms that would have real impacts on future conditions in that country, such as economic growth or honoring of contracts. The large-N findings presented in Chapter 3 controlled for these possibilities econometrically. This chapter, however, will for the most part take snapshots of dynamics within particular organizations at a given time. Even though these agreements are examined in close focus, it is still possible to make inferences about market reaction based on changes in membership and not changes in policy (Alternate Hypothesis 1). The reason for this is that most of the agreements that one might consider particularly "bad company" are South-South arrangements. For the most part, the achievements of those agreements fall far short of their ambitions. Many have remarked on the implementation gap in the majority of regional economic arrangements (Haftel, 2012; Gray, 2014). Lacking strong enforcement mechanisms, true supranationality (wherein the agreements reached on the regional level automatically translate into domestic law), and domestic barriers to implementation both at the political and the infrastructural level, most of these agreements have a relatively poor track record of actual performance.[1] Most of these agreements have not encouraged policy reform among members, so it is reasonably safe to assume that investors are not anticipating future policy changes in their assessments of member states' sovereign risk; rather, the proposed depth of integration only makes an agreement more visible to more investors.

Furthermore, because accession procedures to these organizations are relatively uncompetitive, there are few significant policy changes in the run-up to

---

[1] For more details, see Ravenhill (2008) on the poor performance PTAs in Asia, Söderbaum (2005) on regional agreements in Africa, and Vaillant (2007) on Latin America, to name a few.

accession either. This is very different from the case of the EU accession of the postcommunist countries, which undertook significant economic reforms in order to be considered for and then eventually to move down the path toward EU accession. By contrast, for most other organizations, countries must simply express interest in order to join (Bienen and Mihretu, 2010), and existing members must vote on their acceptance. There are occasions where a new country's membership may be blocked or delayed for political reasons, but these very rarely have to do with that country failing to admit some preestablished set of criteria. Therefore, it is possible to be reasonably confident that market reaction is not being conflated with membership in a given organization with preexisting policy reform.[2]

Another advantage to examining these agreements up close is that they also hold region effects constant. A given change in risk could be interpreted as, for example, a Mercosur effect when it might be a Latin America effect; that is, the heuristic used by investors might apply to an entire region, not just to members of a particular organization. In the tests in Chapter 3, it was necessary to include separate variables that controlled for the factors that moved in tandem within a region. Because this chapter examines individual organizations *within* a given region, however, it is easier to separate out the dynamics associated with organizations from those with regions as a whole.

This chapter proceeds as follows. I first look at the impact for Latin America of joining Hugo Chávez's Bolivarian Alternative for the Americas. ALBA is a good illustration of the ability of international organizations to offer information about members' willingness (not ability) to honor their debt commitments. Although ALBA membership offered significant financial resources to members, it was a clear signal of a given country's sympathies and attitudes toward Western markets. For many countries, joining ALBA was not a particular surprise; for example, with the election in 2006 of the populist Evo Morales to Bolivia, it was clear that that country had taken a turn leftward. Thus, ALBA membership did not offer new information about that country's political orientation to investors. For other countries with less clear ideological bents, however, signing on to ALBA gave investors new insight as to their

---

[2] For both of these reasons, it is not feasible to run a selection model that takes into account the determinants of accession into a given organization and then conditions any change in investor perception on the estimated probability of accession – that is, to examine Alternate Hypothesis 2. Unlike in the case of EU membership – where the EU itself lays out very clearly the procedures for accession – most organizations have no explicit application procedures. The WTO is the only other organization that has such criteria (Copelovitch and Ohls, 2012). Indeed, in the developing world and in most cases of "bad company," countries occasionally exit from these organizations, whereas no country has yet left the WTO or the EU; this is perhaps an indication that membership procedures in these organizations are not especially rigorous or costly in the short term. Additionally, many less-developed countries are members of multiple organizations simultaneously. This means it would be difficult to set up a selection equation that would predict membership in one organization over another.

attitudes toward markets, and risk increased accordingly. Thus, this serves to illustrate that investors can make negative inferences about a new member to an organization where members have bad reputations.

I also examine the dynamics of the formation of two types of economic organizations in Eastern Europe and Central Asia. Russia, Belarus, and Kazakhstan had already established economic links, but in recent years they announced, first, a Customs Union and then a Eurasian Union, which envisaged not just economic but political convergence. This is a good test of the dynamics of the interaction between poor company and the proposed closeness of ties. Even when an identical grouping of countries – which already had a substantial number of economic linkages – announces unions with different levels of ambition, markets react differently to those unions, both because of the public nature of the announcement and the perceived seriousness of the intentions. This shows that investors respond not just to the company a country keeps but to how closely it is kept.

The final section explores another variation along the continuum of organizations that might have impacts on risk. What if a country about whom perceptions diverge joins an economic union? I use the case of China's establishment of free-trade areas in the developing world to demonstrate that the uncertainty in its new trading partners has widened. I demonstrate this by using an ARCH-in-means model, which allows us to model specifically the variance in an asset as well as an estimate of its price.

5.0.1 Event Studies and Uncertainty

The cases here will demonstrate – through empirical analysis as well as firsthand interviews – the reasons why joining economic agreements whose members make for "bad company" would make countries look more risky. This is an empirically more trying task than the positive case. For starters, unlike in the EU, the rules for entry for many of these agreements are far less stringent and less clearly documented, so it is difficult to isolate the processes of entry from preexisting trends in new members. Second, the data for countries in many of these South-South agreements are less thorough, spanning a shorter period of time and with a coarser level of granularity (observations are often monthly rather than daily).

It is possible, however, to take advantage of several features that these cases have over the more thoroughly documented ones. For example, unlike in Europe, in Latin America many countries have a good deal of wealth but high political risk – unlike in developed countries, where those two variables are usually inversely correlated. This affords an opportunity to examine the independent effects of both ability to repay debt (economic strength) and willingness to repay debt (political risk), which in these countries is often orthogonal. We can also look at changes in membership in agreements that have already been established – not accession, as examined previously, but exit.

This chapter primarily uses event studies to determine the effects of the company a country keeps on an empirical basis. Event studies can help give us a sense of market activity surrounding certain events. However, they are most effective for inference when investors are not anticipating a given news development. If investors had long been counting on a particular event, they would price their expectation of that event into a security prior to the occurrence of the event itself. Imagine, for example, an electoral victory where one candidate had for months maintained a clear lead in the polls. If that candidate then prevailed, there might not be much of a market reaction on the actual day of the vote, because investors would have already anticipated victory. It would be difficult to tell, then, if markets were actually unconcerned with the development, or if their reaction were already built into previous changes in the levels of that security (Shleifer, 2000). In these cases, uncertainty had to be relatively high around both the country in question as well as the possibility of its entry into a given agreement.

Furthermore, these events would have to occur in isolation. Much information is available to markets at any given moment, and it is necessary to separate as best as possible the reactions to that exact event rather than to other things that might be occurring in the news. That is, any change in markets sentiment should be attributable to a particular event, or – to take the elections example once again – to some specific element of a politician's platform, and not to any other world or local event that might be occuring at the same time. It is possible, of course, to hold constant general market sentiment on a news day, but it would be helpful to ensure that any change in a country's sovereign debt spreads could be attributable to one event – and, furthermore, that investors were interpreting that event in relatively similar ways (for example, that they viewed an announcement of market friendliness as an increase in the probability that that particular candidate would honor his or her international debt service obligations).

Thus, event studies are most useful in those circumstances when an event is truly unforseen – for example, a sudden natural disaster or a terrorist attack. Such shocks are difficult to come by in the political arena, where politicians reveal their platforms at every opportunity and often hint at policy changes months in advance of their actual enactment. However, if a government official announces an unexpected policy reversal, or if a politician acts against the wishes of his or her party, it would be safe to assume that these events are relatively more of a surprise than most political events. Market reaction surrounding such events could thus be more confidently interpreted as a genuine referendum on the future returns that investors expect as a function of that event alone. Each case described below centers on countries for whom announcement of integration would have been something of a surprise to investors, and would have been an unexpected move for that country. This design also addresses the potential of reverse causation: focusing on uncertain countries and relatively unexpected events inspires more confidence that it is

IO membership that is driving investor perceptions, and not the other way around.

5.1 DEFAULTS AND BAD COMPANY IN LATIN AMERICA

Latin America is rife with both regional arrangements and sovereign defaults. Given that default risk is a reality in the southern hemisphere, it is important to understand how markets price the likelihood of default, which plays a recurring role in emerging-market debt over time. Even in developed countries, defaults took place repeatedly throughout the nineteenth century but tapered off after World War II – as, too, did issuing of sovereign debt generally. The surge of trade in emerging-market debt in fact stemmed in part from a wave of defaults in the 1980s. These abrogations prompted the creation of the Brady Plan, which aimed to restructure bank debt into tradeable, liquid securities. Since 1980, defaults reached their peak in 1992, with fifty-eight countries in default on their foreign-currency-denominated sovereign debt. At the end of 2004, twenty-six countries were in default of their sovereign bonds, totaling some $126 billion in arrears (Reinhart and Rogoff, 2009) – and the majority of those countries were in Latin America.

Default not only imposes severe losses on creditor countries, but also has huge repercussions for the defaulter. Economists typically characterize the cost of default along five dimensions. First, defaults have negative impacts on international trade (Rose, 2002). Second, market access is temporarily restricted for those countries that default. After World War II, all Latin American countries were excluded from international capital markets until around 1960 (Sturzenegger and Zettelmeyer, 2005). In the 1930s, for example, the British government upheld what they called "diplomatic representations" (only lending to countries that had not previously defaulted), threats of trade-related sanctions, and siphoning off a portion of payments for imports from debtor countries to pay off interest (Eichengreen and Portes, 1989). Breaking from those agreements meant not only no loans, but no trade with Britain. Third, the cost of borrowing on international markets increases. Fourth, countries in default usually see capital flight, as foreign investors pull their money out of the country. Fifth, the domestic financial system suffers, as credit and output contract. Thus, effectively pricing the probability of default is primary in the minds of both creditors and the countries who want to borrow money.

A look at Latin America affords an opportunity to examine not only episodes of default but also a preponderance of agreements among states. Regional economic projects have existed in Latin America since the wars for independence in the early 1800s, but they have swept through the region with particular force since 2001. In the 1990s in particular, security, political and economic motivations drove every country to be interested in regional cooperation. Some fourteen integration schemes currently exist in South America, including the Andean

Community, the Latin American Integration Association, and Mercosur.[3] The design of them is largely similar; most strive for greater economic integration and cooperation, which means that most agreements have overlapping man-dates, purposes, and memberships. This is partially because there is "endless talk of regional integration in Latin America, but rather less action."[4] Another commentator described Latin American integration projects as a "crowded field of largely meaningless multilateral entities."[5] Most of these agreements have rather broad goals of cooperation and not much in the way of action plans; even the more rigorous one, Mercosur, achieved the most significant progress in trade liberalization in its early years but stalled once it hit the more sensitive economic sectors, and after financial crises hit Brazil in 1999 and Argentina in 2001 (Caetano and Vaillant, 2004). These overlapping and relatively weak agreements actually make it somewhat easy to examine our argument; given that the vast majority of these agreements seem to have accomplished little in terms of policy, and that their design does not seem to matter for effectiveness, it is very likely that investors would judge these agreements on the basis of their membership content.

Because entry for the most part is not especially competitive, and because, as mentioned earlier, membership in most of these organizations does not require extensive policy change, countries for the most part see little cost in joining multiple economic arrangements. Indeed, every single Latin American country is a member of at least nine and as many as eleven agreements – that is, the average Latin American country is a member of around 70 percent of the total number of agreements on offer for the region. Initially, it might seem that these overlapping memberships would make it difficult to discern the effects of any one particular member. Because most organizations in Latin America are so inclusive, membership in any one organization should not have much of an impact on investor perceptions one way or another. Thus, the organization would have to be relatively smaller or distinct in its mission to enable investors to clearly distinguish it from another organization. This is certainly the case with ALBA.

5.1.1 Investor Perceptions of Chávez's Bolivarian Revolution

Since being elected president in 1998 until his death in 2013, Venezuelan Pres-ident Hugo Chávez was one of the primary political influences in Latin Amer-ica, not only because of his vocal support of leftist policies and his anti-market stance, but also because of Venezuela's oil reserves. Spikes in commodity prices

---

[3] As of 2012, the full list is the Organization of American States (OAS), CELAC, the Association of Caribbean States (ACS), Caricom, UNASUR, the Andean Community (CAN), Mercosur, the Latin American Parliament (LAP), the Latin American Integration Association (LAIA), LAES, Rio Group, SICA, and ALBA.

[4] "The Pacific players go to market," *The Economist*, 7 April 2011.

[5] "CELAC latest lineup within the Americas," *Washington Times*, 19 December 2011.

allowed Chávez to finance many of his social and political projects – although at the cost of greater perceived risk among markets (one analyst commented that "when oil prices fall, it's going to be impossible to get back that lost credibility").[6] Though Chávez in his early years in office followed a relatively centrist program, sticking with the economic guidelines of the IMF and encouraging foreign corporations to invest in Venezuela, he embraced more radical policies in his second presidential term. After a series of attempted coups, alongside a spike in commodity prices that generated significant revenues for oil-rich Venezuela, Chávez began publicly articulating his ideology of a "socialism of the 21st Century," predicated on a rejection of neoliberal economic policies.

A significant part of this ideology was the establishment of the ALBA, which Chávez proposed in 2004 as an alternative to the proposed U.S.-backed Free Trade Area of the Americas. Its founding members were Cuba and Venezuela, with the subsequent addition of Bolivia (2006), Nicaragua (2007), Dominica and Honduras[7] (2008), and Saint Vincent and the Grenadines, Antigua and Barbuda, and Ecuador (2009). At the time of this writing, expansions were still being considered to include Suriname and Saint Lucia.[8] At one point, then-Russian President Dmitri Medvedev visited Venezuela to "discuss and consider our participation in the association's activities perhaps as an associated member," Medvedev said. If ALBA was consistent with Russia's agenda for a multipolar world, "then why not," Medvedev was quoted as saying.[9]

ALBA's benchmark ideology leaned far more to the left than did most other Latin American economic blocs. The organization promoted protection of national companies through favorable government procurement policies and tariffs on imported goods. Foreign companies operating on member states' soil were not acknowledged to have rights. ALBA members got cheap oil through Chávez's Petrocaribe program, which offered preferential rates on oil (at its peak, around 161,000 barrels per day) and pharmaceutical drugs through Cuba's State Center for Quality and Control of Medicines.[10] The year 2009

---

[6] "Chávez's Control of Bank Threatens Economy, Maza says," *Bloomberg*, 22 January 2007.

[7] Honduras exited the organization a year later, as will be discussed in further detail.

[8] It would be ideal to run a two-stage selection model, as in the previous chapter on EU accession, that would condition investor perceptions of Latin American and Caribbean countries on an estimated probability of ALBA membership determined in a first-stage equation. However, this technique is infeasible here because of the relatively few number of countries in ALBA and the recent time frame in which they joined. Additionally, four of the eight current ALBA members do not issue their debt on international markets, meaning that there are no observations for those countries on the dependent variable. For example, in a quarterly dataset of Latin American and Caribbean countries from 1993 to 2010, only 5 percent of observations are coded as 1 for ALBA membership – too few for a standard treatment-effects equation.

[9] "Medvedev meets with leaders of ALBA member-states," *Russia & CIS General Newswire*, 27 November 2008.

[10] "Chávez says Venezuela will meet all of energy needs of leftist allies," *The Associated Press*, 29 April 2007.

saw the establishment of an alternate currency for regional trade – the Sistema Único de Compensación Regional or SUCRE – although that currency is only in use for government-to-government exchanges. Even this move was described in anti-Western terms. "Enough with the dictatorship of the dollar, long live the SUCRE," Chávez announced after signing the relevant legislation.[11]

From the outset, it was clear that ALBA was being viewed internationally not according to its institutional design per se, but rather by its membership content. Media constantly referred to ALBA in terms of the ideology of its members, Venezuela in particular, with such descriptions as "Chávez's touted 'Bolivarian Alternative for the Americas' grouping of revolutionary socialist regimes known as ALBA,"[12] "[Chávez's] alliance of radical countries,"[13] "a group of leftist countries,"[14] "the Chávez Bolivarian paradise,"[15] or "the ALBA bloc of leftist Latin American countries."[16] One analyst, when describing ALBA, commented, "Observer members are Haiti, Iran, and Uruguay. Yes, I double checked on Iran, but seriously, who's surprised?"[17] These quotes all indicate that many pundits viewed ALBA through the lens of the reputation of its most visible members.

ALBA was also not discussed in the Western press in terms of its actual policies – aside from the promised transfers of aid – but instead of the political agendas of their banner members. "The ALBA countries, led by Venezuelan President Hugo Chávez, believe they are engaged in an ideological battle and need to employ every resource within the broad parameters of democratic legitimacy to pursue their political project and prevent what they call the right-wing oligarchs from returning to power," one political analyst was quoted as saying.[18] Another article described ALBA as "much leftist rhetoric, and few specifics."[19] Others called the agreement "a clever mixture of politics and economics, weighted toward the politics."[20] "According to any reasonable definition of the term, this is not a trade agreement," said a political analyst at Inter-American Dialogue in Washington. "It's an attempt to pose a real counterweight to the U.S. role and agenda in Latin America."[21] Contrasting the Central American Free Trade Agreement (CAFTA) with ALBA, one commentator

---

[11] "A Guide to ALBA," *Americas Quarterly*, 5 May 2011.
[12] "Sorry, Che, we blew it," *The Washington Times*, 18 June 2008.
[13] "A challenge for Chávez," *The Guardian*, 30 June 2009.
[14] "Coup rattles Central America," *The Financial Post*, 29 June 2009.
[15] "Time to Move Forward on Foreign Policy," *CBS News*, 8 September 2009.
[16] "Troops snatch President from bed and bundle him out of the country," *The Times of London*, 29 June 2009.
[17] Brian Hasbrouck, *Political Risk Explored*, 21 December 2009.
[18] "Despite Honduran crisis, Nicaraguan President Ortega launches bid to extend his term," *Christian Science Monitor*, 20 July 2009.
[19] "Bolivia Signs Pact With Leftist Allies," *Los Angeles Times*, 30 April 2006.
[20] "Castro, Chávez, Morales Sign Anti-U.S. Pact," *Associated Press*, 29 April 2006.
[21] "Cuba, Bolivia, Venezuela Reject U.S. Trade," *Associated Press*, 29 April 2006.

wrote, "CAFTA is a full-fledged trade agreement that promises new markets and incentives for business, but it is too new to judge. ALBA essentially offers its members the symbolism of Latin American unity and the immediate reality of Venezuelan dollars."[22] Those sentiments highlight the degree to which the economic policies in ALBA were viewed as being secondary to the politics.

Despite the proximity to bad company, the incentives to join ALBA were clear. For example, Bolivia was promised $150 million in transfers and loans to assist rural radio stations and fuel shipments along with other projects. Nicaragua received pledges for $60 million in similar financing, and $21 million was committed to Dominica.[23] This came along with promises of heavily subsidized Venezuelan oil to all ALBA members, which Chávez promised would guarantee the "supply of all [members'] energy needs . . . 100 percent."[24] For cash-strapped countries, these are strong arguments in favor of membership.

Yet even taking into account these financial motivations, many expressed concern that ALBA membership still carried reputational costs in the eyes of the international community. "Watching Hugo Chávez give $500,000,000 per year of 'free' money to [Nicaraguan President] Daniel Ortega; or almost $200,000,000 given to [Honduran President] Manuel 'Mel' Zelaya's government in Honduras to help with his illegal attempt at reelection, it's only natural that [Haitian] President Martelly be attracted by the possibility of more resources for his hurting people," wrote one analyst with regard to Haiti's possible entry into the bloc. "[But] while the siren's call of easy money may seem a panacea for the bureaucracy of the World Bank or USAID, membership in the ALBA will bring [Haiti] into common cause with the world's most destabilizing countries."[25] This illustrates the peer effects incurred by ALBA members, whatever the potential economic gains.

Countries were not unaware of these reputational consequences and of the potential alienation by the international community. But for many of them, the prospect of financial assistance and cheap energy were too attractive to turn down. Dominica, for example, particularly after the devastation wrought by Hurricane Dean in August 2007, turned to ALBA because it "needs an injection of capital," said Alix Boyd-Knights, speaker of the country's House of Assembly at the time. "Yes, we want to have friendly relations with the other countries, but at the same time it cannot be at having friendly relations at any cost, or at a loss to ourselves. You have to be realistic."[26] Similarly, Dominica's then-Prime Minister Roosevelt Skerrit defended ALBA membership as a justified response

---

[22] "Daniel Ortega's new best friend: Hugo Chávez," *Salon*, 8 February 2007.

[23] "Trade group to provide Dominica $21 million," *Associated Press*, 3 September 2008.

[24] "Chávez says Venezuela will meet all of energy needs of leftist allies," *The Associated Press*, 29 April 2007.

[25] "Haiti Should Stay Away From Chávez's ALBA," *Huffington Post*, 12 January 2012.

[26] "Dominica house speaker defends joining Venezuela's ALBA bloc," *BBC Monitoring*, 29 February 2008.

in the face of what he perceived as U.S. inattention. "We have said to the United States it needs to be more responsive to the concerns of the Caribbean region.... A relationship is a two-way communication. If there are people who are prepared to listen to Dominica that's the point."[27] In a subsequent speech, Skerrit expressed gratitude for Chávez's attention, saying, "We shall make no apologies... that President Chávez is our friend and the people of Venezuela are our friends."[28] Thus, it was clear that some countries felt the potential economic benefits of ALBA outweighed the reputational costs.

ALBA Membership: Not New Information for Some

Were markets, in fact, surprised that any of the countries signed on to ALBA – that is, did ALBA membership give markets new information that went against the conventional wisdom about those countries? For some of those members, joining ALBA was simply a confirmation of their leaders' preexisting anti-market tendencies. Cuba had already been operating as a one-party communist state with a largely closed economy for decades, so its leftward leanings were already well established. Its key role in the foundation of ALBA was perhaps even less surprising than Venezuela's participation, given the chilly relationship between the United States and Cuba and Fidel Castro's decades-long mainte-nance of a state-planned economy.

Similarly, for Nicaragua – the poorest nation in mainland Latin America – ALBA membership was just an additional piece of evidence about its leaders' longstanding populist tendencies. Daniel Ortega – who had already served as president from 1985 to 1990 – had been a longtime member of the social-ist Sandinista National Liberation Front. Ortega has been a leading figure in Nicaraguan politics since he led the Sandinistas to overthrow dictator Anasta-sio Somoza in 1979. After being elected president for the second time in 2006 – under claims of widespread fraud from the opposition – one of Ortega's first acts in office was to pay a visit to Iranian President Mahmoud Ahmadinejad.[29] "The revolutions of Iran and Nicaragua are almost twin revolutions," Ortega told the press on the occasion of the visit, "since both revolutions are about jus-tice, liberty, self-determination, and the struggle against imperialism."[30] Thus, Ortega was a leader who had long been in the news, and whose ideological leanings were apparent from the very beginning, so Nicaragua's ALBA mem-bership was likely not a novel piece of information to markets.

Bolivia's membership was also not much of a surprise. The country's pres-ident, Evo Morales, came to power in December 2005 as the party leader for the Movement for Socialism, in the country's first majority victory by a single

---

[27] "Dominica denies backing for Venezuelan integration plan," *BBC Monitoring Latin America*, 1 March 2007.
[28] "Venezuela's Chávez calls for anti-imperialist unity as he woos Caribbean," *Associated Press*, 17 February 2007.
[29] "Nicaragua opposition candidate calls Ortega win 'fraud,'" *BBC*, 7 November 2011.
[30] "Nicaragua e Irán, 'Unión Invencible,'" *BBC Mundo*, 7 June 2007.

party. Morales, an avowed socialist, had promised a break from the country's colonial past, and he used the gains from nationalizing the country's oil, mines, gas, and communications sectors to finance programs to aid the poor. Morales's signing of the agreement, less than four months after he took office, occurred just days after Chávez pulled Venezuela out of the Andean free-trade agreement in opposition to Peru's and Colombia's negotiations of free-trade agreements with the United States. "It's amazing, but new leaders have made me the happiest man in the world," Castro said at the time. "Now, for the first time, there are three of us."[31]

For these countries, then, markets would not react substantially to ALBA membership, because their leaders' leftward tendencies were already well established.[32] Indeed, a comparison of the market reactions in terms of risk confirm this expectation; none of the countries experienced statistically significant abnormal returns surrounding their membership of ALBA. This is most likely attributable to the fact that markets had already priced in their concerns about those countries' anti-market leanings well in advance, and ALBA membership – though a public and negative event – did not provide them with any new information about those countries.

Changes in Risk for Honduras, on Entry and Exit

The other countries in ALBA, however, did not fit this pattern in quite the same way. The case of Honduras provides a good example of a country for which signing onto ALBA was somewhat unexpected – and that signing was followed by an exit that was presaged in the press but not necessarily a sure deal. Honduras had been receiving aid from the United States since the mid-1980s and had been on a path of neoliberal economic reform since the 1990s. When Manuel Zelaya was elected president in 2005, he campaigned as a conservative. The early years of his presidency, however, were marked by attempts to control the media and other abuses of power.[33] Honduras had previously been an ally of the United States, after a long history of accepting economic aid in exchange for anti-Sandinista interventions, but when Zelaya signed on to ALBA in August of 2008, his leanings had clearly changed. He stated at the time that the country did not need permission from any "empire" to join the agreement.[34] This move may not have been altogether unexpected at the time, given Zelaya's attempts to concentrate power, but it was not completely in keeping with the president's initial policy platform. Thus, ALBA membership

---

[31] "Leftist leaders sign 'people's' pact: Trade deal counters U.S. movement," *The Calgary Herald*, 1 May 2006.

[32] Saint Vincent, Antigua and Barbuda, and Dominica are also ALBA members; one might expect that the reputations of small nations such as these without much of a history in capital markets would be negatively impacted by ALBA membership. However, none of these countries issue sovereign debt instruments on international markets, so these claims cannot be tested.

[33] "The Truth Comes Out in Honduras," *Wall Street Journal*, 25 July 2011.

[34] "Honduras signs up to Chávez-led trade bloc," *EuroNews*, 26 August 2008.

might be considered as more of a revelation to markets than in the case of countries that had a more consistent anti-Western stance.

At the time, Honduras's membership in ALBA was controversial both domestically and abroad. As for many of the members, joining ALBA was an attractive financial prospect; in keeping with ALBA's policy of agricultural promotion, Honduras was promised $30 million worth of access loans for farmers, and Venezuela pledged a donation of 100 tractors. Castro also spoke of a program where Cuban teachers would travel around the country teaching reading skills. More importantly, Venezuela also promised to buy bonds worth $100 million for housing programs.[35] The prospect of financial assistance was a powerful argument for Honduras in favor of signing on to ALBA; one paper claimed that "aid benefits (medical and food supplies) are more likely drawing Honduras closer to the controversial bloc rather than any embrace of the bloc's economic and political orientations."[36]

Yet ALBA membership was hotly contested in the country's parliament, on the grounds that ALBA membership would keep Honduras from integrating into the global economy; furthermore, many were skeptical that the promised aid would actually arrive. Cheap oil for ALBA would mean less revenue for Venezuela, because the country would have had to divert its supplies from the United States, where it received premium prices.[37] Opponents of the move were also worried about the reputational cost of joining the agreement. "The key source of concern rests on the diplomatic implications of joining the group. Honduras's main economic and political partner has long been the U.S.," wrote one source. "However, most of the ALBA nations are at odds with the superpower and Honduras's joining the anti-U.S. grouping casts a negative light as to where its diplomatic priorities lie."[38] Others commented that Zelaya's "recent adherence to Venezuelan President Hugo Chávez's Bolivarian Alternative for the Americas (ALBA)... represent a significant political risk."[39]

Once Honduras announced ALBA membership, risk increased by a statistically significant 1.56 percentage points in the thirty days surrounding the event.[40] Even though Zelaya had already been making moves to announce his leftward inclinations, there was still an added increase in risk once he announced close ties with ALBA. Considering that that event had been foreshadowed in the press and preceded a very visible change in government to a more right-wing orientation, this is still a substantial increase in risk.

[35] "Leaning left: Honduras joins a club promoted by Venezuela and Cuba," *The Economist*, 20 October 2008.
[36] "Opposition to Nicaraguan President's Visit Intensifies in Honduras," *Global Insight*, 22 August 2008.
[37] "Chávez says Venezuela will meet all of energy needs of leftist allies," *Associated Press*, 29 April 2007.
[38] "Honduras Joins Leftist Bloc Amid Opposition Concerns," *Global Insight*, 26 August 2008.
[39] "Honduras: Zelaya risks ALBA membership," *Oxford Analytica*, 16 September 2008.
[40] In a sixty-day event window, risk increased by 1.47 percentage points.

Ultimately, Zelaya's closeness to Chávez prompted the business community and the middle class to fear the introduction of socialist populism.[41] After an attempt to change the constitution so that his four-year presidential term could be extended, Zelaya was overthrown in a military coup – the first in Central America since the end of the Cold War.[42] ALBA was even invoked by some local commentators who were critical of Zelaya's moves to the left. "[The government] wanted to turn Honduras over to Chávez," said a local news editor. "Hondurans don't want that."[43] The coup was controversial, and world leaders initially expressed disapproval of the overthrow of a democratically elected leader.[44] However, the new president, Porfirio "Pepe" Lobo Sosa, was quick to convince the international community of the legality of the coup and to reestablish global ties.[45]

Part of this strategy involved relations cooling with ALBA. Shortly after the coup, ALBA countries had agreed to withdraw their ambassadors from Honduras in protest.[46] Chávez and Castro had both been vocally critical of the subsequent election that followed the coup, calling it another example of U.S.-endorsed meddling in Latin American affairs.[47] Chávez – who had allegedly given advisors and logistical support to Zelaya in his attempts to extend his term (a move with which Chávez was familiar, having removed his own term limits in February of that year) – threatened military action if harm befell any of the representatives of the Venezuelan embassy.[48]

Subsequent to the elections, on 16 December 2009, the new president submitted to Honduras's Congress a proposal to withdraw from ALBA on the basis of its "disrespectful treatment" of Honduras.[49] Justifying the decision, Honduran President Lobo claimed that ALBA was "very given to intervening in the internal affairs of other states, [and] the proof is that they wanted to delegitimize the [Honduran] elections.... No agreement should mean submission to another country or its participation in military or political matters.[50]

---

[41] "Lawmakers and Business Leaders Oppose Honduras Joining Leftist Latin American Alliance," *Global Insight*, 4 August 2008.

[42] "Honduran President Is Ousted in Coup," *New York Times*, 28 June 2009.

[43] "Honduran president-elect calls for unity and reconciliation; U.S. plans to work with new government," *Washington Times*, 1 December 2009.

[44] "Obama says Honduras coup illegal," *BBC*, 29 June 2009.

[45] "Honduran president-elect calls for unity and reconciliation; U.S. plans to work with new government," *Washington Times*, 1 December 2009. However, the legality of the coup is still debated; an OAS commission acknowledged that Zelaya was a corrupt head of state but that the coup was not legitimate. See "Honduras Truth Commission rules Zelaya removal was coup," *BBC*, 7 July 2011.

[46] "ALBA withdraws ambassadors from Honduras," *CCTV News*, 30 June 2009.

[47] "Castro slams US-backed 'electoral farce' in Honduras," *Agence France Presse*, 13 December 2009.

[48] "Chávez threatens military action over Honduras coup," *Reuters*, 28 June 2009.

[49] "Honduran de facto government announces withdrawal from ALBA," *Xinhua*, 16 December 2009.

[50] "Honduran elected authorities support withdrawal from ALBA," *Infosur Hoy*, 29 December 2009.

At the time, it was clear that Honduras's Congress – whose members were overwhelmingly sympathetic to the coup – was prepared to approve Honduras's exit from ALBA. The deputy head of the Nationalist party was quoted as saying, "Making an analysis of whether it has brought benefits or not to the country, one would easily conclude that there have been many more detrimental than positive effects; as a result, we would be in agreement with this initiative."[51] The head of the National Party at the time said he "supports the withdrawal from ALBA because Honduras was surprised by its effects: it was offered cooperation [through ALBA], and in practice it became part of a political-military agreement." Another member of Congress claimed that ALBA had "hidden clauses and small print which established a commitment from Honduras in relation to political and military matters.... [ALBA] brought money to the government of president Zelaya, with the agreement to change the model of government and turn it to left-wing totalitarianism."[52]

Interestingly, leaving ALBA was not cast as a move that would significantly affect Honduras's economic situation. Honduras was still part of Petrocaribe – indeed, the oil program covers seventeen members, only eight of which were ALBA members. Furthermore, Lobo stressed that Honduras would still have commercial relations with ALBA member countries on a bilateral basis.[53] This is another indication that any market reaction to ALBA exit would be based on the political, rather than economic, implications of the agreement.

As anticipated, on 10 January 2010, the Honduran Congress voted 123 to 5 to withdraw from ALBA. This move was met with scorn from Chávez, who claimed that Honduras "had already left ALBA and turned its backs on the poorest in Honduras the day the coup took place."[54] But for markets, exiting ALBA was good news. Cumulative abnormal market returns for Honduran government debt, in a thirty-day event window, were a statistically significant drop in risk by .23 percentage points; in a sixty-day window, the overall change was a drop of .10 percentage points.[55] This contrasts with a statistically significant increase in risk of 1.47 percentage points around the signing of ALBA.[56] Markets punished and rewarded, respectively, association and disassociation with ALBA in almost equal measure; upon exiting ALBA, Honduras regained nearly all the confidence it had lost as a functioning of joining the agreement in the first place.

---

[51] Ibid.

[52] Ibid.

[53] "Honduras takes steps to withdraw from ALBA," *El Universal*, 16 December 2009.

[54] "Turning against the poor; Chávez and Zelaya condemn withdrawal from trade treaty as 'right-wing agenda,'" *Morning Star*, 14 January 2010.

[55] Honduras Government Notes up to two years; predicted returns generated as a function of JP Morgan's EMBI for Latin America. *Source*: Global Financial Data; benchmarked against the JP Morgan Emerging Market Bond Index.

[56] For comparison's sake, this was also within a sixty-day window; this time is justifiable given the long durations of the discussion surrounding each event.

The scale of market reaction was relatively small in magnitude, compared with the other events that were taking place in Honduras at the time. ALBA membership could not compare with a dramatic coup, which resulted in a change of risk of around 15 percentage points. However, it is clear that investors saw Honduras's exit from ALBA as good news – and not for economic reasons, but for the company it had chosen not to keep.

Changes in Risk for Ecuador

Ecuador was a more ambiguous case than was Honduras, in terms of the types of expectations markets might have had as to its debt performance and the degree to which ALBA membership updated those expectations in a uniform way. Not only its leader at the time of ALBA membership but also the country's recent history did not have the best of reputation with financial markets. In the last part of the twentith century, the country had a particularly volatile history since the fall of its military dictatorship in 1979. From the mid-1990s up to 2007, the country had gone through seven presidents[57] and a number of economic crises. One of these crises, in 1999, was so severe that the country defaulted on its sovereign debt and subsequently abandoned its own currency, adopting the U.S. dollar as part of a broader package of economic reform.[58] In May 2006 – when Alfredo Palacio, previously the country's vice-president, entered higher office after the previous president, Lucio Gutiérrez, was removed from power by Congress for abuse of power – the United States broke off its FTA negotiations with Ecuador, ongoing since 2006, because of the government's annulment of an operating contract with the U.S.-based Occidental Petroleum Corporation.[59] Clearly, Ecuador was not in the category of what investors would consider good company. One analyst commented, "Everyone knows the bad countries – Ecuador, Venezuela, Bolivia, Argentina – and steers clear."[60]

This trend continued once Rafael Correa was elected president in 2007, on a campaign platform promising a "citizen's revolution" of economic restructuring to provide more funding for social programs directed at the poor and a rejection of economic ties with the United States, including threats to renege on the country's debt commitments.[61] Correa, an economist by training, had briefly served as finance minister under Palacio but had been forced to resign after he publicly denounced the World Bank's withholding of a $100 million

---

[57] One of those presidents, Abdala Bucaram – who in the run-up to elections once climbed down the swinging ladder of a helicopter wearing a Batman costume – recorded an album called *The Madman Who Loves* to encapsulate his campaign promises. He was subsequently deposed by Congress for "mental incapacity." See "President Bucaram, 'A Madman Who Loves' – and Sings," *IPS*, 11 October 1996.

[58] "Ecuador Says It Will Default on Its Foreign Debt," *Wall Street Journal*, 12 December 2008.

[59] "US cancels Ecuador FTA talks because of broken contract," *Associated Press*, 18 May 2006.

[60] "Political Risk: Latin American Markets Brace," *LatinFinance*, March 2010.

[61] "Ecuador Update," KSN Consulting, 6 December 2007.

loan to Ecuador. In a radio address on 15 November 2008, Correa announced, "We'll take until 15 December to decide if we'll keep paying or if we'll fight a legal battle, because those debt renegotiations were a veritable robbery for the country." He added: "We're not playing around. If there is a sufficient basis for us to say: 'we can't pay this debt because it's illegitimate,' that's what we'll do. Let the bond prices fall, let the country risk go up . . . that doesn't interest us at all, that doesn't concern us at all."[62] On 12 December 2008, Correa announced Ecuador's second debt default in less than a decade, on $31 million worth of the government's 2012 bond issues as well as two other global bond issues due in 2015 and 2030.[63] After originally offering bondholders a haircut of 35 cents on the dollar, Ecuador bought back 94 percent of its defaulted bonds in 2009.[64]

Analysts noted at the time that the default was "purely at this point a function of willingness, not ability [to pay]."[65] The debt burden was only 21 percent of its GDP, and the country – an oil exporter – had been benefiting from high commodity prices.[66] "Correa is really, really convinced foreign debt is like the devil and he doesn't have to pay," said the head of emerging-market macroeconomic strategy at Bulltick Capital Markets in Miami. "There's a strong ideological component here."[67] Thus, the consensus was that internal politics motivated Correa's decision to default on the country's foreign debt obligations.

However, Correa had also made some early moves to distance his country from Chávez. After Venezuela left the Andean Community in 2006 in protest of FTA negotiations between the United States and Peru, Colombia, and Ecuador, Correa was vocal in his criticism of the move. In fact, even though Ecuador was being courted to join ALBA, Correa said Ecuador would only do so if Venezuela returned to the Andean Community. The Ecuadorian president also refused the offer of a Venezuelan loan in 2007. Most decisively, however, in what was described as an "unexpected turn of Ecuadorian foreign policy [away from] left-driven regional initiatives,"[68] in June 2008, Correa announced formally that his country would not be signing on to ALBA, citing a lack of concrete, meaningful proposals. This was an event that made many take notice. A U.S. embassy cable noted that "the Ministry of Foreign Affairs stressed that [Ecuador] had no intention of joining ALBA in the short or medium term, as the group does

---

[62] "Ecuador auditing sovereign bonds delays interest payments," *Merco Press*, 16 November 2008.

[63] "Possible scenarios after Ecuador debt default," *Reuters*, 12 December 2008.

[64] It also borrowed $7.25 billion from China, raised taxes on oil companies and banks, and raided the country's pension fund to finance its budget. See "China Loans Ecuador $1 Billion As Correa Plans First Bond Sale Since 2005," *Bloomberg*, 24 January 2012.

[65] "Ecuador defaults on its foreign debt," *Wall Street Journal*, December 12, 2008.

[66] "Lessons from Ecuador's bond default," *Reuters*, 29 May 2009.

[67] "Ecuador Says It Will Default on Its Foreign Debt," *Wall Street Journal*, 12 December 2008.

[68] "Ecuador refuses to join ALBA," *NowPublic News*, 13 June 2008.

not offer any concrete initiatives. . . . ALBA was essentially political and there were no firm proposals or projects presented in any area discussed at the summit. [The minister] noted that he 'did not understand' what ALBA would do."[69]

But this stance against Venezuela did not last long. "The choreography devised to accomplish [ALBA's] objectives is simple: handout petroleum in advantageous terms to countries, 'without' strings attached, and collect the IOUs in terms of progressive political loyalty, until the country has gone from friend to recruit," one analyst wrote. "Some leaders, like Nicaragua's Ortega and Bolivia's Morales, were already ideologically predisposed, while the seduction of Ecuador's Correa took a little more time."[70] On 6 June 2009, Chávez used his weekly radio address to announce that Ecuador would join the agreement in a few weeks' time.[71] At the occasion of Ecuador's accession, Correa announced that "we will join ALBA so that our voices can be heard at international forums saying that we are determined to change the current unjust international order."[72] On the same day, Saint Vincent and the Grenadines, as well as Antigua and Barbuda, also signed on to the agreement.[73]

Figure 5.1 shows cumulative abnormal returns on JP Morgan's EMBI+ Ecuador government bond spreads, where returns are a function of EMBI+ for Latin America.[74]

The increase in risk in the thirty-day window surrounding the event measured at a statistically significant 5.7 percentage points. This is far smaller than the 17-percentage-point increase in cumulative abnormal returns surrounding the default of Ecuador's bonds on 2008. But it is in fact surprisingly large, given that Correa had signaled his intention to default on foreign debt back in his election campaign, and thus his unreliability as a debtor was well known. This indicates that markets took Correa's shunning of ALBA as a positive sign for the country's future trajectory.

El Salvador Stays Out
El Salvador was an example of a country with an ambiguous reputation that actually benefited in the eyes of financial markets from staying out of ALBA. A series of military dictatorships ruled the country from 1931 to 1979. In

---

[69] "Ecuador – No Plans to Join Bolivarian Alternative," U.S. Declassified Diplomatic Cable, U.S. Embassy in Ecuador, 9 May 2007. A U.S. embassy comment on the report stated, "We suspect that these career diplomats are reflecting current GOE policy. That said, this decision will not ultimately be driven by the technocrats. This appears to represent President Correa's calculus at this time, but we would not rule out a change of position in the future."

[70] "The Chávez Adventure in Honduras: From Coup d'Etat to Coup d'Grace?" *Human Events*, 13 July, 2009.

[71] "Ecuador to Join ALBA June 24," *IPS*, 6 June 2009.

[72] "President Rafael Correa Highlights Importance of Ecuador's Integration into ALBA," *Cuban News Agency*, 23 June, 2009.

[73] "Ecuador joins ALBA this week, announced President Chávez," *Mercopress*, 22 June, 2009.

[74] EMBI are denominated in basis points rather than percentage points; hence the different scale.

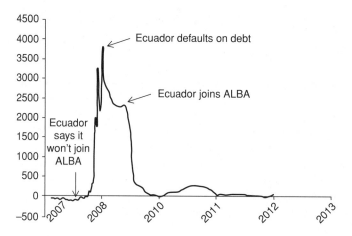

FIGURE 5.1. Changes in Risk for Ecuador.

the 1980s, then-U.S. President Ronald Reagan called El Salvador the southern border of the United States, setting the stage for a decade-long proxy war
between the United States and the Soviet Union, in which 75,000 people died.
The cornerstone of this war was the uprising of a Cuban-supplied, left-wing
guerrilla group called the Farabundo Martí National Liberation Front (FMLN),
which was brutally repressed by a U.S.-backed reformist military junta. In
1989, Nationalist Republican Alliance (Arena), a powerful conservative party,
took office and subsequently controlled the presidency continuously until
2009. Although relative peace and full democracy arrived in 1992, violence
and unrest continued to plague the country; in 2008, El Salvador had the
world's highest murder rate, with more deaths per day than during their civil
wars.

The 2009 elections pitted Arena's presidential candidate, Rodrigo Ávila, a
former police chief, against Mauricio Funes of the FMLN, which had been
considered the most powerful leftist guerrilla organization in the Americas.
Despite FMLN's reputation, Funes campaigned as a centrist, promising to
increase taxes on the rich to fund social programs while pledging economic
reform and the maintenance of the dollar as El Salvador's currency. These
pledges notwithstanding, the selection of Salvador Sánchez Cerén for vice-
president worried many; Sánchez had led a hard-line Marxist faction of the
FMLN during the civil war. Four days after the 11 September 2001 attacks
in the United States, Ceren burned a U.S. flag and congratulated al Qaeda
for punishing the United States for its wrongdoings around the world. Based
on Ceren's reputation, "it is laughable," the *Washington Times* wrote in an
editorial, "when front-man Funes says he will seek closer ties with the U.S. if
elected.... The real winner ... assuming the FMLN prevails, will be Venezuelan dictator Hugo Chávez, [who] has been the FMLN's sugar daddy for

years."[75] The *Economist* wrote that Ceren, the "real muscle" in the ticket, "crystallizes the fears of some Salvadoreans that Mr Funes is a front man for a party still controlled by the far left, which would align El Salvador with Cuba and Hugo Chávez's Venezuela."[76] At best, Funes was thought to be a "wild card."[77] This indicates a high level of uncertainty around Funes's intentions and orientation.

Yet upon entering office with a 51.32 percent win, Funes maintained his centrist platform. He reached out to conservative party leaders and members of the business community, appointing representatives from the financial sector to his economic cabinet. He also maintained good relations with the World Bank, the IMF, and the Inter-American Development Bank, maintaining a market-friendly orientation.[78] At the same time, he appeased the left by expanding social programs – including rural health care and anti-crime measures as well as universal basic education – and giving subsidies to farmers and small businesses. Although he paid a historic visit to Cuba – the first by an El Salvadorian president in fifty years – he stressed that the visit was meant to spur the import of cheap medicines and was not an effort at political closeness.[79] He attempted to advance social-democratic policies in the style of Brazil's Luiz Inácio Lula da Silva, whom he often praised.[80]

But as one newspaper put it, "President Funes's own political ideology is best judged by the company he keeps internationally."[81] Funes had maintained distance between himself and Chávez, and the Venezuelan leader had not attended Funes's inauguration. Nonetheless, there had been significant pressure within his party to deepen ties with Chávez, who had given cheap oil and other financing to FMLN-controlled districts in El Salvador.[82] But on 14 January 2010, Funes formally pledged that he would not bring El Salvador into ALBA. "If the FMLN wants to become part of the ALBA with its mayors, or as a political party it wishes to participate in the efforts that the ALBA governments, parties, and countries carry out, then do it, there's no problem, but this government is not going to do it," Funes said in an announcement. "The FMLN has a certain vision about international relations and about the projects it has decided on at the international level, especially on a regional scale, [and] I do not totally share it. . . . I have decided to work more toward Central American integration, toward consolidating a regional bloc, toward uniting policies and

---

[75] "U.S. needs Latin policy to end neglect, contain threat," *The Washington Times*, 15 March 2009.

[76] "El Salvador's presidential election: A nation divided," *The Economist*, 12 March 2009. The article also quoted a local analyst as saying, "Funes is a democrat, but much of his party is not. . . . A lot of them see democracy as a means to make the revolution."

[77] "Funes Government Considered a Wildcard," *The Nica Times*, 19 May 2009.

[78] "Mauricio Funes: His Way," *Analitica*, 11 February 2010.

[79] "El Salvador's president: So far, so good," *The Economist*, 16 December 2010.

[80] "Left turn: The voters opt for 'safe change,'" *The Economist*, 19 March 2009.

[81] "Mauricio Funes: His Way," *Analitica*, 11 February 2010.

[82] "The FMLN blackmail," *Analitica*, 1 February 2009.

FIGURE 5.2. Changes in Risk for El Salvador.

uniting efforts with the presidents of the region, rather than looking toward other entities such as the ALBA."[83] Funes added that he was looking toward a "greater strategic relationship" with the United States, which is "a government presided over by a Democrat of clear convictions, who has a different vision of the North-South relationship."[84] Indeed, in the following year, U.S. President Barack Obama made El Salvador his only Central American stop on a Latin American tour and praised Funes for his leadership.[85]

Although Funes had always kept Chávez at arm's length, many had expected Funes to bow to party pressure to move further leftward once he entered into office. As one paper described it, "his moves so far have surprised many who expected the leader of the Salvadoran leftists to draw closer to the Venezuelan president."[86] Once he established his distance, however, markets took this as a positive signal.

Figure 5.2 shows the drop in risk that El Salvador received: cumulatively, the drop in risk for spreads on Salvadorian debt[87] was 3.84 percentage points (or 384 basis points). This shows the goodwill that markets extended toward Funes as a result of his distancing from ALBA.

It should be noted that, as before, this boost in market credibility was finite. Because emerging markets did better than expected in 2011–2012, the spread

[83] "Honduras Withdraws from ALBA, El Salvador Won't Join Despite FMLN Support," Venezuelanalysis.com, 18 January 2010.

[84] Ibid.

[85] "In El Salvador, Obama lauds Funes as a model Central American leader," *The Christian Science Monitor*, 23 March 2011.

[86] "Split With the Past," *LatinTrade*, 1 February 2010.

[87] Based on JP Morgan's EMBI+ El Salvador Government Bond Spread (EMBPSLVM), differenced off EMBI Latin America.

for El Salvadorian debt actually increased. The country experienced sluggish growth relative to the rest of Latin America, with only 1.5 percent GDP growth in 2011.[88] Slipping popularity led to a loss of seats for the FMLN in elections in 2012, with the right-wing Arena party holding a majority.[89] So avoiding bad company cannot substitute altogether for good economic fundamentals, but it can at least provide a temporary increase in confidence – and it is possible that joining ALBA would have led to a more entrenched loss of investor confidence than staying out.

In sum, the case of ALBA has illustrated many aspects of the theory. This is an example of an organization that did not necessarily have a high level of proposed integration – although it did announce the establishment of a common currency, those proposals were never implemented – but was populated with arguably the worst of "bad company," considering its foundation by Venezuela and Cuba. Thus, in terms of the interaction described in Chapter 2 and tested in Chapter 3, the weight of bad company did the work here, not the proposed closeness of ties. This organization also was one that was clearly viewed in terms of its membership content and not any measure of policy reform that it promoted; indeed, given that there were no admission criteria, Alternative Hypotheses 2 or 3 – that preexisting policy reform or subsequent enforcement of rules might be driving any market reaction to countries joining the agreement – can be ruled out. Similarly, by examining countries with leaders who had ambiguous commitments to the left, such as Ecuador, El Salvador, and Honduras, where ALBA membership was truly a surprise – or, at least, that different actors had different expectations that could have canceled each other out – Alternate Hypothesis 1, that leaders tended to "select" into agreements that reflected their underlying tendencies, most likely does not hold.

This case also gives further insight into the duration and magnitude of the effect. The company you keep does not affect markets to the degree of a coup (Honduras), or persistently poor economic performance (El Salvador), or a default (Ecuador). But it can still make a difference in the short term, and investors most likely price this knowledge into their future valuation of that country's sovereign assets.

5.2 PERCEPTIONS OF RUSSIA AND THE EURASIAN UNION

The case of the proposed Customs Union among Belarus, Kazakhstan, and Russia, and the subsequently proposed Eurasian Union (with those same three

---

[88] "Official: El Salvador 'not falling apart,'" *Tico Times*, 1 June 2012. The article quoted Funes's top advisor as saying, "El Salvador had the lowest level of growth in Central America despite all the reforms.... We have pretty much tried everything there is to do. We've opened the economy and we've signed free trade agreements, but we still have an economy that does not grow at the rate it needs to grow."

[89] "Separation of powers: Elections in El Salvador and Belize," *The Economist*, 15 March 2012.

countries as founding members), helps gain leverage on a different aspect of the theory: how the proposed level of integration affects investor perception, holding company constant. In the case of ALBA, the policies – or lack thereof – are more or less held equal, and the changes in perceived sovereign risk for some new members could be attributed to the spillover of the poor reputations of Venezuela and Cuba. With regard to the Eurasian Union, the company stayed relatively fixed, but one crucial thing shifted. The level of *proposed* integration, and therefore the public nature of the announcement, varied even though the members did not. This allows leverage on the question of to what degree proposed integration might be driving investor effects, rather than the quality of members. Because both the Customs Union and the Eurasian Union have at the time of writing only been announced and not actually implemented, in this case it is safe to reject Alternate Hypotheses 2 and 3: that preexisting policy reform and subsequent enforcement are driving investor reaction to the proposed unions.

As above, however, investors would only react to these announcements if they represented new information about a country on whom expectations had not already converged. At first glance, it would seem as though none of the countries involved – Belarus, Kazakhstan, and Russia – fit the bill. Belarus is often called Europe's last dictatorship. President Alexander Lukashenka came to power in 1994 and quickly moved to extend the scope of his power as well as his term limits. His rule has been marked by the suppression of free speech and of the opposition. In the mostly closed, largely state-run economy, there are almost no private businesses, and "foreign investors stay away."[90] The country has long had close economic ties with Russia. It benefited from energy price booms in the late part of the 2000s but suffered a downturn in the summer of 2011 when a balance-of-payments crisis drained the country's hard-currency reserves.

Similarly, since the breakup of the Soviet Union in 1991, Kazakhstan had a long period of authoritarian rule and a state-managed economy. Kazakhstan is Central Asia's largest economy, with significant oil, mineral, and metal reserves. The Organization for Security and Cooperation in Europe has criticized the country's elections as not meeting democratic standards. In 2004, Transparency International labeled the Nazarbayev regime as being plagued by "rampant corruption." Accordingly, Kazakhstan had long been shunned by international direct and portfolio investors alike. "The issue of Kazakhstan is political risk," said a fund manager at BlueBay Asset Management. "It's the only risk you cannot quantify. That's why for the best part of three years we haven't invested in any Kazakh deal."[91]

Russia, however, represents a slightly different case – in the late 2000s its political direction was up in the air, and its recent economic history was

---

[90] "Belarus country profile," *BBC*, 23 December 2011.
[91] "Default risks could sour demand for corporate debt," *Reuters*, 26 January 2012.

tarnished. The country had default in its recent history; in 1998, following blowback from the East Asian financial crisis, the Russian government devalued the ruble and declared a moratorium on payment to foreign creditors. Vladimir Putin, a former KGB agent who had been appointed to the post of president in 2000 by outgoing head of state Boris Yeltsin, enjoyed wide popularity as a result of the relative political stability and economic prosperity that Russia saw under his tenure. However, his rule was controversial in the West for his authoritarian style and his suppression of free speech. Putin ended his second presidential term in 2008, to be replaced by Dmitry Medvedev, who positioned himself as a pro-Western moderate. However, Putin was subsequently appointed prime minister, leading some to speculate that he was still the central power in the Kremlin. This suspicion appeared to be validated when, toward the end of his term in office on 24 September 2011, Medvedev officially proposed that Putin stand for the presidency in 2012. Although Putin pledged to continue down Medvedev's path of economic modernization and gradual political reforms, there was uncertainty as to whether Russia would take a different direction; for example, one commentator noted that the tone but not the substance of Russian foreign policy would be likely to change under Putin.[92] Thus, during the time period within which both the newly invigorated Customs Union and the Eurasian Union were announced, Russia's reputation was somewhat in flux, and investors would potentially be responsive to what they perceived as new information on the government's trajectory.

5.2.1 A New Customs Union and a Planned Eurasian Union

Economic integration schemes among some of the former Soviet Union states had long been in existence, including a preexisting free trade area (CISFTA), the Eurasian Economic Community (Eurasec), a Common Economic Space established under the Commonwealth of Independent States (CIS), and a Collective Security Treaty Organization. In fact, a customs union among Belarus, Kazakhstan, and Russia had already been on the books since the late 1990s. Furthermore, after the breakup of the Soviet Union, many of those countries had joined the proposed free-trade area of the Commonwealth of Independent States, an economic organization that was supposed to have established a free-trade area as well as a broader program of economic and political cooperation – although the organization's track record was patchy (Sakwa and Webber, 1999). The CIS was criticized for having "ill-defined, often contradictory strategies, and a lackluster economic base."[93] In fact, the Russian acronym for the CIS is SNG, leading many to nickname the group as the *Soyuz Nizhshykh i Golodnykh* (Union of the Lowly and Hungry). Thus, economic integration had already existed on paper – if not in practice – for many of the former Soviet

---

[92] "Putin Calls For Eurasian Union In Former Soviet Space," *RFE/RL*, 9 October 2011.
[93] "Europe Endless," *Central Europe Review*, 17 January 2000.

Union countries, as well as for Belarus, Kazakhstan, and Russia in particular, in the form of a nominal customs union.

Even the idea of a Eurasian Union itself had been in circulation for several years. In a March 1995 meeting in London, Kazakh President Nazarbaev had proposed the formation of something called a Eurasian Union – but by May, he had already abandoned the idea. In a 2011 speech, one Russian Duma representative claimed that elites had decided to form an Eurasian Economic Community in 2000.[94]

At a tripartate meeting in Minsk in November 2009, Belarussian, Kazakh, and Russian heads of state agreed to form a customs union, to be put in place by July 2010.[95] Then-President Medvedev described the move as "a very significant and long-awaited decision."[96] But the announcement did not receive much coverage: of 292 related news articles on Lexis Nexis in the two-month period surrounding the event, only 7 were from major world publications,[97] and even that one was the BBC Monitoring's regional sources.

By contrast, Putin's subsequent announcement in November 2011 of the eventual formation of a Eurasian Union to be implemented in 2015, following the announcement of his return to the presidency, received a much stronger reaction in the media. Of 723 news articles on that topic in major world publications, 267 – nearly a third – were in major world publications. This illustrates the point that the proposed depth of integration is significant not in terms of the policy reform entailed per se, but of the public nature of the commitment.

Initially, it might seem as though there should have been no market reaction to either announcement, because some level of de jure integration had already existed among the former Soviet Union countries. But news media treated it as a novel event. One paper described the Eurasian Union announcement as "the surprise announcement of a free-trade zone being created in the former communist bloc"[98] – even though CIS member states had already agreed to establish a free-trade area back in 1996. Another paper called the plan "unexpected,"[99] and AFP described the move as a "surprise announcement."[100] Therefore, the announcement of the Eurasian Union was not only more public than that of the Customs Union, but it was also billed as being new information altogether.

---

[94] "Road to Eurasian Union Will Take Five Years," *Izvestia,* 17 November 2011.

[95] "Russia, Belarus, Kazakhstan to create unified economic space by Jan. 2012," *RIA Novosti,* 19 December 2009.

[96] "Russia, Belarus, Kazakhstan agree on customs bloc," *AFP,* 27 November 2009.

[97] Based on a Lexis Nexis search, which describes its category of major world publications as "news sources from around the world which are held in high esteem for their content reliability. This includes the world's major newspapers, magazines and trade publications which are relied upon for the accuracy and integrity of their reporting."

[98] "Vladimir Putin pushes for closer ex-Soviet Union," *Daily Telegraph,* 19 October 2011.

[99] "Putin reveals plan for 'new Soviet Union,'" *The Times of London,* 5 October 2011.

[100] "Snubbed By EU, Ukraine Edges Toward Russia," *AFP,* 19 October 2011.

The prospect of a Eurasian Union was received in both Russia and the West with suspicion on two somewhat contradictory fronts. The first was motivated by the fear – particularly pronounced in the West and in former communist countries that had a history of tense relations with Russia – that the proposed Eurasian Union was the first step of an attempt to reinvigorate the Russian empire. The union was described as "one of Moscow's top foreign policy priorities."[101] Many decried the Eurasian Union for being a means for Moscow to exert influence over former Soviet states,[102] as well as an attempt to lure countries such as Ukraine away from closer ties to the European Union.[103] Interestingly, others saw the Eurasian Union as an attempt to counteract not the European Union but China, which had been investing heavily in the former Soviet Central Asian republics.[104]

The second view – rather at odds with the first – was that the proposal was just another in a series of meaningless agreements in the post-Soviet space. From 1992 to 2005, no fewer than 182 treaties had been signed among the former Soviet Union countries (Willerton, Goertz, and Slobodchikoff, 2012). Very few of them have actually been implemented fully. One article described the pattern since 1992 as follows: "CIS leaders gather and agree in principle on the need for closer cooperation (usually with a few demurrals). Months pass, and the various parties cannot concur on the details of integration. Then the whole cycle begins afresh."[105] For example, the CIS countries signed a treaty establishing an economic union on 24 September 1993, then signed an agreement to unify customs procedures on 8 July 1994, and that same year – on 21 October – established an Interstate Economic Committee with a secretariat in Moscow, not in Minsk, the home of the CIS secretariat. But once the committee met for the first time on 18 November, the member states decided that the agreed-on voting system – which was proportional to market size – gave too much weight to Russia, but at the same time could not agree on delegating powers to the secretariat, leaving the organization powerless to implement any further proposals.[106] In another example, one CIS summit in October 2007 produced seventeen agreements on its own, but one paper noted that "despite the move toward greater integration on paper, it remains

---

[101] "Eurasian Union Proposal Key Aspect of Putin's Expected Presidency," *Stratfor*, 7 October 2011.

[102] "Don't Bet on the BRICs," *BusinessWeek*, 3 November 2011.

[103] One paper wrote, "The name was deliberately chosen. For most of the last century, Eurasia was scarcely a neutral term: it evoked the whiff of racial degeneration, the prospect of civilisation overrun by eastern hordes" (see "Eurasia: the old dream," *The Guardian*, 8 October 2011). Another wrote that "creating a pseudo-Soviet Union in the teeth of encroaching Chinese and American influence would see [Putin] hailed as the man who clawed back the Russian Empire" (see "Vladimir Putin's plan to create a Eurasian Union is about reclaiming the Russian Empire," *Telegraph*, 5 October 2011).

[104] Russia's Eastern Anxieties, *International Herald Tribune*, 17 October 2011.

[105] "Slow Progress For CIS Economies," *Transitions*, 25 February 1995.

[106] Ibid.

uncertain to what extent the agreements will be implemented."[107] With regard to the customs union, another noted that "CIS agreements are often worth more on paper than in practice."[108] Similarly, regarding the free-trade zone within the CIS countries, even Ukrainian President Viktor Yanukovych noted in 2012 that even though the agreement had been in existence since 1994, "this agreement did not exist for practically all the years of independence, and I will say candidly, Russia did not much want to have such an agreement."[109]

Although these two sources of skepticism seem contradictory, they both reinforce the central idea of the book. Observers can be dubious about the proposed Eurasian Union's ability to promote real cooperation, but at the same time fearful of the intent behind the project. This illustrates that many perceptions of proposed closer ties have very little to do with the actual policies that might be entailed, and are instead motivated by mistrust over the political implications of the ways in which members of a group might overtly or covertly influence one another.

As with ALBA, it became clear that the Eurasian Union had more of a political than an economic bent. The organization replicated many preexisting integration efforts and did not "contain anything new; a model of concentric circles of integration – from the Customs Union to the extensive Eurasian Space – has been laid out by the ideologues of the project more than once."[110] Thus, contrary to Alternate Hypothesis 1, it seems unlikely that any investor reaction to the announcement of the organization's formation would have been in anticipation of new policy reforms that the organization would have promoted.

But the proposed Eurasian Union did distinguish itself by the types of countries and politicians that expressed interest in or disdain for it. As with ALBA, there were some intimations that countries were primarily interested in the idea of the Eurasian Union because of the prospect of assistance from Russia.[111] But most of the expressions of support or rejection were political in nature.[112]

---

[107] "Signed, Sealed, and Deliberated," *Transitions Online*, 10 October 2007.

[108] "Kyrgyzstan Rushes into Moscow's Economic Embrace," Eurasianet.org, 20 October 2011.

[109] "Ukrainian president interviewed on relations with Russia, political situation," *Rossiyskaya Gazeta*, 19 March 2012.

[110] "Russian PM's integration idea seen as ongoing 'prudent regionalization' policy," *Gazeta*, 10 October 2011.

[111] One Web site wrote, "Now they have signed up to the Customs Union – the impoverished Kyrgyzstan, which virtually has no economy whatsoever and is ready to accept any financial aid from anyone at all, [would like to join]. . . . Everyone is prepared to live on Russian money, but no one is ready to hand over to Russia full control over local assets or even over its own sponsorship money." "Russian website pessimistic about Putin's plans for 'empire from test tube,'" *Gazeta*, 24 October 2011.

[112] Armenia did lodge a practical complaint; the prime minister said that the country would not be interested in joining because "in practice, there are no examples of a country joining a customs union with which it has no common border because the whole thing loses its economic meaning [without such a border]." "Armenian Premier: No Plans To Join Russia's 'Eurasian Union,'" *RFE/RL*, 8 December 2011.

Georgian President Mikhail Saakashvili, who had long tried to position Georgia as a West-friendly nation and whose country had engaged in military conflict with Russia, was vocal in his attempts to distance himself from the Eurasian Union, stating that the project represented "the most savage idea of Russian nationalists."[113] At the other end of the spectrum, politicians in Moldova's breakaway republic of Transdniestr – which still allies with the defunct Soviet Union, down to a preponderance of Lenin statues in its cities[114] – spoke out in favor of the organization. One politician said, "We should enter this union at least economically, if not politically, although it's the political aspect that interests us in the first place. The people I talked to [in Moscow] do not think it's impossible."[115] In the middle, Ukraine – split between pro-EU sentiments in the country's west and a more Russian and Central Asian orientation in the east – prevaricated on membership. Government officials tried to express interest in the Eurasian Union without alienating the EU; at a conference entitled "Ukraine on the crossroads: the EU and/or the Eurasian Union," Prime Minister Viktor Yanukovych told organizers, "Before our meeting I was about to suggest a small amendment: you were right to put the word 'and' between the EU and the Eurasian Union but I would remove the 'or'," adding, "Ukraine has never contrasted one economic organization with the other and we cannot do that."[116] Thus, it appears that members were positioning themselves to the EU with respect to the political and reputational implications that membership would have.

As before, for countries that already had solid reputations – for better or for worse – with markets, there would not be much of a change in investor perception, as the news of the Eurasian Union would not provide markets with new information about those countries' intentions. Both Belarus and Kazakhstan had long and visible histories as regimes with poor reputations, so no change would be expected in those countries' risk levels. Russian politics, however, were at the time of announcement of both agreements in a period when expectations of the government's future behavior were certainly not uniform. Although Medvedev had made strides toward economic reform and Western rapprochement, and even though Putin had promised to continue those policies, his reinstatement as president after having already served two terms cast doubt on his future intentions. Thus, the theory would predict that Russia's public declaration of closer ties with Belarus and Kazakhstan would result in increases in risk for that country, to some extent with respect to the Customs Union but to a greater extent for the more visible Eurasian Union. Even though

---

[113] "Eurasian Union Proposal Key Aspect of Putin's Expected Presidency," *Stratfor*, 7 October 2011.

[114] "Trans-Dniester 'Nation' Resents Shady Reputation," *New York Times*, 5 March 2002.

[115] "Moldova's breakaway republic of Transdniestr should join Eurasian Union," *Ukraine General Newswire*, 28 November 2011.

[116] "Ukraine never contrasted EU with Eurasian Union," *Ukraine General Newswire*, 17 May 2012.

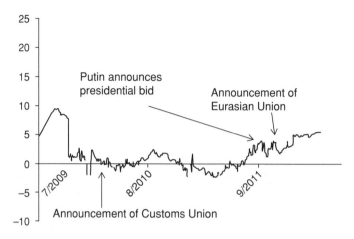

FIGURE 5.3. Changes in Risk for Russia.

the goals and eventual membership space of the Eurasian Union were more ambitious than those of the Customs Union, the fact that these types of unions had a long history of being proposed but not implemented makes this case a reasonably close approximation of a natural experiment, in which the proposed level of integration varies but the company does not.

Figure 5.3 shows the cumulative abnormal returns for three-month treasury bill yields for Russia, with attention drawn to the announcement of the Customs Union (on January 1, 2010) and the Eurasian Union (on 18 November 2011), as well as Putin's announced return to the presidency.[117]

Russian sovereign debt saw no statistically significant abnormal returns for a sixty-day window surrounding the announcement of the Customs Union.[118] However, the announcement of the Eurasian Union was associated with an increase in risk of .35 percentage points (standard deviation .05). This indicates that on balance, Russia's reputation worsened temporarily among investors with the announcement of the Eurasian Union. By contrast, there was no statistically significant reaction to the announcement of the customs union among those same countries. This test does not show what exactly investors were reacting to, but given fact that the only committed members (Belarus, Russia, and Kazakhstan) had already announced a customs union in the previous year, to no noticeable reaction, and given the poor reputation for implementation among previous post-Soviet integration schemes, investors likely responded to the political direction that Russia seemed to be taking, in contrast to Medvedev's pro-Western leanings. That Putin was choosing to ally himself with Kazakhstan

---

[117] Spreads on Russian three-month treasury bills benchmarked against three-month German treasury yields. *Source*: Global Financial Data.

[118] Abnormal returns were -.01 (standard deviation .07)

and Belarus and to shore up links among the former Soviet Union countries shows that he was choosing company that investors found suspicious.

5.3 WHEN COUNTRIES LEAVE A "BAD COMPANY" ORGANIZATION

This section shows the further influence of the company a country keeps by examining what happens when a relatively good-quality member leaves an organization of mixed reputation. Exit from international organizations occurs relatively infrequently. Usually, the perceived political cost of exit means that countries tend to simply skip paying their membership dues but remain in the organization. There are some exceptions to this; for example, Chile had been a member of the Andean Community since its inception in 1969 but withdrew in 1976, claiming that it produced unfavorable political situations on the domestic front, but data limitations prevent examination of the impact of this move. Additionally, in 2006 Venezuela left the Andean Community in protest of the bloc's attempts to establish a free-trade agreement with the United States.[119] However, even without Venezuela, the Andean Community was still encumbered with the anti-market Bolivia and Ecuador; according to one analyst, "when Venezuela left, Bolivia just stepped into its role."[120] Peru's foreign trade minister at the time, Mercedes Araoz, commented that even without Venezuela, the Andean Community consisted of "two countries with a marked leftist tendency – Ecuador and Bolivia – and two more open countries, Colombia and Peru."[121] Thus, the political content of the organization did not improve significantly and would be expected to provoke little investor reaction.

However, the case of COMESA and SADC in sub-Saharan Africa does afford an opportunity to explore whether – as in the case of Latin America – markets look favorably at countries that divest themselves of bad company. Both blocs comprise many of the same members, but SADC has the benefit of being spearheaded by South Africa, which is not only the continent's biggest market but is also among the countries with high perceived quality of governance. The Southern African Development Coordination Conference[122] was first formalized in July 1981, subsequently evolving into the Southern African Development Community in July 1992. South Africa joined SADC in 1994, followed by Mauritius (August 1995), the Democratic Republic of Congo (September 1997), Seychelles (1997), and Madagascar (2005). With GDP

---

[119] Venezuela's official letter of exit read in part: "In general the Free Trade Treaties possess the same neo-liberal concepts as the Free Trade Area of the Americas, translating into injustice, inequality, exclusion, minority privilege, discrimination and destruction of the principles of equality and progression in the guarantee and enjoyment of rights, establishing new forms of colonialism."

[120] Interview, Ricardo Paredes, COMEX-Peru, 10 July 2009.

[121] "Will Ecuador turn toward Mercosur?" *World Trade Review*, 31 January 2007.

[122] Members included Angola, Botswana, Lesotho, Malawi, Mozambique, Swaziland, Tanzania, Zambia, and Zimbabwe.

per capita at $3,152 in 2006, SADC is gradually building a southern African free-trade area, which is supposedly set to mature into a common market by 2015 (its planned transition to customs union by 2010 has yet to materialize).

COMESA had a largely similar structure, minus South Africa and with a few more countries, such as Egypt.[123] The treaty establishing COMESA was signed on 5 November 1993, and was ratified a year later, on 8 December 1994. At the time of its founding, COMESA member states included fifteen of the twenty-three countries that the United Nations had designated as least developed, and currently have an average GDP per capita of around $1,800. The organization has had a difficult time meeting its own deadlines. It was supposed to establish a totally free-trade area initially by 2000, but presently only eleven of the twenty-one members have eliminated their internal barriers, and nontariff barriers remain widespread. The planned customs union for 2004 has not yet materialized, although it is currently scheduled for 2008. Member countries were supposed to have reduced their tariffs by 80 percent as of October 2006, but only five members managed to do so. Monetary union was originally envisaged by 2025. But at the bloc's eleventh summit in November 2006, the main rallying cry was for doing away with nontariff barriers and for adopting "good governance and amicable coexistence."[124] The average political quality for the organization was thus a bit worse – but COMESA had also lost its status as a potential partner in EU trade negotiations. [125]

In the late 1990s, the EU was in the process of beginning to negotiate Economic Partnership Arrangements to its former colonies to extend the nonreciprocal preferences it had extended to its former colonies; those preferences were being lifted in order for the EU to be compliant with the WTO. The EU had previously granted preferences to many of its former colonies under the so-called

---

[123] Members included Burundi, Comoros, Democratic Republic of the Congo, Djibouti, Egypt, Eritrea, Ethiopia, Kenya, Libya, Madagascar, Malawi, Mauritius, Rwanda, Seychelles, South Sudan, Sudan, Swaziland, Uganda, Zambia, and Zimbabwe.

[124] "Africa's main bloc calls for slash of non-tariff barriers, end conflicts," *Agence France Presse*, 16 November 2006.

[125] Mozambique also withdrew from COMESA in 1995, specifically citing its desire to integrate more closely with SADC. For its part, Seychelles announced in July 2003 that it would pull out of SADC as of 1 July 2004, saying that the high membership fees ($500,000 per year) were not offset by parallel benefits. When it left the bloc in 2004, Seychelles had failed for some time to pay its membership dues and was subsequently penalized by being denied the right to speak during SADC meetings ("Seychelles to pull out of SADC, IOR regional cooperations," *Agence France Presse*, 7 July 2003). Unfortunately, because Seychelles only began issuing its debt on international markets in 2006, that case also must regrettably remain untested. Namibia also announced on 16 May 2003 that it would pull out of COMESA (though according to restrictions imposed by the treaty, its withdrawal did not take effect until May 2004, even though the country stopped participating in COMESA activities). Namibia had not been part of the free-trade area within COMESA. At the time, a Namibian official said that "SADC was a more important building bloc than COMESA" ("Namibia Pulls Out of COMESA," *The Namibian*, 16 May 2003). However, Namibian debt is only available on a monthly basis, which is too infrequent for event analysis.

Cotonou agreement, but the WTO had granted them a finite waiver to do so, because those preferences went against the WTO principle of trade reciprocity. Thus, since 2002, the EU has been involved in attempts to negotiate free-trade areas with much of the developing world, as an explicit part of its development strategy. Its most aggressive efforts were directed toward its former colonies, but simultaneously it has attempted to establish free-trade areas in Latin America. It has directed far less energy toward East and South Asia, with proposed links limited to "an informal process of dialogue and cooperation." The EU initially tried to promote a regional approach in its trade negotiations, particularly with the EPAs. It grouped the African-Caribbean-Pacific (ACP) countries into four regional subgroupings in Africa, attempting to negotiate directly with many of the trade agreements already in place. It echoed this approach, with similar results, in Latin America. But disagreements among the members of the various agreements meant that even the provisional agreements that managed to be signed were concluded with individual countries.

Many critics viewed these measures as an attempt on the part of the EU to privilege foreign investment over African growth priorities; a typical criticism called the EPAs "a threat... to the right and capacity in general of African countries to develop their economies according to the needs of their people and their own national, regional and continental priorities."[126] "It will kill off any ambitions for regional integration within and across Africa and South-South relations with other developing regions," another analyst said.[127] EU Trade Commissioner Peter Mandelson and EU Development Commissioner Louis Michel refuted these charges, saying, "The problem is that EU businesses and investors have too little interest in these regions, not that they have too much."[128] They also pointed out that openness would benefit Africa far more than Europe, given that the continent makes up such a small percentage of EU trade.

Nonetheless, the EPA negotiation was at the forefront of Tanzania's consideration of its overlapping memberships in African trade agreements – as well as the "high membership costs" of being in both COMESA and SADC and a "lack of economic gains" – when it exited the organization in October 2000.[129] The EU had expressed interest in conducting an EPA with only one of Africa's RTAs. The EU finally launched its EPA negotiation with the SADC on 8 July 2004. Under this arrangement, individual SADC members could negotiate their own EPA with the EU, and six of the fourteen were doing so, including Angola, Botswana, Lesotho, Mozambique, Namibia, and Swaziland, with South Africa taking part in the negotiation as an observer. Tanzania, in

---

[126] "Stop Economic Partnership Agreements, Civil Societies Cry Out," *Africa News*, 17 September 2007.
[127] "Speakers Denounce EPAs as Hurdles to Africa's UN Goals," *InterPress Service*, 11 April 2009.
[128] "Nobody is Pushing Free Trade, EU Chiefs Urge." *The Guardian,* 30 October 2007.
[129] "Tanzania Reaffirms Decision to Quit COMESA," *Africa News*, 16 August 2000.

fact, was denied the right to negotiate because of its overtures to COMESA as well as its overlapping membership in the East African Community Customs Union. "I cannot see any economic advantage of being a member of more than one [trade] bloc," the EU head of trade was quoted as saying with respect to Tanzania. "Countries have to identify the center of gravity when it comes to regional integration. Economic advantages can only be accrued if a country remains within one customs union."[130]

One interview with a trade advisor at COMESA revealed that "this was at at a time when Tanzania was trying to make some kind of point internationally.... We were negotiating with them to stay, but it became this kind of exercise in face-saving, and when they backed out despite our efforts we lost a lot of credibility."[131] Another confirmed that "SADC had always been a more coherent unit, and when Tanzania and Namibia left it really became the center of gravity in terms of regional organizations."[132] Similarly, another interview subject stated that "it is hard to take COMESA seriously when it can't even incentivize its more important members to stay in it," and that this downgrading in credibility "didn't have so much to do with trade as with the overall image [of COMESA]."[133]

Tanzania's economic policies and even potential gains from trade did not change much as a result of leaving COMESA. It maintained bilateral agreements with its main trading partners in COMESA, so as to counteract any trade losses.[134] Because SADC's FTA already zero-rated 85 percent of Tanzania's tariff lines, Tanzanian traders maintained nearly the same leverage as did those in COMESA.[135] Additionally, Tanzania was not unambiguously of much lower political risk than many other African countries; its World Bank governance score at the time of its pullout was ranked in the forty-first percentile in Africa. Although corruption and electoral misconduct were common, the country – unlike many in Africa – had little history of internal or external violent conflict, except the 1979 war with Uganda. Therefore, Tanzania had reputational gains to be made as a result of leaving the organization.

It is more difficult to do a precise event study in this case, because of the frequency of observations for African countries. Because the capital markets are not deep, data are often only available on a quarterly or monthly basis, and many of the countries do not issue their debt on international markets at all. Furthermore, a parallel counterfactual is difficult to establish, because there are no African countries that issue sovereign bonds that are not included in one of these two trade agreements. Similarly, it is infeasible to test the differences

---

[130] "EU advises Tanzania to stick to one economic agreement," *The Guardian,* 21 January 2005.
[131] Author interview, Mwansa Musonda, Senior Trade Advisor, COMESA, 2 December 2008.
[132] Author interview, Jay S. Salkin, Advisor, Research Department, Bank of Botswana, 25 November 2008.
[133] Author interview, Charles Harvey, University of Botswana, 28 November 2008.
[134] "Tanzania to Ensure Trade With COMESA After Pullout," *Xinhua,* 6 September 2000.
[135] "Tanzania Will Not Rejoin COMESA," *The Citizen,* 8 July 2008.

in means between countries in the two trading blocs as a function of market reaction to different shocks. This is because the RTAs have a strong overlap in membership, and most of Africa's nonmembers do not issue their debt on international financial markets.

Nonetheless, an event study of abnormal returns surrounding Tanzania's exit from COMESA indicates an improvement in investor perceptions of the country. In a thirty-day event window surrounding its exit, Tanzania received a statistically significant drop of risk of .21 percentage points[136] following its withdrawal from COMESA. If the event window is widened to sixty days, the drop in risk is .92 percentage points and is also statistically significant.[137] This could have been attributable to its departing poor company or – with the prospect of the EU signing an EPA with SADC, where it still retained membership – signing on to potentially better company. But Tanzania did look better to investors after it pulled out of an agreement where members had a lower overall quality of governance. Though this is far from a definitive test of the consequences of membership, this should serve as an indication of the change in perceptions that investors have as a result of membership in organizations with poor-quality members.

5.4 INCREASES IN UNCERTAINTY: CHINA'S REACH INTO EMERGING MARKETS

So far, this chapter has examined the impact of countries with decidedly poor reputations proposing economic unions. But what happens when a country that has a mixed reputation signs onto agreements with emerging markets? This section further investigates the dynamics of international affiliations by examining the impact of China's free-trade associations. This case tests the middle point of the curve in the theoretical graph in Chapter 2, where a country whose political risk is in the middle of the spectrum joins relatively loose economic unions. There might be no overall changes in risk for the signatories, but that may simply be because investor reactions diverge to the extent that they cancel each other out. That is, some investors might see this as a sign of increased risk, but an equal number might regard this as a risk-decreasing prospect. If there are an equal number on both sides, the opposing effects will negate each other, such that the observed effect is zero. However, if that were the case, the standard errors around these estimates will increase even if there is no notable change in risk itself.

Particularly since the global economic crisis has hamstrung markets in the United States and Europe, more and more eyes are turning to China, which has continued to make significant inroads to increase its ties in emerging markets. Even prior to the financial crisis, China had been investing heavily in Africa and

---

[136] Test statistic is 2.78; greater than 1.96 indicates statistical significance.
[137] Test statistic is 2.32; greater than 1.96 indicates statistical significance.

India, particularly in the form of direct investment in commodities. At present, China is currently carrying out feasibility studies, negotiating or actually implementing FTAs with more than twenty countries or regions, mainly in the Asia-Pacific region. It has has so far established fourteen FTAs: ASEAN (2002), Hong Kong (2002), Macau (2003), Thailand (2003), Niger (2005), Chile (2006), Pakistan (2006), New Zealand (2008), Peru (2008), and Singapore (2008). It is currently in FTA negotiations with Australia, Pakistan, the Southern Africa Customs Union, the Gulf Cooperation Council, Iceland, Norway, and Costa Rica, with plans to eventually open deals with Japan, India, Taiwan, and South Korea.

The reception to China's FTAs has been particularly cautious in emerging markets in Asia. Officials in countries such as Myanmar – which itself has little to lose in terms of political credibility – have made a point of expressing their enthusiasm for Chinese investment.[138] Other nations seem wary of Chinese domination of the region, while mindful of the potential gains of access to Chinese markets, particularly given the slowdown in U.S. and European demand.[139] Similarly, investor reception of the FTAs has been mixed. One portfolio investment bulletin argued that an FTA between Taiwan and China would be "a major positive for Taiwan."[140] According to a spokesperson for European chambers of commerce, China's proposed FTAs "'changed the whole strategic equation' in some companies' business model. This was because the FTAs were complex and, in some cases, still unpredictable."[141] One ratings agency said that, at least for South Korea, the FTA would not affect the country's credit rating one way or another, because greater political problems dwarfed the potential effects of the agreement.[142]

Thus, anecdotal evidence suggests that this relatively low level of integration with a country of questionable political quality is insufficient in consolidating investor opinion one way or another. This proposition can be examined systematically. Here, because the level of proposed integration is relatively low (a free-trade area rather than a common market, as in Mercosur), even though China's political risk is relatively high, acceding countries would not necessarily see a systematic drop in risk levels, but rather an increase in the uncertainty surrounding their debt instruments. That is, investors' individual perceptions of the merit or demerit of integration with China would be mixed; some might view it as positive whereas others would be wary of the country's future trajectory. Thus, the standard errors surrounding those assets would increase

---

[138] "Chinese headed for Asia," *China Daily*, 9 November 2004.

[139] "Whether you call the FTA Asean+1 [Asean-China] or China+1 [China-Asean], the implication is very different, in the political and economic sense, about who is the most powerful partner in a multinational company's eyes in terms of trade and investment," one Thai official said. "China FTAs 'need careful thought,'" *The Nation*, 9 November 2004.

[140] "Sell in May and Go Away?" *Emerging Markets Briefer*, 15 May 2009.

[141] "Foreign investors alarmed by FTAs," *The Nation*, 23 September 2004.

[142] "Fitch Ratings: free trade agreement not to result in rating upgrade for S Korea," *Euromoney*, 6 April 2007.

TABLE 5.1. *ARCH-in-Means Test of China FTAs as a Predictor of Uncertainty*

	A.	B.
Constant (β)	-1.24^{***}	-1.26^{***}
	(0.56)	(0.57)
Inflation	2.34^{***}	2.29^{***}
	(0.56)	(0.71)
Reserves	-1.12^{**}	-1.01^{*}
	(0.62)	(0.58)
China	0.21	0.62
FTA	(0.39)	(0.38)
σ_ϵ	0.32	0.45
	(0.19)	(0.29)
Constant (σ)	1.41^{*}	1.91^{**}
	(.70)	(.97)
China	–	1.21^{**}
FTA		(.58)
ϵ^2_{t-1} ARCH(1) term	0.46	0.48
	(0.23)	(0.22)
N	120	120
LL	1289.57	1109.21
χ^2	11231.31	10245.01
Prob χ^2	0	0

Pooled ARCH-in-means results regressions using averaged bond spreads for eleven countries negotiating FTAs with China. Test statistic (in parentheses) must be greater than the absolute value of 1.96 to indicate statistical significance; those that make the cutoff are indicated with a *.

as a function of their closure of an FTA with China. Specifically, the variance of investor perceptions would rise. I performed a Perron (1989) test to see if the date of closure of the FTA with China marked a structural break in the assets in question. Those tests did not prove significant – although this is unsurprising, given that the prediction here is not for a systematic change in risk *levels* but in a widening of the *variance* in risk.

For the dependent variable, I collapsed the monthly spreads on three-year sovereign debt, benchmarked against U.S. treasury bills, into averages so that they constitute a single series. The data run from January 1999 to January 2009, with averages for the ASEAN countries (agreement negotiations concluded in 2005), Hong Kong (2003), Thailand (2003), Chile (2005), Pakistan (2006), Peru (2008), and Singapore (2008).[143] Table 5.1 shows the results, first of a specification of the variance term that, along with an autoregressive term,

---

[143] Macau and Niger do not issue their debt publicly and are excluded from this analysis, as is New Zealand, which is not an emerging market.

excludes an indicator of the conclusion of the Chinese FTAs as a predictor (Model A), and then a specification that includes the FTA indicator (Model B). The mean equation in both cases uses the standard controls employed in previous models.

As anticipated, conclusion of FTAs with China are in fact associated with greater variance of risk perceptions of the countries in question. Once the indicator for negotiations is included, the coefficient on the variance (the constant of σ) increases and becomes statistically significant; additionally, the FTA indicator itself is positively associated with variance. This confirms the expectation that China's FTAs have to some degree increased the uncertainty surrounding the countries to whom it is linking itself. On a larger scale, this demonstrates that when a state with ambiguous levels of political risk forms mid-level economic unions, even though the point estimates of a recipient countries' risk might not change, the differing investor opinions will evidence themselves in greater variance around default expectations. Of course, that uncertainty can subsequently be resolved, but in the short term, investors have differing perceptions of the implication of signing onto cooperation agreements with China.

5.5 CONCLUSION

This chapter examines the flip side of the benefits of joining an agreement with good-quality members such as the EU, as Chapter 2 shows. By the same logic, as is demonstrated on the aggregate level in the previous chapter, some agreements actually make their members look more risky and increase the levels of uncertainty about a country's direction, particularly if there is a high level of proposed integration with members who themselves have high levels of political risk. To explore these dynamics, this chapter takes a mutlifaceted approach to exploring the rationales behind investor aversion to regional trade agreements that bring bad company together, with case illustrations as well as event analysis and techniques to estimate not just the levels of risk but the uncertainty surrounding those estimates.

Countries whose reputation was not already dire saw an increase in risk from signing onto Hugo Chávez's Bolivarian Alternative for the Americas. Similarly, when Putin signaled a new direction in Russian foreign policy by announcing the formation of the Eurasian Union, risk associated with Russia increased. Additionally, even low levels of integration with a member of questionable political quality can have an impact on emerging markets. Even if risk does not increase directly, the variance around their assets does increase, meaning a greater level of market uncertainty as to that country's trajectory. China's conclusion of free-trade areas in emerging markets illustrates this phenomenon. The African case demonstrates this as well, as country risk for Tanzania as well as Namibia dropped once they exited COMESA, even if they may have left their former trading partners somewhat in the lurch.

Is this reaction rational? That is, does joining agreements with poor-quality members actually make a country more likely to default on its debt, or is the perceived increase in risk unwarranted? Chapter 4 demonstrated – with the case of Hungary's budget crisis, and the violations of the Stability and Growth Pact – that investors were relatively relaxed about breaches of rules in the EU (perhaps too relaxed, judging by the sovereign risk panics that unfolded in Europe in 2008). By the same token, investors tend to be overly skittish in their reactions to indications of "bad company" in emerging markets.[144]

Even though there are potentially good reasons for investors to be nervous about close unions with unstable neighbors, investors still seem to react to these organization in excess of those reasons. One factor is the possibility of contagion: countries who trade heavily with their neighbors can absorb the volatility in their neighbors, in the form of the loss of markets for their goods in the event of an exchange-rate shock. But what I demonstrate here is investor reaction to changes in the membership or integration status of several institutions, even well before the real signs of proposed integration, or of contagion, will have materialized. This indicates that new perceptions of a country based on the company it keeps will occur even before any potential changes in that country have actually occurred. Chapter 6 goes on to explore the limits of those changes in perception.

---

[144] Hilscher and Nosbusch (2010) show that investors in emerging markets are sensitive not just to the levels but to the volatility of economic indicators, particularly to shocks in the terms of trade.

6

How Risk for Core Members Changes on IO Expansion

When emerging markets join international organizations, the effects are clear: investor perceptions of risk rise or fall depending on the reputations of the other members of the organization. But what happens to those existing members once new countries join their ranks? Does the reputation of a group of good members take a hit if a less reputable member comes in? When do bad reputations overwhelm good ones, and whose reputation in a given organization might suffer? And how might those effects be disentangled – do investors rationally fear contagion if a new member gets into economic trouble, or are they making irrational assumptions about an old member's trajectory, based on the type of company it keeps?

International organizations frequently expand, yet very little research has been directed toward the consequences of IO enlargement. Scholars who support the view that treaties are endogenous strategies often claim that institutions are chosen from an infinitely large set of possible treaties and may be chosen based on likely compliance.[1] That is, heads of state will not expend their energies negotiating agreements that will not be upheld by members. This view holds that the institutions that we observe in the world should not take on risk – but this chapter provides evidence that letting in new members does precisely that.

This chapter examines the implications of the central hypothesis by looking at the repercussions of admitting new members to an organization. "The company you keep" can run in both directions; that is, existing members may take on some of the risk of newer members. When risky countries join a group, they can increase the perceptions of risk of the more stable members, as demonstrated by the case of Germany in various rounds of EU expansion.

---

[1] See, for example, Snidal (1994); Downs, Rocke, and Barsoom (1996); Pahre (1997); de Mesquita (2000). For an opposing view, see Przeworski (2004).

This is an observable implications of the central hypothesis as well as a matter of core concern to international organizations. Many organizations in the world are weighing the costs and benefits of expansion, and this chapter presents evidence that letting in new members can come at a cost to existing ones.

The tests presented here also help unpack the mechanism behind this effect on core members. There is some degree of rational assessment in the changes in risk, to the extent that taking on an unhealthy new member may effect the other members of the organization's ability to repay their own debt. Economic contractions in the eurozone, for example, have not only weakened the central currency but also put pressure on the richer countries to bail out distressed members. If a country spends down its reserves to bail out an errant member of its club, it then has less cover if it runs into economic trouble itself. Similarly, if membership in an economic organization means that trade ties have strengthened among member states, then an economic contraction in a member might mean that that country's citizens have less purchasing power with which to buy their neighbor's exports; the problem is worsened if that country's currency falls in value, making neighbors' exports even more expensive. That said, the tests that follow show that investors react to those shocks in a disproportionate manner. Furthermore, investors seem to make inferences about core members' *willingness* to pay back their own debt based on the inclusion of certain types of members.

This chapter proceeds as follows. First, I establish the broad effects of expansion on existing members of an organization. The next section shows that letting in riskier countries can make old members look more risky. Every round of EU expansion has brought a slight increase in risk perceptions for Germany. This is a trend that has reversed somewhat; since the European sovereign debt crisis in 2009, risk levels for German paper have actually decreased somewhat, as demand for the safe haven of German debt has increased even as the value of the euro has slipped.[2] But over the course of EU expansion, investors have ascribed slightly greater risk to Germany as the EU enlarges, though that reaction is not the result of any one common attribute of those countries. These tests show that members of an organization can see their good reputations weaken somewhat when more risky members join their clubs.

The subsequent sections try to assess further whether investor reaction anticipates changes in an existing member state's ability or willingness to uphold its foreign debt obligations. I examine the case of Mercosur to establish the material risks that members run when their associates experience economic crises. These consequences are at least partially a result of economic contagion – that is, shifts in countries' terms of trade that make them vulnerable to shocks in their trading partners, and therefore may affect their ability to

---

[2] "German Bonds Rally as Euro Weakens," *Bloomberg*, 6 August 2012.

service their debt.[3] This partially supports the theory put forward in Alternate Hypothesis 2 – that changes in a country's economy as a result of membership in international organization may underly subsequent changes in risk. The gains in cheap energy that Mercosur countries would receive from Venezuela's entry into the bloc seem to have been outweighed by the perceived instability of countries who are now further indebted to the anti-Western Chávez. This also provides support for the central hypothesis – that the ideological impact of the company a country keeps can spill across its borders. An illustration from Uruguay shows that markets reacted in disproportion to the potential contagion effects.

Finally, I show how the seal of approval offered by the EU has eroded since the "big bang" round of enlargement. Countries opening negotiations after 2004 experienced much weaker drops in risk than did the postcommunist countries. This stems in part from uncertainty about those countries' prospects for actually entering the EU – and that uncertainty has only grown more profound since the economic crisis in Europe. Unlike in previous rounds of enlargement, membership is no longer an inevitable outcome following opening accession negotiations. The example of Turkey, including interviews with officials in those countries, confirms this phenomenon. But it is also the case that once riskier members join an organization, the variety of members dilutes the strength of the seal of approval.

The jumps in risk for existing member states upon expansion to include riskier members points to a puzzle for IO theory: if expansion can lead to a weakened reputation for a group as a whole and core members in particular, why, then, would members of international organizations ever agree to letting in new members? The theory proposed in this book does not explicitly take this issue on, but in the conclusion I provide some context for the many factors that go into member states' calculations when it comes to organizational expansion. Those factors may in many cases offset the risks of taking on weaker members.

6.1 INVESTOR RISK TO CORE MEMBERS: GERMANY AND EU ACCESSION

When an international organization takes on members with high uncertainty, it can dilute the credibility of the stronger members of the organization. This proposition can be examined by looking at default risk associated with enlargement on core members. Chapter 4 demonstrated some of the reputational gains that the postcommunist countries made once they joined the EU. But did those

---

[3] A potentially interesting test along those same lines would have been to track yields in the ASEAN member states when the poorly governed Laos and Myanmar joined in July 1997. Unfortunately, ASEAN's expansion occurred right at the onset of the East Asian financial crisis. While a spike in risk premia could be anticipated at that time, it would be difficult to argue in good faith that that surge was a result of the expansion of ASEAN and not to the financial panic hitting the region at that time.

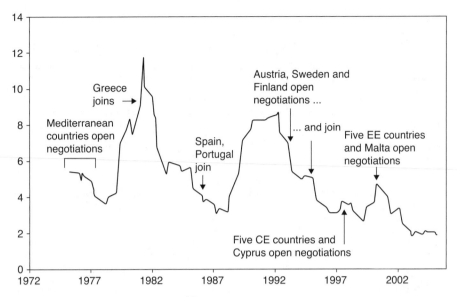

FIGURE 6.1. German Treasury Yields, 1975–2006.

gains come at the expense of preexisting EU members? As the anchor economy and the primary architect of the monetary system, Germany is the country that would experience the biggest impact on its sovereign paper concurrent with new entrants to the club.[4] Germany has the strongest economic reputation among the countries in the EU; expansion could have brought the country economic gains as it stabilized potential markets for trade and investment, but there were also potential risks of having less reputable members in the club. That is, it is possible that investor perceptions of risk in Germany increased slightly over different rounds of enlargement. These are risks that are acute in the eurozone crisis, as much as the pressure for financial bailouts falls on Germany.

A look at the raw data gives a somewhat ambiguous picture; Figure 6.1 shows quarterly yields on German treasury bills since 1975, with indicators for steps along the road to EU expansion. Note that higher values are an indication of higher levels of risk. Although German risk trended mostly downward in this period – consistent with the pattern of U.S. treasury bills and other secure assets prior to the financial crisis of 2007 – there are some movements that are consistent with overall market volatility. The two largest spikes in the early 1980s and early 1990s result from the global debt crisis and the Exchange Rate Mechanism (ERM) crisis, respectively. The dip in risk in 1987 could have

---

[4] This works out practically as well; all models in the section to follow were also run on the "Big Three" countries: France, Germany, and the United Kingdom. Germany was the main driver of the effect.

come with the change in institutional rules in the European Monetary System that came about from the Basle-Nyborg agreement (Gardener and Perraudin (1992). There is no easily discernable pattern on the effects of EU expansion; particularly, the inclusion of the postcommunist countries seems to coincide with spikes in risk, but this is amid an environment of overall volatility.

Although there is no immediately perceptible change in risk for Germany at the time of expansions, this proposition can be tested more systematically. To this end, I assemble quarterly data on Germany's treasury bill yields, from the first quarter of 1970 to the fourth quarter of 2005.[5] To control for serial correlation in time-series data, I use an ARIMA model with autoregressive and moving average terms, such that forecasts are a linear function of past observations and nonlinear functions of the coefficients, and preceding estimation errors are taken into account when estimating subsequent values.[6] To enable linear estimation and in keeping with standard techniques in finance, I take the natural log of the dependent variable; predicted values and substantive interpretations are translated back into original units.

I include controls standard to models of bond yields, including overall output (measured in euros); inflation of consumer prices; the trade-weighted real exchange rate, adjusted to consumer prices; and total government debt. These are taken from the vast literature on finance that includes an equally vast number of explanatory variables; these are widely agreed to be the most robust predictors (Min, 1998; Edwards, 1998). To ensure that the EU accession variables are not picking up on preexisting economic activity between Germany and the rest of the EU, I also control for lending to the countries in the EU 25. I control for exogenous and endogenous shocks by constructing a dummy variable with values of 1 for the quarters around the ERM crisis and central bank intervention of 1992 and the global debt crisis of the early 1980s, and 0 otherwise.

I evaluate changes in the nature of the European Union in several ways. First, I create four variables that count the number of countries with whom the EU has formally opened membership negotiations; the number of countries that are in the process of accession to the EU; and the number of full EU members in a given quarter. The EU variables themselves are straightforward; membership ranges from 6 to 25, and negotiation and accession from 0 to 12.[7] For the euro variable, those numbers are also dependent on the progress of the euro project itself. I define the cut points as the first quarter of 1979, when the Economic and Monetary System and the Exchange Rate Mechanism were

---

[5] These range from 11.77 (in the third quarter of 1981) to 1.82 (in the second quarter of 2002), with a mean of 5 and a standard deviation of 2.17.

[6] I assume an AR1 process and MA 1 and 4, as is common for quarterly data.

[7] Once countries are in the process of ratifying the accession treaty, they are not counted as negotiators; similarly, once they become members, they are not counted as being in the accession stage. Thus, particularly the accession variable has a rather large number of zeros, given that countries usually ratify the accession treaty within a year or two.

TABLE 6.1. *Changes in German Risk Levels as a Function of New Member Accessions*

Constant	2.552***	2.52***
	(.723)	(.71)
Output	3.23	−3.91
	(2.64)	(2.94)
Inflation	1.102**	1.185***
	(.359)	(.342)
Real exchange rate	−.0048	−.006
	(.0048)	(.0047)
Government debt	−.12**	−.13**
	(.04)	(.04)
Shocks	.29	.23
	(.09)	(.10)
Lending to EU 25		−5.73**
		(1.90)
Number of ERM countries	−	−.007
		(.007)
Number negotiating	−	.03***
		(.006)
Number acceding	−	.0043
		(.003)
Number of members	−	.043***
		(.009)
AR	.935	.954
	(.026)	(.02)
MA L1	.41	.495
	(.078)	(.091)
MA L4	.139	.135
	(.10)	(.097)
σ	.081	.07
	(.0054)	(.0051)

Dependent variable is the natural log of yields on German treasury bills, quarterly from 1972 to 2005. ARIMA estimations with robust standard errors in parentheses. ***$p < .001$, **$p < .05$, *$p < .10$. $N = 139$.

established, with six countries; the first quarter of 1992, when the Maastricht treaty establishing convergence criteria was signed by ten countries; the first quarter of 1999, which witnessed the formal transition of the ERM to the euro, with eleven countries; and the first quarter of 2002, when euro notes and coins were formally introduced in twelve countries.[8] The results of this basic specification are shown in Table 6.1.

[8] Arguably, other cut points could be included into the measure, but it is hard to see how their omission would bias the results.

Of the domestic economic variables, inflation and government are the two big performers. Higher levels of inflation are associated with increases in German debt yields that are statistically significant, at the .005 level. Higher levels of government debt coincide with similarly significant decreases in treasury yields; this is perhaps a reflection of greater demand for treasuries.[9]

Turning to more international variables, as expected, the more countries that are negotiating or actually inside the EU, the greater Germany's risk levels. These effects are statistically significant at the .001 level for the stages of initial negotiation and of membership. The number of members at the accession stage is not statistically significant at the conventional levels. This is consistent with research on the impacts for EU accessor countries, as well; the biggest impact for accessors comes at the stage of negotiation. One might expect, too, that different processes may be at work when it comes to Germany; investors may build into their pricing Germany's commitment of admission to the union at the time of negotiation, but membership brings different strains to stronger economies that are factored into debt pricing.

For a substantive interpretation of these results, consider the effect of varying the numbers of negotiators and members. Holding all other variables at their means, moving from one to two negotiators (as occurred from 1976 to 1979, when first Greece, then Portugal, then Spain) increases German yields by .06 (from 1.03 to 1.09). Moving from six to twelve negotiators (as occurred during the "big bang" in 1999, when many of the postcommunist countries were brought onto the negotiating table in the run-up to their eventual accession), predicted treasury yield rises from 1.2 to 1.43 percent. Under the same procedure, moving from nine to twelve EU members, as occurred with the membership of Greece, Portugal, and Spain in the mid-1980s, makes for a predicted increase in German yields of .20; moving from fifteen to twenty-five, with the accession of the post-communist countries, Cyprus and Malta, has a predicted increase in yields of 1.02 percentage points. The last is a particularly sizeable jump; by contrast, yields increased at the advent of the ERM crisis in 1992 by 3.16 percentage points. This indicates that investors perceived greater risk to Germany for the "big bang" enlargement than for other expansions.

To enable comparisons across the different units in which the independent variables are measured, Table 6.2 shows the effect on German securities of a change in one standard deviation for each of the variables. These indicate that, save for inflation, the numbers of countries negotiating or inside the EU do have substantively significant effects, second only to inflation.

But what aspects of these acceding countries reflect poorly on Germany? In order to control for what aspects of EU expansion might make Germany's own

---

[9] It should be noted that debt often works differently in predicting the yields of developing countries; whereas in OECD countries, high levels of debt mean high demand and thus lower yields, in developing countries, debt is often a sign of a government's inability to raise revenues domestically, and often is associated with higher yields.

TABLE 6.2. *Effects of One Standard Deviation Change of IVs*

Output	−0.86
Inflation	1.11***
Real exchange rate	−0.97
Government debt	−0.71**
Shocks	0.36
Lending to EU 25	−0.99
Number of ERM countries	−0.02
Number negotiating	1.09***
Number acceding	1.03
Number of members	1.07***
Number of ERM entrants	0.98

***p < .001, **p < .05.

default risk look somewhat greater, it is necessary to consider characteristics of economies that might generally point to instability and eventual default. Some of these areas come straight from the Maastricht criteria. I measure the effects of different economic characteristics of the EU hopefuls along six dimensions. Theoretically, both the stage of negotiation as well as the economic indicators of the countries under consideration have an impact on German treasury bills, but the summed amount takes into account the number of countries at any given stage of accession – which has already been demonstrated to be significant.

The first consideration is the wealth of acceding nations: in the most recent round of expansion, the twelve countries that entered the EU in May 2004 had a GDP of around 40 percent lower than the EU average. The effects of low GDP on risk to Germany are indirect: they would be intermediated through labor market mobility (if workers from poorer countries sought higher wages in the richer countries) or by direct transfers to those countries from the ECB central budget. The former arguably has benefits of its own, but because treasury bill rates reflect the stability of a country's economy, these changes in flows would have at least short-term destabilizing effects.

Countries that are already regarded as having a high likelihood of default would themselves increase Germany's default risk. High amounts of government debt, as well as high interest rates, have been shown to drive up yields in developing countries (Edwards, 1986). Thus, overall levels of debt, as well as the rate at which governments borrow, would be a good indication of default risk and, by extension, of the need for possible future bailout.

On the more positive side, EU expansion has also brought more dynamic economies into the EU; average growth rates in the new entrants in 2004 were 4.6 percent, compared with an overall average of 2.2 percent in the Euro area at the same time. It is therefore reasonable to expect that faster-growing economies might improve the overall economic soundness of the EU and actually reflect positively on Germany's levels of risk.

I also include a variable for whether acceding countries were signing on to the euro. Adoption of the euro, for those that choose to do so, is a cornerstone of the single market; it eliminates exchange-rate risk and presumes a single monetary policy for all members. EU countries have entered the ERM at different schedules, or not at all. During ERM talks, France made its entry conditional on Germany's, so that the Bundesbank could not conduct its own monetary policy outside of a European system.[10] With the crisis in the eurozone, investors might have been particularly attentive to whether new entrants would be joining the single currency.

Finally, high-inflation countries might have been a particular cause for concern among investors. Inflation remains one of the strongest predictors of debt yields; it reflects not only the stability of the economy but also the government's ability to effectively leverage monetary policy. While the aftermentioned five variables relate to a country's liquidity and solvency, inflation is a reflection of a country's macroeconomic fundamentals. As such, drastic changes in consumer prices indicate uncertainty not only in an economy's present but also in its medium-term future, because policy measures such as currency revaluation may be necessary to keep inflation under control. Like exchange rates, they also indicate a country's ability to finance its foreign-owned loans with domestic currency. Many defaults are in fact precipitated by inflationary runs; think of Argentina in 1999 or Turkey in 2001, most recently.

In Table 6.3, I again perform an ARCH-in-means analysis on yields on German bunds, but I group countries that were in various stages of EU integration in any given year, and add their values for six different economic characteristics: debt as a share of GDP; GDP per capita, inflation, economic growth, average interest rates, and real-effective exchange rate. For example, in 1994, when three countries (Austria, Finland, and Sweden) were negotiating for EU admission, their added inflation levels (the third column) were 11.54. Summing the values takes into account both the number of countries and the economic characteristics those countries have.

No dimension measured here seems to be consistently doing all the work in these regressions, with most of the coefficients not achieving conventional levels of statistical significance. In terms of the characteristics measured here, are averages more important than the overall numbers? Note that the summed dimensions shown in Table 6.4 only find statistical significance below .05 levels for inflation among accessors and ERM members, as well as for interest rates in EU members and in ERM participants. None of the summed dimensions for negotiators are significant here. For the averages, higher levels of GDP

---

[10] The United Kingdom joined ERM1 in 1990 but withdrew in September 1992 after a speculative crisis; Denmark and Sweden did not join in 1999, when the eurozone officially came into existence, confirming their rejection in referendums in 2000 and 2002, respectively.

TABLE 6.3. *German Risk and Attributes of New Members, on Six Dimensions*

	Debt	GDPpc	Inflation	Growth	Interest	REER
Constant	2.51***	2.48***	2.14***	2.62***	1.79**	2.12***
	(.697)	(.72)	(.77)	(.75)	(.73)	(.79)
Output	−1.03	−1.31	3.02	−2.01	−1.19	−1.98
	(2.66)	(2.47)	(2.71)	(2.74)	(2.24)	(2.12)
Inflation	1.11***	1.17***	1.12***	1.15***	1.24***	1.19***
	(.36)	(.36)	(.38)	(.36)	(.34)	(.36)
Government debt	−1.12***	−1.20***	−1.18***	−1.20***	−1.19**	−1.21***
	(.51)	(.47)	(.46)	(.47)	(.48)	(.51)
Real exchange rate	−.0043	−.004	−.004	−.005	−.001	−.003
	(.0046)	(.004)	(.005)	(.005)	(.004)	(.004)
Lending to EU 25	−.44	−.50	−.30	−.49	−.47	−.43
	(.21)	(.26)	(.23)	(.28)	(.19)	(.21)
Negotiator	.05*	.008	−.06	.03	.05	.04
	(.027)	(.005)	(.06)	(.05)	(.06)	(.03)
Accessor	−.03	.004	.21**	.004	−.046	.03
	(.03)	(.0093)	(.08)	(.009)	(.07)	(.02)
Member	.02	.001*	.002	.001*	.042**	.04
	(.04)	(.0007)	(.14)	(.0007)	(.017)	(.022)
ERM	−.044	.03	.023***	.001	.01**	.02
	(.06)	(.02)	(.008)	(.001)	(.004)	(.01)
AR	.938	.93	.933	.938	.91	.92
	(.02)	(.02)	(.02)	(.02)	(.03)	(.03)
MA L1	.417	.41	.409	.416	.44	.42
	(.09)	(.08)	(.09)	(.07)	(.10)	(.10)
MA L4	.153	.14	.141	.161	.122	.123
	(.08)	(.11)	(.108)	(.10)	(.097)	(.10)
σ	.079	.08	.08	.0792	.078	.08
	(.0053)	(.005)	(.005)	(.005)	(.005)	(.006)

Dependent variable is the natural log of yields on German treasury bills, quarterly from 1972 to 2005. Column 1 groups EU negotiators, accessors, and members by their levels of external debt; Column 2, by those countries' GDP per capita; Column 3, by their inflation levels; etc. ARIMA estimations with robust standard errors in parentheses. ***$p < .001$, **$p < .05$, *$p < .10$. N = 139.

per capita both in negotiators and in members seems to be associated with increases in risk – a puzzling result. What is striking in these tables is that economic dimensions do not seem to capture what was going on in our first set of results; there is some significance of EU expansion that goes beyond what is being measured here.

If anything, the significance of the raw numbers of countries along the road of accession compared with the relative insignificance of particular economic aspects of those countries might indicate a few things. First and most obvious is omitted variable bias: there might be other aspects of those countries to which investors are reacting, such as their political stability or their institutional quality. It is also possible that the rise in yields associated with enlargement has less to do with the attributes of individual members and more to do with changing institutional dynamics in an enlarged EU. With a greater number of members from which to wrangle consensus, German preferences – typically preferences that investors like – might have a harder time holding sway.[11]

Recall the literature in political science on how new members, or members with differing preferences, hamper efficiency in EU institutions. This is in concert with the vast literature on political constraints and veto players, which argues that an increased number of bodies with different preferences at the decision-making table will make policy change more difficult (Tsebelis, 2002; Henisz, 2004). This theory has been used to predict no shortage of outcomes, including infrastructure deployment (Henisz and Zellner, 2006), attraction of foreign direct investment (Roberts, 2005), and monetary policy (Keefer and Stasavage, 2002). However, this literature would predict that enlargement would produce an *overall* decrease in efficiency, which ought to resonate across all members. There is nothing to explain the different effects for acceding members – who all experienced sharp decreases in default risk – and for Germany, where accession was associated with an increase in default risk.[12] Testing for ideological differences among new member states would be feasible for the more recent rounds of admitted countries, but most ideology data does not extend back much farther than the 1990s.

The implication of the veto players literature, however, is that more actors with greater variance in their policy positions means that policies become more difficult to change. The policy positions that might be of particular concern to investors, however, would likely be economic. In the run-up to admission, new entrants are, at least in theory, supposed to sign on to a single monetary policy. Past adherence to these policies would already be reflected in the economic dimensions that I have measured earlier.

It is possible, at least, to eliminate certain variables from further consideration; new entrants' levels of government debt and exchange rate stability seem to have no impact on Germany. The dimensions that have the highest levels of statistical significance across the most models are inflation and interest rates. Holding all other variables at their means, increasing summed inflation by one standard deviation for accessors and ERM entrants increases German treasury bill yields by 1.99 and .99, respectively; the same procedure for summed interest rates for members and ERM members increases yields by 3.77 and .10, respectively. More than any other variables tested here, these two represent past instability and past risk; thus, it could be that greater levels of uncertainty associated with new entrants bring up uncertainty about Germany as well.

---

[11] That depends on where power comes from in EU negotiations, as discussed in Slapin (2006).
[12] Veto players theory might, however, explain the decrease in volatility experienced by new members, which may be a function of policy stability.

In summary, although the exact dynamics of the effect are hard to pin down, the changes in risk for emerging markets as a result of the company they keep are not entirely zero-sum. Germany seems to have absorbed some degree of the risk of more unstable members entering the EU. I only measured these levels of risk in the pre-financial crisis period, but certainly this observation is relevant in terms of the financial crises sweeping southern Europe, Latvia, Hungary, and Ireland. One of the contributing factors of those crises was that the European Central Bank (and, implicitly, Germany) guaranteed sovereign paper for all those countries in the eurozone. This meant that, in very real terms, Germany did shoulder the risk associated with those countries' fiscal policies. This is evidence that risky company is not without cost; even before the financial crisis hit, Germany took on at least some of the instability associated with new EU members. And now that those countries' finances are in doubt, it looks set to take on much more.

6.2 MERCOSUR: CONTAGION, CAN'T PAY, AND WON'T PAY

This section examines the effect on members of organizations when their members suffer economic as well as political crises. To this end, it tackles the task of separating the signals of a country's ability and willingness to pay back its debt once it joins new trade agreements by using several different methods. Investors ought to react not only to signs of economic trouble but also to signs of a lack of willingness to repay debt. The best test case would be looking at agreements with countries that are wealthy, who are perfectly capable of servicing their debt in financial terms, but for political or other reasons have given an indication that servicing their foreign debt obligations may not be their top priority. These types of examples can clearly separate the inferences that investors make about a country's willingness to pay as a function of the company it keeps, versus how new trade partners affect a country's ability to service its debt.

Contagion is all the more probable if countries have close economic ties with unstable countries. If one country in a trade alliance undergoes a currency crisis, healthier countries in an RTA will see demand for their exports dry up, because those goods automatically become more expensive. This can have deep economic repercussions in the healthy countries, often driving them to a liquidity crisis themselves.[13] Indeed, contagion has been argued to be one of the primary risks of increased trade ties (Rose and Spiegel, 2002). Once a country deepens trade with a neighbor, it is more susceptible to currency crises in its trade partners, because their exports will become more expensive to countries whose currency plummets. This suppressed demand can hit those countries hard and many economic papers have examined contagion effects (Calvo and Mendoza,

---

[13] For a review of the liquidity crisis literature, see Detragiache and Spilimbergo (2001).

1993; Calvo, Izquierdo, and Talvi, 2003, 2006; González-Rozada and Yeyati, 2008). In economic terms, this can mean the exhaustion of export markets, which then prevents hard currency from coming into a trade partner; in terms of investor psychology, financial crises in one country are often accompanied by sudden stops in international capital flows for an entire region. Indeed, many articles have shown that increased trade ties can increase volatility in a country (Rodrik, 1997, 1998; Kim, 2007).[14]

The case of Mercosur illustrates several points along the ability-willingness continuum. With a combined population of 250 million (some 63 percent of South America's total) and a combined GDP of $1 trillion (about 76 percent of the region's total), the Southern Cone Common Market, or Mercosur, is the third-largest RTA in the world in terms of country size. Mercosur's founding members – Argentina, Brazil, Paraguay, and Uruguay – signed the association treaty on 26 March 1991, in part as a riposte to the formation of NAFTA. Chile had been invited to join Mercosur but turned down those invitations, not wanting to jeopardize its chances of entry into NAFTA at that point. Brazil's and Argentina's economic crises in 1999 and 2001 are examples where, as a result of currency devaluations in their trade partners, nearly all the countries in question suffered because of their increased economic ties with those countries. This shows some degree of rational calculation behind the jumps in risk for members of the same organization. However, a description of Uruguay and its restructuring of its debt after the Argentine default will show that investors overreacted in terms of their assessment of Uruguay's ability as well as its willingness to come to an agreement with its creditors in tough economic times. Additionally, Venezuela's announcement of planned closer ties to the union increased the average political risk associated with members, as evidenced by a demonstration of movements in risk for Mercosur countries following political shocks in Venezuela.

It should be noted that, interestingly, these reactions take place even though Mercosur has, by most reports, fallen very short of its integration goals (Caetano and Vaillant, 2004). Although trade among the member countries has increased, nontariff barriers to trade continue unchecked, and the member countries have yet to effectively implement a common external tariff despite being a customs union on paper.[15] One critic charts this to "a gap between what is said, what is agreed, and what is effectively applied by countries in their domestic legal systems" in Mercosur (Vaillant, 2007). Mercosur brought benefits to members primarily in the mid-1990s, when Argentina's and Brazil's macroeconomic cycles were in sync and when a boom in commodity prices brought in substantial revenues, but after the Brazilian economic crisis in 1999 and the collapse of Argentina's currency board in 2001, the organization has

---

[14] But see Gray and Potter (2012), who argue that volatility decreases with close trade networks.
[15] Author interview, Coen van Iwaarden, Cámara de Comercio Argentino-Holandesa, 21 July 2009.

stagnated. Mercosur has fallen far short of establishing a common regional market, and in the late 1990s intraregional trade actually declined (Aggarwal and Espach, 2004). Indeed, Latin America more generally exhibits a somewhat surprising lack of convergence on most economic indicators, given the large number of regional integration projects underway there (Serra et al., 2006). This further supports the proposition that international organizations change perceptions disproportionate to the actual changes that those organizations induce.

6.2.1 Possible Contagion Effects: Ability to Pay

This section examines changes in risk when members of an organization actually do experience economic crises and default. Since its formation, the two largest Mercosur members – Brazil and Argentina – experienced some of the most dramatic financial crises of the last two decades of the twentieth century. Member countries' susceptibility to the ill effects of these crises has been a topic of much discussion in Latin America. Trade was particularly pronounced between Brazil and Argentina, and many worried that the exposure left countries susceptible to contagion effects. "With Mercosur, the regional distribution of pain from one nation's financial problems is now transferred from one member state to another like a rapidly mutating virus, rather than being more readily contained as it was in earlier eras" wrote one observer (Guira, 2005).

Brazil was the first country to experience a crisis after Mercosur's inception. Part of Felipe Cardoso's "Plan Real" to implement market structural adjustments and economic reforms was the introduction of a newly valued currency with a crawling peg to the dollar to contain the inflation that the country had experienced prior to the 1994 "tequila crisis" (Evangelist and Sathe, 2006; Sanya and Mlachila, 2010). Portfolio investment surged in the country in the 1990s. But in the wake of the East Asian and Russian financial crisis and subsequent pressure on the real, Brazil dropped its semifixed exchange rate on 13 January 1999. Brazil accounted for nearly a third of Argentine exports in 1998, but after the devaluation of the real made Argentine goods more expensive, Argentine exports to Brazil experienced a 28 percent drop the following year.

Subsequently, following a decade of strong economic performance and overenthusiastic portfolio investment, Argentina was also forced to abandon its currency board, which had been adopted in 1991 to combat inflation and impose fiscal discipline (Sanya and Mlachila, 2010). High growth in the late 1990s was accompanied by high volumes of portfolio investment as well as government spending. But after a loss of confidence in the economy triggered a run on deposits, Argentina defaulted on $95 billion of debt in 2001, one of the biggest defaults of the past century.[16] The Argentine peso went from a fixed

---

[16] See Blustein (2004) for an excellent account of the Argentine crisis.

TABLE 6.4. *Cumulative Abnormal Returns Around Debt Crises in Mercosur*

Country	Brazil Crisis	Arg. Crisis	Paraguay Crisis	Uruguay Crisis
Argentina	154.89*	927.38*	12.21*	9.83*
	(2.41)	(2.80)	(2.22)	(2.90)
Brazil	189.92*	59.92*	48.20	67.23
	(2.84)	(4.23)	(1.48)	(1.23)
Paraguay	38.62*	31.42*	124.28*	23.78*
	(2.00)	(23.32)	(12.78)	(4.93)
Uruguay	69.42*	96.65*	97.37*	132.26*
	(2.01)	(14.98)	(19.23)	(43.90)
Non-Mercosur countries	35.52*	39.29*	8.29	4.98
	(1.99)	(2.42)	(2.12)	(1.78)
Difference in means	77.69***	239.55***	70.15**	58.27**
Standard error	20.31	92.20	32.12	24.12

Cumulative abnormal returns for Mercosur members (in rows) surrounding defaults or renegotiations (in columns). Test statistic (in parentheses) must be greater than the absolute value of 1.96 to indicate statistical significance; those that make the cutoff are indicated with a *.

one-to-one rate with the U.S. dollar in January 2002, to a low of .26 to the dollar in June of that year.

The decrease in purchasing power that results from currency devaluation and inflatin effectively reduces a country's market size. Thus, potential investor penalties of other Mercosur countries when one of their members defaults could be argued to be a rational response to increased pressure on their reserves. For example, Argentina receives 14 percent of income from within-Mercosur exports while Brazil only 7 percent – thus, Argentina tends to be more adversely effected by Mercosur-member shocks than by Brazil.

Because both of these crises were currency crises, Mercosur members would experience contagion effects purely as a function of their increased trade ties. A devalued currency would mean that imports would become relatively more expensive in the wake of a financial crisis; thus, exporters to Brazil or Argentina would suddenly see a reduction in demand for their goods and would be stuck without hard currency coming into their economy. That is, investor reaction to these crises would reflect a changed assessment of Mercosur members' ability to honor their own debt obligations.

In fact, Paraguay defaulted on $25 million worth of foreign currency bonds in early 2003, paying back some $9 million in the subsequent years, after a new administration headed by Nicanor Duarte Frutos took power. Uruguay also nearly defaulted on its debt obligations, as will be discussed in greater detail below.

Table 6.4 illustrates the affect on Mercosur members, compared with other countries in Latin America, of Brazil's currency crisis in 1999, Argentina's default in 2001, Paraguay's default in June 2003, and Uruguay's near-default in September 2003. As described in the previous chapter, I use event analysis to test the cumulative abnormal returns or losses that investors experienced around the crises. The event windows are fifteen days, with ten in the run-up to the event and five in the aftermath, because the dates of the default were advertised in advance.

Following Argentina's default in 2001, it was the other members of Mercosur that felt the pain most acutely. In all of the aforemention crises, Mercosur members suffered greater increases in risk than non-Mercosur countries, and those increases are statistically significant at the .05 level or below. In terms of sovereign risk, the crises seemed to have hurt the smaller members more than the larger ones.[17] This is consistent with expectations of contagion – but were those reactions actually warranted? The section that follows argue; that this reaction was disproportionate to the difficulties Mercosur members actually experienced, by examining the case of Uruguay's debt restructuring after the Argentine financial crisis.

6.2.2 Uruguay's Debt Restructuring

The case of Uruguay's near-default following the Argentine crisis is a good example of how even an emerging market that has a good reputation can be tainted by the company it keeps. Of all the Mercosur countries, Uruguay is considered to have suffered the most extreme contagion effects from the Argentine crisis, partially for structural reasons. Uruguayan banks had high exposure to Argentina and Brazil; around 40 percent of the country's bank deposits came from nonresidents in the 1990s, and about 80 percent of those were Argentines. Once Argentina imposed a freeze on foreign bank accounts (the "corralito"), Uruguayan accounts took a serious hit. Markets forgot Uruguay's history of repaying its debts in the time of the Argentine crisis.

After Argentina's massive default in 2001, investors reacted in extreme fashion. The country saw a run on its Uruguay's currency and bank deposits – by July 2002, 38 percent of bank deposits had left the country – which ended up draining 80 percent of the country's foreign reserves (Plaza and Sirtaine, 2005). In response, the government announced that it would let go of the Uruguayan peso's peg to the dollar – and the peso immediately depreciated by nearly 30 percent. Uruguayan bond spreads over U.S. *treasuries* peaked at 3,000 in July 2002. In March 2003, Fitch downgraded Uruguayan assets to 'CCC-' from 'B-' and predicted a possible default, because the country had virtually no access

---

[17] However, the effects persisted in larger economies outside of the demonstrated event windows. Brazilian yields peaked at about 2,400 in the run-up to the 2002 elections, as markets feared that the favorite to win, the left-leaning Luiz Inacio Lula da Silva, would drive Brazil to default as well.

to capital markets.[18] Similarly, Standard & Poor's docked its rating to 'SD' in May of that year.[19]

During the crisis, government officials passed a raft of policies aimed at reassuring investors. These included new regulatory frameworks for the financial system as well as bank reforms. But the crucial event was a debt restructuring that took place on 10 April 2002, overseen by Salomon Brothers. The restructuring involved a $1.5 billion loan from the U.S. Treasury, an IMF loan to shore up reserves, and a renegotiation of the terms of nineteen different bond issues, contingent on the implementation of bank reforms. There was high-level U.S. involvement on this deal; "it was consistent with our new policy to deal with contagion: [to] help countries who were following good policies and who were not the cause of the crisis," the former U.S. Undersecretary of Treasury for International Affairs later said (Taylor, 2007).

During this process, Uruguayan officials had to remind investors that it was the only country in Latin America that had never defaulted on interest payments during the "Brady-bond" restructuring that bailed out Latin American countries in the 1980s (Steneri, 2004). "Certainly we were affected as far as deposits [after the Argentine crisis], but the market reaction was far more extreme [than warranted]," says a representative from the Uruguayan stock exchange. "It was only after we reminded them that we actually had a good history of debt repayment and that we were really wanting to make a deal that [markets] calmed down." The debt renegotiations incorporated several investor demands – including investor refusal to take a haircut in terms of the principal – and though its financial troubles were not over, the country did avoid all-out default. Only 7 percent of the country's bondholders opted out of the restructuring plan, which involved either five-year payment extensions or substituting for a new, more liquid bond that would be worth somewhat less on the market. "Uruguay was given a second chance because of its tradition and because it acted prudently in a moment of extreme crisis, not because the debt dynamics have improved," said one analyst.[20] That is, even if the country's ability to service its debt had been compromised, it had to remind investors that its willingness remained intact, despite assumptions made as part of its membership with Mercosur.

One Uruguayan former trade official claimed that, in fact, in terms of sovereign bonds, Mercosur was a negative for Uruguay rather than a positive – not just during the crisis but in the long run. "All the time that we were issuing our debt on markets, we were trying to convince people that we weren't like Brazil or Argentina – especially Argentina – but the Mercosur affiliation

---

[18] "Fitch Downgrades Uruguay to 'CCC-' Negative Outlook; Warns Default Likely," *Business Wire*, 12 March 2003.

[19] Standard & Poor Report, "Sovereign Defaults: Heading Lower into 2004," 18 September 2003.

[20] "Uruguay: A Well-Executed Model for Debt Workouts," *Bloomberg*, 29 September 2003.

made that difficult."[21] An academic agrees: "The difficulty with an organization like Mercosur for a smaller country is that we aren't very well-known in financial markets, and investors make assumptions about the way we behave based on how Argentina and Brazil behave."[22]

That said, Mercosur has undoubtedly provided benefits to its smaller members. Uruguay had been extremely protectionist in the run-up to Mercosur's founding, and significant liberalization did take place under Mercosur's auspices, albeit reciprocal rather than unilateral opening (Connolly and Melo, 1994; Caetano and Vaillant, 2004; Garriga and Sanguinetti, 1995). Nonetheless, Uruguay has expressed dissatisfaction with the trading benefits that Mercosur has provided, particularly since Brazil and Argentina have pressured Uruguay not to establish external FTAs, such as with the United States.[23] In March 2006, Uruguayan finance minister Danilo Astori complained specifically about it being blocked from U.S. FTAs, saying that thanks to Mercosur, "Uruguay's problem is that [it] depends only on the goodwill of Brazil and Argentina" (Wheeler, 2007). The country has also complained of the lack of dispute resolution in the organization, such as in its attempts to construct a pulp mill in a river between it and Argentina. Negative investor assumptions are perhaps another drawback of the organization – even in the presence of actual fallout from economic crises in neighbors, investor reaction may at least initially be out of proportion to what is merited.

6.2.3 Mercosur's Ideological Orientation: Willingness to Pay

This section demonstrates investor reaction to political shocks in Mercosur. I show that investors make inferences about other Mercosur members' willingness to pay, based on shocks primarily in Venezuela – not yet a full member but a vocal negotiator – as well as in Argentina. Venezuela, an oil-rich country, should have improved its trading partners' *ability* to service its debt by providing it with cheap energy, but if investors responded to political shocks in that country by penalizing other Mercosur members, that would mean that its entry had an impact on the group member's perceived *willingness* to honor their debt commitments.

Meetings of heads of state in regional trade organizations tend to be dry affairs, yielding little more than handshakes or deadlocked talks. The January 2007 meeting of the Mercosur heads of state in Rio de Janeiro got off to a livelier start. Before the summit even began, Hugo Chávez, the authoritarian leader of Venezuela, the bloc's newest member, had this to say, after arriving at

---

[21] Author Interview, Marcel Vaillant, Dept. of Economics, University of the Republic, Montevideo Uruguay, 11 July 2009.

[22] Author interview, María Inés Terra, Facultad de Ciencias Sociales-UDELAR, 13 July 2009.

[23] Author interview, Cecilia Durán, Uruguayan Ministry of Foreign Affairs, 17 July 2009.

a Copacabana Beach hotel: "They say I came to poison [Mercosur], that Chávez came to contaminate it. Not at all. Neo-liberalism was what contaminated us to death."[24] Later at the summit, Bolivia's President Evo Morales joined his Venezuelan ally in saying Mercosur needed "profound reforms" of the anti-market variety – even while requesting full membership in the bloc. Bolivia also wanted to make its membership conditional on being allowed exemption from the common external tariff, a measure that would have undermined much of the economic benefit of the union.[25]

Brazil's trade- and market-friendly President Luíz Inacio Lula da Silva closed the two-day summit proclaiming, "There has never been such a promising polit-ical climate for the integration of Mercosur." But markets were beginning to have a different view of that proposed integration. "Mercosur already was in very serious trouble," said one Latin America analyst at the time. "It just seems to be in great danger of turning into a political forum for bashing the market economy."[26] *The Economist* called Venezuela's potential admission to the bloc "a challenge to Mercosur's identity.... Mercosur claimed to stand for open trade and regional integration led by the private sector; in 1996 it committed itself to 'the full respect of democratic institutions.' Mr. Chávez is a fan of none of these principles."[27] Two days later, Venezuela had nationalized its central bank, leading another investor to comment that "Mercosur is no longer about trade. The new joiners don't have much to trade – they are even opposed to free trade, it seems. The organization is more and more political, and to some degree anti-American."[28] Commentators held similar fears about Bolivia's candidacy; one paper commented that "as a potential Mercosur mem-ber, Bolivia would, like Venezuela, create a political risk of the kind inherent to nationalist governments that proclaim ill-defined socialism."[29]

The accession of Venezuela is a good example of a country that had signif-icant ability but questionable willingness to service its foreign debt. Economi-cally, the advent of Chávez's Venezuela to Mercosur should have been a boon for all its members. Chávez provided for nearly all the members' trade in cheap oil, and would have potentially served as a valuable export market as well. One bond trader who previously worked for a credit-ratings agency remarked that at his former job, country risk was the order of the day, "but now it's all about liquidity.... If trade with Venezuela is going to help the current account [of existing members], that's enough for me."[30] And yet other investors have questioned Venezuela's willingness to repay its debt, even if it has the cash to do so. After that country's default on its sovereign debt in 1902, the aggrieved

[24] "Chávez denies attempt at radicalizing Mercosur," *El Universal*, 18 January 2007.
[25] "South American unification elusive at Mercosur summit," *Associated Press*, 19 January 2007.
[26] "Unification Remains Elusive at Mercosur," Associated Press, 22 January 2007.
[27] "An ominous step," *The Economist*, 10 December 2005.
[28] "Does Mercosur have a political agenda?" *Council on Hemispheric Affairs*, 1 February 2007.
[29] "Bolivia's New Status Puts Pressure on Mercosur," *Interpress Service*, 18 January 2007.
[30] Author interview, Phillipe Sachs, JP Morgan, 10 May 2006.

TABLE 6.5. *Cumulative Abnormal Returns as Venezuela Negotiates with Mercosur*

Country	Return	Test Stat
Argentina	−8.74*	3.88
Brazil	24.12*	4.80
Paraguay	−3.20	1.80
Uruguay	−12.23	−1.83
Venezuela	−5.91	−2.11
Difference in means	−7.48	
Standard error	2.26	

Cumulative abnormal returns for Mercosur members surrounding Venezuela's negotiations. Test statistic (in parentheses) must be greater than the absolute value of 1.96 to indicate statistical significance; those that make the cutoff are indicated with a *.

parties unleashed their navies to blockade the ports until the debts were repaid. It defaulted eight more times over the twentieth century.

Indeed, initial market response favored the prospect of Venezuela's entry into Mercosur. Table 6.5 depicts investor reaction in a five-day window around Venezuela's first signing of an association agreement with Mercosur, on 16 June 2006, through calculating cumulative abnormal returns around the event, compared with an asset's previous performance. What event analysis does not allow us to do is to control for other factors that might be driving the relationship. How, for example, would it be possible to distinguish between contagion effects associated with being in Mercosur particularly and the effect of being in the region as a whole?

To address at least in part this question, I show the returns for the Mercosur countries and the non-Mercosur countries in Latin America, as well as a difference in means between the two groups. If that difference reliably does not include zero, then there is indeed a distinction between Mercosur countries and other countries in the region, no matter to what that difference may be attributable.

Investors responded positively to the entry of Venezuela, with significant drops in risk associated with Uruguayan, Paraguayan, Venezuelan, and Argentine bonds, in descending order of magnitude. Brazilian bonds actually experienced *gains* in risk that were statistically different than zero. This is reminiscent of Germany's increased risk at the entry of new states to the EU. In the face of Venezuela's potential entry to the trading bloc, the pro-market Lula di Silva – who commandeered the bloc's largest economy – would perhaps see decreased influence. Paraguay and Uruguay, the smallest economies in the group, saw a boost in their credibility upon Venezuela's entry, probably attributable to the prospect of increased liquidity. Regardless, even with the gain in risk for

Venezuela, there is a difference in risk between Mercosur and non-Mercosur countries of 12.20 percentage points – not a huge change in substantive terms, but statistically significant.

It is probable that investors had already factored in close relations between Argentina and Venezuela, as indicated by the relatively small drops in risk for Argentina relative to the two smaller economies. Following the Argentine default of 2001, a dizzying turnover of leaders produced in 2003 an eventual president, Nestor Kírchner, who since his election expanded a populist platform. In 2005, he oversaw a massive restructuring of $103 billion worth of debt, which had investors settling for a repayment of 30 cents on the dollar – a deal on which the international financial institutions did not look kindly, even though more than 75 percent of bondholders accepted the terms. After the restructuring, it turned out that Argentina need not fear isolation from international markets. Venezuela was flush with cash because of the surge in prices of oil, one of its primary exports. Eager to exert regional influence as well as to engage in a bit of arbitrage, Chávez moved in to Argentina's rescue. Over 2006, Chávez raided $580 billion of the country's central bank's reserves to buy some $3.1 billion in Argentine bonds.[31] On 13 October 2006, Argentine country risk was at its lowest level in ten years – although Venezuela was its primary backer, and the share of Western holders of Argentine debt had decreased. But for Brazil – the largest market and the member with the most credibility – risk increased somewhat as a function of the planned closer ties with Chávez.

6.3 WHEN NEW MEMBERS CHANGE THE BRAND OF THE ORGANIZATION

Beyond the effects on core members themselves, how does the inclusion of risky members change the way the whole organization appears to outsiders? Once organizations expand to include more risky members, expectations about the meaning of inclusion in those organizations would start to vary. The heuristic power of international organizations only works if most individuals interpret membership in those organizations in a similar manner. If organizations expanded to include too many divergent members, investor perceptions might themselves diverge, and there would be less of a clear effect on risk levels for new applicants to the organization. The current rounds of EU enlargement afford an opportunity to examine this proposition.

---

[31] He went on to sell $2.4 billion of those bonds to a hand-picked group of Venezuelan banks at a $309 million profit. "Any operation that hands out $300 million discretionally, regardless of the mechanism, is a clear incentive for corruption," said one Venezuelan analyst. "The Chávez play," *The Economist*, 28 October 2006.

6.3.1 Attenuated Effects in Current Enlargement Negotiations

This section further examines the limits of the EU seal of approval by considering the effects of negotiations for current EU candidates. I offer evidence that the EU effect is attenuating, through event studies of the opening of negotiations with Turkey, Croatia, and Macedonia. This could result from two different mechanisms. The first is that, as the EU grows larger and more diverse, the EU that those countries are potentially signing onto is very different than the rich-country club of the early 1990s. This points to the fragility of institutions' ability to transfer confidence, even one whose effects are strong. The second possible mechanism is that – particularly after the accession in 2007 of Bulgaria and Romania, which EU publics as well as the Commission viewed after the fact as being too soon – the probability of admission of the current round of EU applicants is far lower than for previous rounds. However, it should be noted that the event studies below were taken *before* the admission of Bulgaria and Romania, when the real bad news about accepting underprepared members began to sink in.

The new additions in this table are the results from Croatia, Turkey, and Macedonia's opening of negotiations, formally on 17 December 2005. Where in the twentieth century no country had opened negotiations without eventually getting into the club, two of these countries had negotiations frozen: Croatia in 2005 (though the negotiations ended up being suspended for only nine months), and Turkey in November 2006. Following a dispute over access of Cypriot ships to Turkish ports, Brussels suspended negotiations indefinitely, in a move that many thought was a pretext for deeper, underlying concerns about Turkey's joining the union, even if it had met all the on-paper requirements (and more, in fact, than previous entrants had had to meet). On 8 November 2006, the EU published a report entitled "EU Enlargement Strategy and Main Challenges," which was critical of nearly all countries' prospect on the path to enlargement, largely for political reasons. The report cited Turkey's dispute with Cyprus, Croatia's failure to comply with the war crimes tribunal in The Hague, and Macedonia's slow progress with reforms. It also made reference to the EU's "absorption capacity," stating that "at present, it appears unlikely that a large group of countries will in future accede simultaneously."[32] This stood in contrast to previous EU language, which had implied that the countries could accede in a subsequent round of enlargement, and many took this language as an indication of the lack of political will for further EU expansion. Starting in November 2007, the EU began to refer to the negotiation process as "open-ended" and announced that negotiations would most likely take at least ten to 15 years. In a Brussels summit in December 2008, France – which then chaired the EU presidency – would only use the term "intergovernmental

---

[32] "Enlargement Strategy and Main Challenges," *EC Communication*, 8 November 2008.

TABLE 6.6. *Event Analysis of Opening EU Negotiations: Decreased Potency with an Expanded EU*

	Big Bang	Turkey	Croatia	Macedonia
Announcement of	−4.33*	−1.19*	−3.23*	−2.21*
Negotiation	(1.99)	(2.10)	(2.01)	(2.09)
Opening of	−4.24*	1.21*	−2.25*	−.78*
Negotiation	(2.01)	(2.21)	(2.36)	(1.95)
8 November 2006	−	4.58*	2.11*	1.01*
EU Report		(2.21)	(1.98)	(2.34)

Event analysis of cumulative abnormal returns surrounding different stages of EU negotiations. Results for the "big bang" countries show pooled returns for the sixteen countries that joined the EU in 2004 and 2007. Test statistics in parentheses; stars indicate statistical significance, where the statistic exceeds the absolute value of 1.96.

conference" rather than "accession conference" to describe a meeting at which two new chapters were scheduled to be opened, and official documents surrounding the meeting did not refer to accession as the goal of negotiations.[33]

Table 6.6 indicates the reaction of investors for each of the three candidate countries in thirty-day windows around the publication of that report, along with the initial announcement of the opening of formal negotiations and the subsequent initiation of negotiations. These latter two results are contrasted with those for the "big bang" round of enlargement in 2004.

Consistent with the results in the table, note that the cumulative abnormal returns of the "big bang" countries opening negotiations are by far greater than that in the other rounds. This should also serve as a robustness check of the results presented in Chapter 4. Note, too, that the three most recent candidates for enlargement do receive statistically significant drops in risk associated with the opening of negotiations and the previous announcement of negotiations. However, compare the drop in risk received by the "big bang" countries and the newer potential entrants. The returns for "big bang" countries are almost twice the size of those associated with announcements of opening of negotiations for Macedonia, Croatia, and Turkey ten years later. Similarly, it should be observed that there are slight *increases* in risk levels for countries following the publication of the unfavorable EU report – the first indication that the latest round of enlargement would not continue in the same manner as the previous ones.

This reaction could be a function of many different phenomena, not all mutually exclusive. One is that investors may not believe that the more recent negotiating countries are ever going to gain full membership in the EU. Where up through the "big bang" of enlargement, no country that opened negotiations had been denied entry, here the opening of negotiations may not be nearly as

---

[33] "No Good News for Turkey from EU Summit," *Turkish Daily News,* 12 December 2008.

credible a signal of eventual membership. Particularly with very visible public reluctance to admit Turkey, as well as "enlargement fatigue" throughout the union, investors may well assume that the EU's gestures toward the latest batch of candidates are not as sincere as in previous rounds of enlargement.[34]

Furthermore, the EU of today is a vastly different entity than that of the mid-1990s, when the Central European and Baltic states joined. Then it was a union of relatively rich countries, with average GDP per capita at $25,000 a year. With twenty-seven members in 2007, internal divisions over foreign policy, and a proven unwillingness to enforce its own rules, the signal from the EU supply side may not be nearly as strong. The current financial crisis – which has exposed severe economic weaknesses in Hungary, the Baltic countries, Bulgaria, and Romania – has further problematized the EU's previous image as an economic stronghold.

6.3.2 Turkey's EU Candidacy

This section offers a descriptive analysis of one of the current candidate countries. Turkey's candidacy for the EU is another case that shows how the power of the EU's seal of approval exists separately from the merits of the country itself, similar to the ENP as well as to the Croatia anecdote that opened the chapter. This country had not only already undertaken an extensive economic reform program prior to EU accession but also faced the prospect of closing every chapter in the *acquis* while still being denied ultimate EU membership. Investors reacted minimally to reform outside of the EU process as well as to the prospect of going through the motions of EU accession without the prize at the end.[35]

Since the 1980s, Turkey had turned from state-led growth toward openness and liberalization. Encouraging foreign investment had been a key component of Turkey's growth. By the mid-1990s, the Turkish government relied heavily on short-term debt, issuing government securities on international markets, as well as supplying domestic banks with high-interest bonds. But Turkey suffered a financial crisis in February 2001, triggered by an upset in confidence after then-President Ahmet Necdet Sezer accused then-Prime Minister Bulent Ecevit of not doing enough to fight corruption in the banking system. Within just a few months, the value of the Turkish lira had dropped 50 percent, domestic interest rates shot up to 3,000 percent, and inflation reached nearly 70 percent at its peak. More than $70 billion worth of portfolio investment fled the country in a matter of months.

---

[34] Interestingly, the "big bang" enlargement seems to have been regarded as much more of a sure thing; when the French rejected the EU constitution, spreads between Polish government bonds and German government bonds hardly budged.

[35] See also Mosley and Hardie (2007), who argue that, unlike in the Italian case (Favero et al., 2000), investors in Turkey reacted not just to economic fundamentals but to the probability of EU membership.

In the run-up to the crisis, Turkey had been in the midst of a $12 billion IMF program, aimed at reducing the state's reliance on deficit spending. In 2002, the IMF approved a rescaled $8 billion loan centered on an adjustment program that promised to decrease budget deficit, overhaul the banking system, and speed up privatization. Turkish authorities devalued the lira and introduced new banknotes in January 2005, made its central bank independent, and increased the autonomy of financial regulatory agencies. Although unemployment as well as current- and capital-account deficits persisted, the government's commitment to the reform program paid off in terms of economic growth.

Thus, when Turkey opened EU negotiations in December 2005, its economy was already in relatively sound shape. In fact, the chapters of the *acquis* dealing with services provision, company law, financial services, and statistics were among the first to be closed, because Turkey's economic reforms had already put them in line with most of the Commission's requirements.[36] But when negotiations were halted, the mandate came from the European Council to freeze talks until the Cypriot issue was resolved. Even though the opening of the chapters on economic and monetary policy was initially blocked by French President Nicolas Sarkozy, the Commission opened those chapters in December 2008, along with the chapter on Information Society and Media.

In fact, after negotiations were suspended, the EU made it clear to Turkey that the country could well close every chapter of the *acquis* but still be denied membership.[37] Event studies of the opening of the three chapters mentioned previously, as well as of the 20 December 2007 opening of the chapters on Health and Consumer Protection and on Trans-European Transport, showed no statistically significant investor reaction. This is perhaps indicative that investors see the opening of chapters as no guarantor of progress down the road toward accession, and that without that ultimate prize, the negotiations are meaningless.

Experts confirm this idea. One official who worked with the EU negotiations said, "It is stalled, and the stalling is costing us ... because people within Turkey are aware that it's largely political, but from the outside [investors] can only see this very bad signal."[38] Another expert adds that "in fact Turkey has made quite a bit of progress on economic matters, and the serious investors know that, but the ones that are more superficial are easily discouraged by our lack of progress with the EU."[39]

The case of Turkey, then, demonstrates just how tenuous the effect of good company can be. Even though Turkey had already undertaken significant

---

[36] Interview, Julien deSmedt, European Commission Directorate General for Enlargement, 7 June 2008.

[37] Interview, Atila Eralp, METU, 8 June 2008.

[38] Author interview, Nilgun Arisan, Secretariat General for the EU Affairs, Foreign Ministry of Turkey, 15 May 2008.

[39] Author interview, Galip Yalman, METU, 16 May 2008.

economic reforms under the auspices of the IMF, and even though its negotiations with the EU were put on hold for political, not economic, reasons, portfolio investors displayed remarkable skittishness. Of course, investors could have also been reacting to the diminished possibility of future economic gains for Turkey as a result of being excluded from EU membership. Nonetheless, this example indicates the heuristic element of the company a country keeps: even though economic evidence of a country's well-being may be in full display, investors are still sensitive to the signals it receives from an institution such as the EU.

6.4 CONCLUSION

This chapter has demonstrated the costs to existing member states of letting in new members. When emerging markets enter into economic agreements, they absorb the risk levels of the other members of those organizations. But preexisting members can lose some of their good standing among portfolio investors when they take a member of poor repute into their fold. The case of Germany prior to the 2009 financial crisis shows the slight jumps in risk for a core member, as does the example of Venezuela's moves toward Mercosur and its effects on the preexisting members. Additionally, countries that are now negotiating with the expanded, more diverse EU do not experience the same drops in risk as did those in earlier rounds of enlargement. This shows that, even if one holds the level of proposed integration constant but varies the average political quality of members, the magnitude of the drops in risk are not as large as when average political quality is higher in a smaller, more homogenous EU. The mechanisms behind this phenomenon have some basis in a fear of economic contagion, but there is some heuristic element to investor reaction as well; for example, in a broader EU, the "brand" has been degraded somewhat.

This raises the question of why any organization would bother to let in risky new countries in the first place. If existing members stand to lose credibility from expansion to weaker members, why does it take place? This is a complex question that many other researchers have addressed. Some argue that members who stand to lose from IO expansion receive payoffs in exchange for their acquiescence (Schneider, 2009); others make claims about the optimal number of members for a given group of countries (Stone, Slantchev, and London, 2008), or on how a lack of credibility and uncertainty about the benefits of integration can lead to expansion (Konstantinidis, 2008). In short, the politics and economics behind IO enlargement are intricate. In many cases, the changes in risk perception of existing members could be offset by other economic gains or political benefits.

That said, there is certainly a point past which the costs of enlargement – among which increased risk is one – will outweigh the benefits. At the time of proposed expansion to the postcommunist countries, many had argued that most of the advantages of enlargement would accrue to the new members, while the old members would be stuck with the budgetary burdens of enlargement (Baldwin, 1994, 1997; Winters and Wang, 1994). Despite those costs, Germany itself had arguably much to gain from initial enlargement; it had a relatively large amount of trade with the Central European countries and also stood to benefit from opportunities for FDI (Hofhansel, 2001). Indeed, after the fall of the Berlin Wall, Germany had been one of the strongest advocates for enlargement, in part because of its desire to make amends for Nazi atrocities in Eastern Europe (Lasas, 2008). Then-Chancellor Helmut Kohl had argued in the early 1990s that, now that geopolitical conditions had changed, the EU "should not, for God's sake, disappoint the trust that these countries have put in us" (Baun, 1997) and should encourage further expansion.

But the recent economic crises in Europe have changed Germany's tune somewhat. Chancellor Angela Merkel has argued that the EU needed to "consolidate" before it can admit any new members. Germany subsequently blocked Montenegro – which had submitted its membership application in December 2008 – from proceeding further along the road toward negotiations[40] and vetoed Serbia's EU candidacy in December 2011.[41] Clearly, there are limits to the levels of risk that countries are willing to shoulder as they expand their clubs. The findings presented here should factor into those calculations that countries make when they consider the trade-offs to enlargement.

The crisis in the eurozone also demonstrates the nuances of IO expansion and risk. In cases such as Mercosur, where member states had long histories of crisis and abrogation of their debt payments, it only took the proposed accession of one risky member to tip risk levels for Brazil. But for organizations such as the EU, where many members have solid reputations, the changes in risk are cumulative. It can take a lot of bad news from a lot of members to actually tip the reputation of an organization from good to bad. The rational design literature implies that as uncertainty about states' true preferences increases, organizations will become more restrictive in their membership (Koremenos, Lipson, and Snidal, 2001) – and indeed, the defections in the eurozone and the delays around enlargement for the current EU indicate that this is already happening.

---

[40] "Is Germany Closing The Door On Further EU Enlargement?," *RFE/RL*, 28 March 2009.
[41] "German veto threat to Serbia's EU candidacy," *European Voice*, 1 December 2011.

7

Conclusion

This book has argued that emerging markets can improve or darken their futures through the ties they make in the international community. All else being equal, portfolio investors pay attention to the company that a country keeps – and how closely that company is allegedly kept. Default risk can be magnified across the members of an international economic organization, particularly when it comes to determining a country's willingness, not its ability, to pay its debt.

Chapter 2 laid out the theoretical foundation for why international economic organizations change perceptions of emerging markets' future behavior. Drawing from sociology and management theory, I argue that the membership content of international organizations will change investor perceptions of country risk – separately from anything that those organizations ask countries to do, or enforcement of behavior, or propensities for countries to join other like-minded groups. In part as a heuristic, the reputations of better-known members will spill over into perceptions of other members of an international group. The changes in risk perceptions will vary depending on the proposed closeness of the association (a proxy for the public nature of the announcement and the seriousness of its intensions) and the extremity of its members' political quality. Political risk, I argue, is an indicator of an emerging market's willingness, not ability, to service its debt – and this information is especially valuable in pricing emerging-market sovereign risk.

Chapter 3 put this theory to the test. For more than 100 emerging markets from the 1990s to 2008 – a period where portfolio investment reached record highs – as well as a smaller annual sample reaching back to the 1980s, risk perceptions of emerging-market sovereign debt are sensitive to the political risk of the other members in an international economic organization. Where proposed integration with good-quality members is high, risk decreases; high integration with poor-quality members sees increases in risk for member states – a relationship that is robust and strong in magnitude across specifications. This effect is undiminished by controlling for economic or political changes that might have occurred in the country and is independent of any legal characteristics of the organization that might foretell the possibility of enforcement of rules. This is compelling evidence that the reputations of the members of an organization have the power to change investor expectations of emerging markets' future behavior.

Chapter 4 showed the effects of "good company" by looking at the EU expansion, paying particular attention to the postcommunist countries. I demonstrate the heuristic nature of this effect by showing that investors react most strongly when Brussels signs off on policy reforms in accession countries – not when those countries actually implement those reforms. This effect is distinct from selection processes (that is, that the EU simply picks winners), from actual policy reforms or changes in economic fundamentals in accessor countries, or from the anticipation of enforcement of rules (as is demonstrated by the relative lack of investor reaction when countries broke EU rules). These findings offer intriguing micro-level insights into the psychological impacts of international organizations. Additionally, now that the average political quality of the EU has been diluted through enlargements, the drops in risk for emerging markets currently negotiating for membership are far less than they were during previous rounds of enlargement. These cases take advantage of the natural variation even within the same organization to show how investor perceptions change once good-quality organizations vary in terms of either the levels of integration offered by their members or if the average quality decreases as a function of a larger number of more diverse members.

Chapter 5 investigated the dynamics of bad company associations by examining investor reaction to entry into, and exit from, proposed economic associations where members had a high level of political risk. The Bolivarian Alternative for the Americas and the Eurasian Union had proposed a high level of integration but had not gotten off the ground in any meaningful way, indicating that investors react to the proposed integration separately from actual policy change in those countries. For countries where uncertainty is high, signing onto those agreements indicated to investors their potential trajectory. Risk increased when governments announced their allegiance with countries where political risk was high, and it decreased when they broke ties with those organizations. I also showed, through the case of COMESA in Africa, that when good-quality members exit an organization, investors regard them as less risky. Finally, the example of China's free-trade associations demonstrated that when a country of mid-level risk initiates loose economic ties with emerging markets, the estimates of risk for those markets may not change, but the variance of investor perceptions increases.

Chapter 6 looked at the effects of enlargement on core members to the organization. Up until 2008, default risk for Germany has increased slightly as a function of rounds of EU enlargement. Similarly, even in the presence of economic contagion as a result of the 2001 default in Argentina, markets temporarily forgot Uruguay's good reputation for servicing its debt and penalized it for its associations with Argentina via the Mercosur trade agreement. Additionally, when Venezuela started angling for membership in Mercosur, Brazil looked somewhat worse off to investors. Finally, there is evidence that the EU "brand" is becoming weaker: new candidate countries are not experiencing the same drops in risk as did the postcommunist countries. This chapter offers new evidence about the consequences of organizational expansion and suggests that, in contrast to claims found in the endogenous cooperation literature, institutions may indeed incur additional risk when taking on new members.

These changes in investor perception do not always match the realities on the ground. The empirical chapters demonstrated *less* convergence on good or bad behavior alike than what market reactions might indicate. That is, the scale of investor reactions to countries' membership in various international organizations is often not matched by those countries' subsequent and future performance. Nonetheless, there is an extent to which these reactions can become self-fulfilling prophecies. If access to capital becomes cheaper for countries as a result of lower risk premia, they can better finance their own economic growth; similarly, countries that can only borrow abroad at prohibitive rates can get stuck in development traps, unable to take advantage of international markets for their borrowing needs. Thus, countries should certainly pay attention to the factors that influence their cost of borrowing abroad, whether those influences are justified or not.

These alternatives go beyond estimating the probability that a politician in an emerging market is sincere in his or her intentions to repay the country's debt. It can also include estimating the likelihood that even an earnest government will be derailed from its economic track, by domestic political opposition or by exogenous shocks, either in the form of natural disasters or – importantly – other investors losing their confidence in a country's creditworthiness. These estimations, as centuries of burst bubbles and subsequent capital flight attest, may end up being way off base. Those who believe in market efficiency think that over- or undervaluation of share prices is offset by arbitrage on the part of sophisticated investors. But believers in behavioral finance think that smarter investors are often unable or unwilling to correct sentiment traders, especially when there are constraints to arbitrage (Shleifer and Vishny, 1997; Subramanian, 2007). Initial miscalculations can have persistent effects on the collective understanding of an asset's worth.

The case of the East Asian financial crisis illustrates this point. Those countries were neither as solid as investment activity might indicate in the run-up to the crisis, nor as abject as the subsequent capital flight might indicate (Blustein, 2006). Most investors now agree that overconfidence in the East Asian economies gave them much lower interest rates than were merited by their economic fundamentals, and that investor panic over the balance sheets of South Korea and Thailand shot risk levels up to much higher than was deserved. Indeed, investment is often driven by herd behavior; it can be as profitable if not more profitable to invest in a healthy country than to invest in a country that other investors think is healthy.

Nonetheless, even such over- or underestimations can be very profitable for investors if their timing is right. Financial crises are often accompanied by rousing critiques of the idea that markets are efficient or rational. However, some theorize that even though stocks or assets may be overvalued, it may still be rational for investors to follow market sentiment, because bubbles can have self-fulfilling effects (Diba and Grossman, 1988; Froot and Obstfeld, 1991; Santos and Woodford, 1997; Lei, Noussair, and Plott, 2001). Investors can insulate themselves from significant short-term losses by dumping their holdings, provided that they are not at the lowest point of market sentiment. Similarly, they can make big gains by buying into perhaps inflated assets, as long as they are not at the peak of market enthusiasm. Thus, even estimations that do not reflect the fundamentals of an economy – erring on the side of overly optimistic or pessimistic – can still be an equilibrium, because investors can profit even from asset prices that are off base.

7.1 IMPLICATIONS

The theory presented in this book has powerful ramifications for studies in international development. I argue that the reputations of international economic organizations can be driven less by their economic or institutional features than by the perceived quality of their members. Those reputations, in turn, kick back into investors' perceptions of new members. Emerging markets that are seen as being suddenly more credible as a function of the company they keep will be able to tap funds relatively easily, thus giving them greater opportunity for growth and development. Many scholars and practitioners have struggled to offer advice to developing countries hoping to attract international capital at favorable rates. The advice this book would give to policy makers is nuanced but important. My argument does not seek to undermine the evidence in favor of economic integration, either at the regional or at the international level. Fully weighing the potential merits of closer economic ties with one's neighbors against the ramifications of "the company you keep" in the eyes of investors is not the intention of this argument. Indeed, it is possible that the gains from trade even with neighbors of dubious repute may outweigh the potential loss of credibility in international capital markets. Many studies have indicated, for example, that Uruguay and Paraguay have benefitted tremendously from enhanced market access to Brazil and Argentina as a function of their membership in Mercosur. Even with the potential accession of unstable Venezuela and the attendant increase in investor risk, as demonstrated in Chapter 5, those economic gains may well swamp the costs of the increased premiums that investors now demand to hold Uruguayan or Paraguayan debt.

But policy choices always involve trade-offs. Thus, ministers of economy and trade may want to take a hard look at the membership composition of agreements that may bring no real integration, only bad friends.

This boost in political credibility can be important for developing countries. Recent work in both the policy and the academic field points to the primacy of domestic institutions in economic development. In the development literature, emphasis is shifting from the urgency of so-called first-generation economic reforms, such as liberalization, stabilization, budget constraints, and privatization, to a new focus on institutions and governance. These "Type Two" or "second-generation" reforms aim at reducing corruption, improving regulations, ensuring independence of monetary and fiscal institutions, and strengthening the judiciary (Rodrik, 2003; Svejnar, 2002). These are the reforms that are targeted at ensuring a decrease in political risk. But such reforms are often slow to materialize and not very visible. The findings in this book imply that if institutions that guarantee certainty – such as political stability and legal enforcement – are thin on the ground at home, at least one aspect of their positive effects can perhaps be imported from abroad, through membership in certain types of international institutions. Similarly, countries can unwittingly absorb the political risk from their close affiliates, in the eyes of investors. This demonstrates that membership in certain international organizations may bring benefits – or, conversely, impose costs – well beyond those that were initially conceived by the literature on international organizations.

Since the stalemate of the Doha round of multilateral talks, free-trade agreements have sprung up among countries all over the world. Though this book did not examine this phenomenon in systematic detail, the theory as well as some of the evidence presented here suggests that even though FTAs promise relatively low levels of integration, investors should also respond positively to these economic links, depending on good political quality of the larger market. And anecdotal evidence does suggest that this may be the case. For example, one trader estimated that Peruvian stocks rose around 15 percent when the country was negotiating its free-trade area with the United States.[1] Another former trade official said that "the US FTA is a great brand for us – it's the gold standard of international agreements, great advertising."[2]

Additionally, countries are increasingly trying to exert their influence through their participation in international organizations. In addition to angling for a seat in Mercosur, Chávez had also planned to build a Bank of the South, in no small part to provide what he viewed as an ideological alternative to borrowing from the World Bank or the International Monetary Fund, as well as a regional organization (the Bolivarian Alternative of the Americas, or ALBA) to rival NAFTA. China has announced that it will spend $150 million to expand the African Union headquarters and to build residences

---

[1] Interview, Ernesto Delgado, BBVA Fondos Continental – Lima, 9 July 2009.
[2] Interview, Ricardo Parredes, COMEX-Peru, 10 July 2009.

for that organization's senior officials. The country has also secured itself a seat at the conference tables of COMESA, SADC, and ECOWAS.[3] Understanding how such moves impact the credibility of the countries in these organizations is crucial in our grasp of the dynamics of international organization.

Countries do face choices in the company they keep, and often those choices are not trivial. As Chapter 5 discussed, Ukraine was dithering on signing onto the Eurasian Union in part out of concern that an orientation toward Russia would hurt its chances of furthering integration with the European Union. But in October 2011, EU representatives postponed a high-level meeting with Ukraine's President Viktor Yanukovych, in protest over the jailing of a prominent opposition leader. In response, Yanukovych, announcing that he was "irritated by how [he] was being treated in Brussels," signed a CIS trade agreement just a few hours later. "Europe will not help us, and we need points of agreement with Russia right away," he said.[4] Such choices are complicated ones for heads of state, and reputational concerns may be just a part of the calculation. The arguments presented in this book seek to quantify as well as theorize those reputational effects.

These cases offer us important lessons in two respects. First, they afford us a deeper understanding of how international institutions confer benefits or drawbacks on their members, and thus how international cooperation works. Perhaps more importantly, they offer cautionary lessons to policy makers in developing countries. My findings suggest that for emerging markets, the role of an international community may be as important as, or even more important than, instruments such as domestic institutions, policies, or laws in providing assurance and credibility. This is powerful advice for would-be reformers, who are routinely thrown out of office on the cross of failed or incomplete policy measures. Take the case of the European Union. Many postcommunist countries spent the better part of the 1990s adopting measures that would convince foreign investors of their commitment to reform. Currency boards stopped the government from taking the printing presses into their own hands and ensured a commitment to low inflation. Some governments flew in international specialists to help write the constitutions. But the impact of signing on to formal EU negotiations dwarfed these efforts in terms of investor confidence. Thus, policy makers might do better to focus their energies on cozying up to the right international institutions – that is, those with deep ties and high-caliber members.

Of course, such institutions are not readily on offer, and in fact are completely inaccessible to some regions of the world. A country can only pick its agreements to a limited extent. States obviously cannot choose from any going international or regional organization: Eritrea cannot hope to join NAFTA, and Bolivia cannot sign on to the EU. But they can frequently make choices about

---

[3] "China's Rise – Hope or Doom for Africa?" *New Vision Uganda*, 26 May 2007.
[4] "Ukraine leans closer toward Russia-led customs bloc," *Agence France Presse*, 19 October 2011.

to which trade agreement within their region they want to belong. Africans, for example, can choose between membership in the South African Development Community and the Common Market for Eastern and Southern Africa, among others. Latin Americans can select between the Andean Community and the Bolivarian Alternative for the Americas. European nations can elect whether or not to apply for consideration for EU membership. Thus, controlling for region, nations do have some autonomy in choosing the organizations to which they want to belong, and these choices can have significant consequences for how those nations are perceived on international markets.

Recall the case of the European Neighborhood Policy, which at first glance could have offered some solace to nations on the periphery of the EU. Though that afforded countries in North Africa and the Newly Independent States an allegiance with Eastern Europe, markets paid it no heed, because those countries were expressly denied full membership in the EU club. What hope, then, for countries in Africa or the Middle East, with no possibility of integrating into an exclusive and tightly bound club?

Even though Somalia can never join the EU, there are lessons for the types of institutions that countries eager to capitalize on Western investment ought not to form. Chile's eventual refusal to join Mercosur now looks prodigious, based on not only the Brazilian currency crisis and the Argentinian default, but also the membership of anti-market Venezuela and, potentially, Bolivia. Thus, the kinds of institutions that give markets confidence are the ones that put developing countries with groups that are farther along the development path. Of course, the danger for those developed countries is that close linkages with risky countries may somewhat damage their own credibility, as is evidenced with the case of Germany in Chapter 4. More stable nations that deepen their ties with less-developed countries do so at some risk. The credibility of newly integrating states will increase, but it comes at the expense of the countries with better records. Scholars are increasingly attempting to measure change in international institutions, as well as those changes' impact on various outcomes, either for cooperative environments or for members themselves.[5] This shows one way in which changes in membership can dilute the boost in credibility for new members or enhance risks for existing ones.

This is an important lesson to consider as more and more regional alliances emerge. Research on the benefits developing countries' integration into the global economy has largely focused on the benefits they can extract from multilateral trade. But with multilateralism teetering after the near-collapse of the Doha talks of the WTO, new trading blocs are on the rise, and this book has

---

[5] On broader outcomes, see, for example, Acemoglu and Robinson (2006) on how regime change may or may not affect economic institutions; on how legalization of trade regimes produces asymmetrical outcomes for member nations, see Busch and Reinhardt (2003) and Lacarte-Muro and Gappah (2000), who argue that the bureaucratization of the WTO has made it more difficult for developing countries with low administrative capacity to file complaints.

demonstrated that these institutions can herald in unanticipated benefits or costs in the form of sovereign risk.

Though the lack of resolution of the Doha round means that the future of multilateral trade negotiations is uncertain, consider the potential benefits for developing countries of smaller, more targeted trading blocs with stable countries at the helm. Although the U.S. creation of the Free Trade Area of the Americas has stalled, it is the kind of organization that might provide Latin American countries with credibility on financial markets – more so than the newly unwieldy Mercosur, whose most recent members are flush with oil money but are stridently anti-market. Conversely, the potential creation of an Asian trading bloc that would unite Australia, India, and China – with high levels of proposed integration, to include an Asian Development Bank (ADB), to develop an Asian Currency Unit (ACU) as part of a comprehensive Asian Monetary Fund – may depend on the political credibility of the country at the helm.

Additionally, regional and international organizations themselves are changing their roles. A truism about institutions is that they are "sticky"; that is, their structures and assumptions tend to linger on even in the face of a much-changed environment.[6] Nonetheless, international institutions can undergo significant changes over their lifetimes. The institutional structure itself might evolve, as the Generalized Agreement on Tariffs and Trade ossified into the more formal World Trade Organization. The roles the institutions play might be transformed; the World Bank and the IMF, for example, were originally designed to perform tasks quite opposite to what they do now (the Bank was meant to provide liquidity, the IMF medium-term loans). Or the number of members might change, and the characteristics of new members may alter the way that a particular institution works and is perceived – especially when it comes to the founding members of the original institution. This project has shown one way in which institutions might evolve to be more likely to help emerging markets break free of development traps.

Finally, what has this story told us about the potential for institutions to transfer their norms and reduce unpredictability? Recall that the argument focused not on instability per se, but rather on investors' *perceptions* of instability. And markets are notorious for getting things wrong. As long as countries have been able to borrow abroad, they have defaulted on their debt; Latin America's first go at this came in the 1820s and has kept up as recently as Argentina's crash in 2001. Similarly, investors have rushed to judgment on the merit of a particular investment, and backpedaled in double time, throughout history. The bump in credibility given to countries that keep good company abroad need not reflect actual changes that have gone on in those countries. Chapter 4 showed that the most of those changes, in terms of policy reform or an overall propensity to be included, could have been factored in by markets

---

[6] See Ikenberry (1988) on the persistence of postwar Western order.

well in advance of those countries' entry into a stable RTA. And there is little reason to believe, theoretically or empirically, that countries would instantly absorb grand norms of good behavior. Scholars in constructivism argue that the internalization of norms is a slow process that can take generations (Moravcsik, 1995).

It should further be noted that the center of gravity in terms of portfolio investors may be shifting. For much of the last century, New York and London have been the hubs of most of the world's bond trades. But recent years have seen the proposed emergence of regional bond markets. Venezuela's Chávez had been an active proponent of a local bond market as part of his proposed Bank of the South. Furthermore, the ASEAN countries as well as China, Japan, and South Korea have been tabling a proposal for an Asian common bond market; this would cement China's position as a regional provider of capital. Having pools of investors that are based not just in Wall Street and the City of London, but also in Caracas and Beijing, might change the uniformity of investor reactions to certain types of events. One can imagine that regional bond markets might have a higher threshold for political risk than what is currently exhibited, or that the calculations that investors in non-OECD countries might differ from those of their Western counterparts. Along those lines, Chávez and Kirchner in July 2006 announced that they would issue a joint sovereign bond, a move unprecedented in capital markets. Analysts viewed the so-called Bond of the South as more of a political than an economic move, aimed at spurring deeper financial linkages in the region. Kirchner described the bond as the "construction of . . . a financial space in the south that will permit us to generate lines of finance which answer our regions' and societies' needs."[7] One might expect that such a bond would be less elastic to political risk.

At the same time, I hope to have demonstrated that the short-term boost afforded by stable institutions can help developing countries make the transition from being high-uncertainty countries to more stable ones. This is not an illustration of the transformative powers of institutions. It is a more modest claim, but still powerful. Membership in the right international organizations can buffer emerging markets from exogenous shocks, as demonstrated in the case of the Hungarian budget crisis in Chapter 4. If investors keep their cool, the domestic political fallout from those shocks can be greatly mitigated. Even in the face of riots and burning cars in Budapest, there were no speculative attacks on the currency or sell-offs of Hungarian debt. Thus, in the event of a government crisis, publics may punish even those governments that admit to lying "morning, noon, and night," as with Gyúrcsány in Hungary, not by hurling them out of office, but by taking them at their word to improve and holding them more accountable in the future. This is one key difference between a developed and a developing country: electoral institutions and heads of

---

[7] "Latin Allies Form a Political Bond," *Financial Times,* 12 July 2006.

government are not hurled out the window at the first sign of crisis, but instead are allowed to run their course within the confines of the system. Thus, the best an emerging-market government can do to ensure stability at home is to quiet panic abroad. The company a country keeps is crucial in this effort. The example of the continued Hungarian budget crisis – which did little to shake investors' calm prior to the global financial crisis of 2007 – provided some evidence that the faith investors place in organizations with quality members is overstated. But if the "halo effect" afforded by association with stable nations turns out to be a self-fulfilling prophecy, few developing countries will question how they got there.

The rate at which governments have access to capital can have huge welfare implications for emerging economies. Portfolio investment is increasingly important to countries that are moving from lower to middle stages of development. When they lack the means to raise sufficient revenue on their own, developing countries have traditionally turned to the IMF or the World Bank. As countries graduate from IMF programs they potentially gain more autonomy. Russia and Thailand have pursued means of early debt repayment, and Indonesia and Pakistan are among those now contemplating the move. Asian countries that were burned by the region's neoliberal financial crisis in 1997 are building up large cash reserves so that they will not have to go back to the Fund in times of economic downturn. As countries become wealthier as a result of earlier competitiveness, and as prices of production and labor rise, their attractiveness to foreign direct investors may decrease.[8] Many countries then shift to capital-market development as a form of financing. Yields on government debt often run parallel with overall levels of stock-market activity, as more companies become listed and equity revenues increase. Lower yields signify a more stable investment and a better-developed capital market, which means that more individual households can have access to capital-market borrowing. Thus, yields on government debt are a substantive concern for countries that are trying to better develop their access to financing – for governments and individuals alike – on world markets. To some extent, the global economic crisis has dampened the appetite for emerging market bonds. Risk aversion and deleveraging have pushed bonds in many emerging markets up and sparked capital flight. Even though many emerging markets have suffered as a result of the global economic contractions, their access to funding at the bilateral, regional, and multilateral level as well as high volumes of reserves have to some extent cushioned them from the global financial crisis.[9]

On the other hand, ministers of economy should consider the trade-offs involved in both the associations that they join as well as who they let into

[8] See Drake (1997); de Soto (2001) on the spread of credit to middle-income countries and the subsequent emergence of a middle class.
[9] "Most Emerging Market Sovereign Ratings Unaffected by Temporary Global Funding Shortage," *SeeNews*, 5 November 2008.

their existing unions. For countries both inside and outside international organizations, accession involves many conflicting considerations. Core members contemplating expansion of an organization confront many political and economic trade-offs in doing so; sometimes expansion to include riskier members can have dramatic consequences for the more stable members, as is evidenced now by the eurozone crisis. But EU enlargement was driven not just by the risk of new members, but also by geopolitical considerations and projections of convergence. Similarly, countries signing on to organizations spearheaded by riskier members may do so because of projected economic gains, even in the face of a worsened reputation among portfolio investors. I have not attempted to evaluate economic gains more generally from agreements, but certainly some of the associations that increase risk in the eyes of investors may bring short- or long-term improvements in GDP. But government officials should be mindful of factoring in possible changes to their risk profile in exchange for the benefits – economic, political, or otherwise – of closer union with other nations.

By the same token, this research has shown that all the members of a given organization are part of its overall risk profile. Just as emerging markets can take on the risk associated with members of an international organization, so too can more developed nations see their risk levels change somewhat once these organizations expand, as was seen in the case of Germany. This tension echoes throughout the current debates in the EU over future enlargement, and to ASEAN as its members consider the accession of China. An organization's identity comes directly from its members, and investor risk is only one aspect of that identity. International organizations in no small part represent ways in which countries define their regional space, their alliances, and their own profiles. This book has demonstrated how those profiles change as a result of membership, and not always for the better. Future architects of international economic organizations should take heed.

Bibliography

Abbott, Kenneth W. and Duncan, Snidal. 1998. "Why States Act through Formal International Organizations." *Journal of Conflict Resolution* 42(1):3–32.

Acemoglu, Daron and James A. Robinson. 2006. "De Facto Political Power and Institutional Persistence." *American Economic Review* 96(2):326–330.

Acemoglu, Daron, Simon Johnson, and James A. Robinson. 2002. "Reversal of Fortune: Geography and Institutions in the Making of Modern World Income Distributions." *Quarterly Journal of Economics* 17:1231–1294.

Achen, Christopher. 2000. "Why Lagged Dependent Variables Can Suppress the Explanatory Power of Other Independent Variables." Paper presented at the annual meeting of the American Political Science Association.

Achen, Christopher H. and W. Phillips Shively. 1995. *Cross-Level Inference*. Chicago: University of Chicago Press.

Adler, Michael and Bernard Dumas. 1984. "Exposure to Currency Risk: Definition and Measurement." *Financial Management* 13(2):41–50.

Aggarwal, Vinod and Ralph Espach. 2004. "Diverging Trade Strategies in Latin America: An Analytical Framework." In *The Strategic Dynamics of Latin American Trade*, eds. Vinod Aggarwal, Ralph Espach, and Joseph Tulchin. Stanford, CA: Stanford University Press, pp. 2–24.

Ahlquist, John. 2006. "Economic Policy, Institutions, and Capital Flows: Portfolio and Direct Investment Flows in Developing Countries." *International Studies Quarterly* 50:681–704.

Akemann, Michael and Fabio Kanczuk. 2005. "Sovereign Default and the Sustainability Risk Premium Effect." *Journal of Development Economics* 76:53–69.

Alesina, Alberto, Enrico Spoloare, and Romain Wacziarg. 2003. "Trade, Growth, and the Size of Countries." Harvard NOM Working Paper No. 03-14; Harvard Institute of Economic Research Working Paper No. 1995; Stanford GSB Working Paper No. RP1774.

Allen, John. 2005. *Apartheid South Africa: An Insider's Overview of the Origin and Effects of Separate Development*. Bloomington, iUniverse Books.

Alter, Karen. 2008. "Delegating to International Courts: Self-Binding vs. Other-Binding Delegation." *Law and Contemporary Problems* 71:37–76.

Alter, Karen and Sophie Meunier. 2009. "The Politics of International Regime Complexity, 7 Perspectives on Politics." *Perspectives on Politics* 7:13–24.

Alter, Karen J. 2000. "Explaining Variation in the Use of European Litigation Strategies: EC Law and UK Gender Equality Policy." *Comparative Political Studies* 33(4):316–346.

Amihud, Yakov and Haim Mendelson. 1986. "Asset Pricing and the Bid-Ask Spread." *Journal of Financial Economics* 17:223–249.

Anderson, Benedict. 1991. *Imagined Communities*. London: Verso.

Ang, Adrian U-Jin and Dursun Peksen. 2007. "When Do Economic Sanctions Work? Asymmetric Perceptions, Issue Salience, and Outcomes." *Political Research Quarterly* 60(1):135–145.

Aspara, Jaakko. 2009. "Aesthetics of Stock Investments." *Consumption Markets and Culture* 12(2):99–131.

Aspara, Jaakko. 2010. "How Do Institutional Actors in the Financial Market Assess Companies' Product Design? The Quasi-rational Evaluative Schemes." *Knowledge, Technology & Policy* 22(4):241–258.

Avery, Christopher and Peter Zamsky. 1998. "Multidimensional Uncertainty and Herd Behavior in Financial Markets." *The American Economic Review* 88(4): 724–748.

Axelrod, Robert. 1981. "The Emergence of Cooperation among Egoists." *American Political Science Review* 75:306–308.

Axelrod, Robert. 1984. *The Evolution of Cooperation*. New York: Basic Books.

Axelrod, Robert. 1997. *The Complexity of Cooperation: Agent-Based Models of Competition and Collaboration*. Princeton, NJ: Princeton University Press.

Baily, W. and Y. Peter Chung. 1995. "Exchange Rate Fluctuations, Political Risk, and Stock Returns: Some Evidence from an Emerging Market." *Journal of Financial and Quanitative Analysis* 30:541–561.

Balassa, Bela. 1961. *The Theory of Economic Integration*. Homewood, IL: Richard D. Irwin.

Baldwin, Richard E. 1994. *Towards an Integrated Europe*. London: CEPR.

Baldwin, Richard E. 1997. "Concepts and Speed of an Eastern Enlargement." In *Quo Vadis Europe*, ed. Horst Siebert. Tübingen: J.C.B. Mohr, pp. 73–95.

Baldwin, Richard E. 2007. "Managing the Noodle Bowl: The Fragility of East Asian Regionalism." ADB Working Paper Series on Regional Economic Integration No. 7.

Banerjee, Abhijit V. 1992. "A Simple Model of Herd Behavior." *The Quarterly Journal of Economics* 107(3):797–817.

Barnett, Michael and Martha Finnemore. 2004. *Rules for the World: International Organizations in Global Politics*. Ithaca, NY: Cornell University Press.

Basu, S., S. Estrin, and J. Svejnar. 2000. "Employment Determination in Enterprises under Communism and in Transition: Evidence from Central Europe." *Industrial and Labor Relations Review* 58(3):353–371.

Baturo, Alexander and Julia Gray. 2009. "Flatliners: Ideology and Rational Learning in the Adoption of the Flat Rate Tax." *European Journal of Political Research* 48:130–159.

Baun, Michael. 1997. "Germany and EU Enlargement into Eastern Europe." Working Paper.

Bearce, David. 2007. *Monetary Divergence*. Ann Arbor, MI: University of Michigan Press.

Bearce, David H. 2002. "Monetary Divergence: Domestic Political Institutions and the Monetary Autonomy – Exchange Rate Stability Trade-Off." *Comparative Political Studies* 35:194–220.

Bearce, David H. and Stacy Bondanella. 2007. "Intergovernmental Organizations, Socialization, and Member-State Interest Convergence." *International Organization* 61:703–733.

Bearce, David H. and Sawa Omori. 2005. "How Do Commercial Institutions Promote Peace?" *Journal of Peace Research* 42(6):659–678.

Beatty, Randolph P. and Jay R. Ritter. 1986. "Investment Banking, Reputation, and the Underpricing of Initial Public Offerings." *Journal of Financial Economics* 15:213–232.

Beaudry, Paul and Franck Portier. 2006. "Stock Prices, News, and Economic Fluctuations." *American Economic Review* 96:1293–1307.

Beaulieu, Emily, Gary W. Cox, and Sebastian Saiegh. 2012. "Sovereign Debt and Regime Type: Reconsidering the Democratic Advantage." *International Organization* 66(04):709–738.

Beck, Nathaniel and Jonathan N. Katz. 1995. "What to Do (and Not to Do) with Time-Series Cross-Section Data." *American Political Science Review* 89:634–647.

Beck, Paul Allen and M. Kent Jennings. 1991. "Family Traditions, Political Periods, and the Development of Partisan Orientations." *Journal of Politics* 53:742–763.

Becker, Howard. 1963. *Outsiders: Studies in the Sociology of Deviance.* New York: Collier Macmillan.

Ben-Haim, Yakov. 1998. "Sequential Tests Based on Convex Models of Uncertainty." *Mechanical Systems and Signal Processing* 12:427–448.

Benartzi, Shlomo and Richard H. Thaler. 2001. "Naive Diversification Strategies in Retirement Saving Plans." *American Economic Review* 91(1):79–98.

Benartzi, Shlomo and Richard H. Thaler. 2007. "Heuristics and Biases in Retirement Savings Behavior." *Journal of Economic Perspectives* 21(3):81–104.

Bernhard, William and David Leblang. 2002. "Political Processes and Foreign Exchange Markets: The Forward Exchange Rate Bias." *American Journal of Political Science* 46:316–333.

Bernhard, William and David Leblang. 2006. "Parliamentary Politics and Foreign Exchange Markets: The World According to GARCH." *International Studies Quarterly* 50:69–92.

Bernhard, William J. and Tracy Sulkin. 2009. "Cosponsorship and Commitment." Working Paper.

Berry, Frances Stokes and William D. Berry. 1990. "State Lottery Adoptions as Policy Innovation: An Event History Analysis." *American Political Science Review* 84:395–415.

Beyers, Jan. 2005. "Multiple Embeddedness and Socialization in Europe: The Case of Council Officials." *International Organization* 59:899–936.

Beyers, Jan and Guido Dierickx. 1998. "The Working Groups of the Council of the European Union: Supranational or Intergovernmental Negotiations?" *Journal of Common Market Studies* 36(3):289–317.

Bhagwati, Jagdish. 1996. "Trade and the Environment: Does Environmental Diversity Detract from the Case for Free Trade?" In *Fair Trade and Harmonization: Prerequisites for Free Trade?*, eds. Jagdish Bhagwati and Robert Hudec. MIT Press, pp. 159–223.

Bienen, Derk and Mamo E. Mihretu. 2010. "The Principle of Fairness and WTO Accession: An Appraisal and Assessment of Consequences." Society of International Economic Law Working Paper 2010/29. London School of Economics and Political Science.

Biglaiser, Glen and Karl DeRouen. 2007. "Following the Flag: Troop Deployment and U.S. Foreign Direct Investment." *International Studies Quarterly* 51: 835–854.

Biglaiser, Glen and Joseph L. Staats. 2012. "Finding the 'Democratic Advantage' in Sovereign Bond Ratings: The Importance of Strong Courts, Property Rights Protection, and the Rule of Law." *International Organization* 66(3):515–535.

Blustein, Paul. 2006. *And the Money Kept Rolling In(And Out): The World Bank, Wall Street, the IMF and the Bankrupting of Argentina*. New York: Public Affairs.

Boas, Morten. 2000. "The Trade-Environment Nexus and the Potential of Regional Trade Institutions." *New Political Economy*: 415–432.

Boerzel, Tanja. 2001. "Non-Compliance in the European Union: Pathology or Statistical Artefact." *Journal of European Public Policy* 8(5):803–824.

Boerzel, Tanja A. 2005. "Mind the Gap! European Integration between Level and Scope." *Journal of European Public Policy* 12(2):217–236.

Boerzel, Tanja A., Tobias Hofmann, Diana Panke, and Carina Sprungk. 2010. "Obstinate and Inefficient: Why Member States Do Not Comply with European Law." *Comparative Political Studies* 43(11):1363–1390.

Bondanella, Stacy. 2009. "Intergovernmental Organizations and the Determinants of Member State Interest Convergence." PhD thesis University of Pittsburgh.

Bordo, Michael D. and Hugh Rockoff. 1996. "The Gold Standard as a 'Good Housekeeping Seal of Approval'." *Journal of Economic History* 56:389–428.

Bourename, Naceur. 2002. "Regional Integration in Africa: Situation and Prospects." In *Regional Integration in Africa*. Paris: OECD, pp. 17–43.

Brada, Josef C. and Ali M. Kutan. 2001. "The Convergence of Monetary Policy between Candidate Countries and the European Union." Economic Systems 25(3), pp. 215–231.

Brambor, Thomas, William Roberts Clark, and Matt Golder. 2006. "Understanding Interaction Models: Improving Empirical Analyses." *Political Analysis* 14(1): 63–82.

Broker, Gunter. 1993. *Government Securities and Debt Management in the 1990s*. Paris, Washington, DC: Organization for Economic Cooperation and Development, OECD Publications and Information Centre.

Brune, Nancy and Alexandra Guisinger. 2007. "The Limited Role of MNCs in Promoting Financial Liberalization in the Developing World." Working paper for Global Challenges to U.S. Business Conference.

Bulow, Jeremy and Kenneth Rogoff. 1989. "A Constant Recontracting Model of Sovereign Debt." *Journal of Political Economy* 97(1):155–178.

Busch, Marc and Krzysztof Pelc. 2010. "The Politics of Judicial Economy at the World Trade Organization." *International Organization* 64(2):257–280.

Busch, Marc and Eric Reinhardt. 2003. "Developing Countries and GATT/WTO Dispute Settlement." *Journal of World Trade* 37(4):719–735.

Busch, Marc L., Eric Reinhardt, and Gregory Shaffer. 2009. "Does Legal Capacity Matter? A Survey of WTO Members." *World Trade Review* 8(4):559–577.

Bussie, Matthieu and Christian Mulder. 2000. "Political Instability and Economic Vulnerability." *International Journal of Finance and Economics* 5:309–330.

Büthe, Tim and Helen V. Milner. 2008. "The Politics of Foreign Direct Investment into Developing Countries: Increasing FDI through International Trade Agreements?" *American Political Science Review* 52:741–762.

Caetano, Gerardo and Marcel Vaillant. 2004. "Qué MERCOSUR y qué Uruguay se necesitan? Apuntes para entender requerimientos recíprocos." Working Paper No. 1504, Department of Economics, University of the Republic-Uruguay.

Calvo, Guillermo A., A. Izquierdo, and E. Talvi. 2003. "Sudden Stops, the Real Exchange Rate and Fiscal Sustainability: Argentina's Lessons." In *Monetary Unions and Hard Pegs*, ed. Alexander V. Mélitz and G.M. Von Furstenberg. Oxford: Oxford University Press, pp. 150–181.

Calvo, Guillermo A., A. Izquierdo and E. Talvi. 2006. "Sudden Stops and Phoenix Miracles in Emerging Markets." *American Economic Review* 96(2):405–410.

Calvo, Guillermo A. and Enrique G. Mendoza. 1993. "Rational Contagion and the Globalization of Securities Markets." *Journal of International Economics* 51(1):79–113.

Campello, Daniela. 2008. "Do Markets Vote? A Systematic Analysis of Portfolio Investors' Response to National Elections." Working Paper.

Campello, Murillo. 2006. "Debt Financing: Does It Hurt or Boost Firm Performance in Product Markets?" *Journal of Financial Economics* 82:135–172.

Campos, Nauro F. and Fabrizio Coricelli. 2002. "Growth in Transition: What We Know, What We Don't, and What We Should." William Davidson Institute Working Paper Series.

Campos, Nauro F. and Roman Horvath. 2006. "Reform Redux: Measurement, Determinants and Reversals." IZA Discussion Papers.

Cantor, Richard Martin and Frank Packer. 1996. "Determinants and Impact of Sovereign Credit Ratings." *Economic Policy Review* 2(2):37–54.

Cappelen, Aadne, Fulvio Castellacci, Jan Fagerberg, and Bart Verspagen. 2003. "The Impact of EU Regional Support on Growth and Convergence in the European Union." *Journal of Common Market Studies* 41:621–644.

Carter, Richard, Rick Dark, and Ajai Singh. 1998. "Underwriter Reputation, Initial Returns, and the Long-Run Performance of IPO Stocks." *Journal of Finance* 53:285–311.

Carter, Richard and Steven Manaster. 1990. "Initial Public Offerings and Underwriter Reputation." *The Journal of Finance* 45:1045–1067.

Case, Anne and Lawrence Katz. 1991. "The Company You Keep: The Effects of Family and Neighborhood on Disadvantaged Youths." NBER working paper no. 3705.

Chakrabarti, Avik. 1999. "Foreign Direct Investment and Host Country Interaction." Occasional Paper No. 69, Export Import Bank of India.

Chapman, Terrence. 2009. "Audience Beliefs and International Organization Legitimacy." *International Organization* 63(4):733–764.

Checkel, Jeffrey T. 1999. "Norms, Institutions, and National Identity in Contemporary Europe." *International Studies Quarterly* 43(1):84–114.

Checkel, Jeffrey T. 2001. "Why Comply? Social Learning and European Identity Change." *International Organization* 55(2):553–588.

Checkel, Jeffrey T. 2005. "International Institutions and Socialization in Europe: Introduction and Framework." *International Organization* 59(4):801–826.

Chen, M. and J.A. Bargh. 1997. "Nonconscious Behavioral Confirmation Processes: The Self-Fulfilling Consequences of Automatic Stereotype Activation." *Journal of Experimental Social Psychology*.

Cheong Chan, Yue, Andy C.W. Chui and Chuck C.Y. Kwok. 2001. "The Impact of Salient Political and Economic News on the Trading Activity." *Pacific Basin Finance Journal* 9:195–217.

Cialdini, R.B., R.J. Borden, A. Thorne, M. Walker, S. Freeman and L. Sloane. 1976. "Basking in Reflected Glory: Three Field Studies." *Journal of Personality and Social Psychology* 34:366–375.

Claessens, Stijn and Simeon Djankov. 2002. "Privatization Benefits in Eastern Europe." *Journal of Public Economics* 83(3):307–324.

Claessens, Stijn, Simeon Djankov, and Daniela Klingebiel. 2000. "Stock Markets in Transition Economies." Financial Sector Discussion Paper No. 5.

Clark, William Roberts. 1998. "International and Domestic Constraints on Political Business Cycle Behavior in OECD Economies." *International Organization* 1(52):87–120.

Codogno, Lorenzo, Carlo Favero, and Allessandro Missale. 2003. "Yield Spreads on EMU Government Bonds." *Economic Policy* 18:503–532.

Cole, Harold and Patrick Kehoe. 1998. "Models of Sovereign Debt: Partial versus General Reputations." *International Economic Review* 39:55–70.

Connolly, M.B. and J. De Melo. 1994. *The Effects of Protectionism on a Small Country: The Case of Uruguay*. Washington, DC: World Bank Publications.

Copelovitch, Mark and David Ohls. 2012. "Trade, Institutions, and the Timing of GATT/WTO Accession in Post-Colonial States." *The Review of International Organizations* 7(1):81–107.

Corcosa, A., J.P. Eckmannbc, A. Malaspinasb, Y. Malevergnede, and D. Sornette. 2002. "Imitation and Contrarian Behaviour: Hyperbolic Bubbles, Crashes and Chaos." *Quantitative Finance* 2(4):264–281.

Cortell, Andrew P. and James W. Davis. 2000. "Understanding the Domestic Impact of International Norms: A Research Agenda." *International Studies Review* 2:65–87.

Cortell, Andrew P. and James W. Davis Jr. 1996. "How Do International Institutions Matter? The Domestic Impact of International Rules and Norms." *International Studies Quarterly* 40(4):451–478.

Cowhey, Peter F. and Jonathan D. Aronson. 1993. *Managing the World Economy: The Consequences of Corporate Alliances*. New York: Council of Foreign Relations Press Inc.

Crawford, Jo-Ann and Roberto V. Fiorentino. 2005. "The Changing Landscape of Regional Trade Agreements." WTO Discussion Paper 8, WTO, Geneva.

Dai, Xinyuan. 2005. "Why Comply? The Domestic Constituency Mechanism." *International Organization* 59:363–398.

Dai, Xinyuan. 2006. "The Conditional Nature of Democratic Compliance." *Journal of Conflict Resolution* 50:690–713.

Dasgupta, Susmita, Benoit Laplante, and Nlandu Mamingi. 1998. "Capital Market Responses to Environment Performance in Developing Countries." World Bank working paper.

de Mesquita, Bruce Bueno. 2000. "Popes, Kings, and Endogenous Institutions: The Concordat of Worms and the Origins of Sovereignty." *International Studies Review* 2(2):93–118.

de Soto, Hernando. 2001. *The Mystery of Capital*. London: Black Swan.

Demirgüç-Kunt, Asli and Vojislav Maksimovic. 1998. "Law, Finance, and Firm Growth." *Journal of Finance* 53:2107–2137.

Detragiache, Enrica and Antonio Spilimbergo. 2001. "Crises and Liquidity: Evidence and Interpretation." IMF Working Paper 01/2.

Deutsch, Yuval and Thomas W. Ross. 2003. "You Are Known by the Directors You Keep: Reputable Directors as Signaling Mechanism for Young Firms." *Management Science* 49(8):1003–1017.

Diamonte, R.L., J.M. Liew, and R.J. Stevens. 1996. "Political Risk in Emerging and Developed Markets." *Financial Analysts Journal* 52:71–76.

Diba, Behzad and Herschel I. Grossman. 1988. "Rational Inflationary Bubbles." *Journal of Monetary Economics* 21:35–46.

Dinkić, Mladjan. 1995. *The Economics of Destruction: Can It Happen to You?* Belgrade: VIN.

Dollar, David and Aart Kraay. 2001. "Growth Is Good for the Poor." The World Bank Policy research working paper no. 2587.

Donno Panayides, Daniela. 2010. "Who Is Punished? Regional Intergovernmental Organizations and the Enforcement of Democratic Norms." *International Organization* 64(4):593–625.

Downs, George, David M. Rocke, and Peter Barsoom. 1996. "Is the Good News about Compliance Good News for Cooperation?" *International Organization* 50: 379–406.

Doxey, Margaret. 1980. *Economic Sanctions and Economic Enforcement, 2e.* Oxford: Oxford University Press.

Doxey, Margaret. 1987. *International Sanctions in Contemporary Perspective.* New York, Macmillan.

Drake, P.J. 1997. "Securities Markets in Less-Developed Countries." *Journal of Development Studies* 13:73–91.

Dreher, Axel, Noel Gaston, and Pim Martens. 2008. "The Global Village and the Social Aspects of Globalisation." Futures.

Dreher, Axel and Stefan Voigt. 2008. "Does Membership in International Organizations Increase Governments' Credibility? Testing the Effects of Delegating Powers." 08-193 KOF Swiss Economic Institute, ETH Zurich.

Drezner, Daniel. 1999. *The Sanctions Paradox: Economic Statecraft and International Relations.* Cambridge: Cambridge University Press.

Duina, Francesco. 2008. *The Social Construction of Free Trade.* Princeton: Princeton University Press.

Düllmann, Klaur and Marc Windfur. 2001. "Credit Spreads Between German and Italian Sovereign Bonds: Do Affine Models Work?" *Canadian Journal of Administrative Sciences* 17(2):166–179.

Eaton, Jonathan. 1996. "Sovereign Debt, Repudiation and Credit Terms." *International Journal of Economics and Finance* 1:25–35.

Edwards, Sebastian. 1986. "The Pricing of Bonds and Bank Loans in International Markets: An Empirical Analysis of Developing Countries' Foreign Borrowing." *European Economic Review* 30:565–589.

Edwards, Sebastian. 1998. "Interest Rate Volatility, Contagion and Convergence: An Empirical Investigation of the Cases of Argentina, Chile and Mexico." *Journal of Applied Economics* 1(1):55–86.

Eichengreen, Barry, Ricardo Hausmann, and Ugo Panizza. 2003. "Currency Mismatches, Debt Intolerance and Original Sin: Why They Are Not the Same and Why It Matters." NBER Working Paper No. W10036.

Eichengreen, Barry and Ricardo Hausmann. 1999. "Exchange Rates and Financial Fragility." NBER Working Paper 7418.

Eichengreen, Barry and Ashoka Mody. 1998. "Interest Rates in the North and Capital Flows to the South: Is There a Missing Link?" *International Finance* 1:35–57.

Eichengreen, Barry and Richard Portes. 1989. "Dealing with Debt: the 1930s and the 1980s." In *Dealing with the Debt Crisis*, eds. Ishrat Hussein and Ishac Diwan. Washingon, DC: The World Bank, pp. 69–88.

Engle, Robert, David Lilien, and Russell Robins. 1987. "Estimation of Time Varying Risk Premia in the Term Structure: The ARCH-M Model." *Econometrica* 55:391–407.

Erb, Claude B., Campbell R. Harvey, and Tadas E. Viskanta. 2000. "Understanding Emerging Market Bonds." *Emerging Markets Quarterly* 4:7–23.

Eulau, Heinz and Jonathan W. Siegel. 1981. "Social Network Analysis and Political Behavior: A Feasability Study." *Western Political Quarterly* 34:499–509.

Evangelist, Mike and Valerie Sathe. 2006. "Brazil's 1998-1999 Currency Crisis." Working Paper University of Michigan.

Fabozzi, Frank J. 2001. *The Handbook of Mortgage-Backed Securities*. Chicago: Probus Publishing.

Fang, Songying. 2009. "The Informational Role of International Institutions and Domestic Politics." *American Journal of Political Science* 52:304–321.

Favero, Carlo A., Francesco Giavazzi, Fabrizio Iacone, and Guido Tabellini. 2000. "Extracting Information from Asset Prices: The Methodology of EMU Calculators." *European Economic Review* 44(9):1607–1632.

Fearon, James. 1998. "Bargaining, Enforcement, and International Cooperation." *International Organization* 52(2):269–305.

Fearon, James. 1994. "Signaling versus Balance of Power and Interests." *Journal of Conflict Resolution* 38:236–269.

Ferguson, Niall and Moritz Schularick. 2006. "The Empire Effect: The Determinants of Country Risk in the First Age of Globalization 1880–1913." *Journal of Economic History* 2:283–312.

Fernandez, Raquel. 1997. "Returns to Regionalism: An Evaluation of Non-Traditional Gains from RTAs." NBER Working Paper No. 5970.

Finnemore, Martha. 1996a. *National Interests in International Society*. Ithaca, NY: Cornell University Press.

Finnemore, Martha. 1996b. "Norms, Culture, and World Politics: Insight from Sociology's Institutionalism." *International Organization* 50:325–347.

Finnemore, Martha and Kathryn Sikkink. 1998. "International Norm Dynamics and Political Change." *International Organization* 52:887–917.

Finnemore, Martha and Kathryn Sikkink. 2001. "Taking Stock: The Constructivist Research Program in International Relations and Comparative Politics." *Annual Review of Political Science* 4:391–416.

Fowler, James H. 2006. "Connecting the Congress: A Study of Cosponsorship Networks." *Political Analysis* 14:456–487.

Franck, Thomas M. 1990. *The Power of Legitimacy among Nations*. Oxford: Oxford University Press.

Fratianni, Michele and John Pattison. 2001. "International Organizations in a World of Regional Trade Agreements: Lessons from Club Theory." *World Economy* 24(3):457–488.

Frieden, Jeffrey A. 1991. "Invested Interests: The Politics of National Economic Policies in a World of Global Finance." *International Organization* 45(4):425–451.

Froot, Kenneth A. and Maurice Obstfeld. 1991. "Intrinsic Bubbles: The Case of Stock Prices." *American Economic Review* 81:1189–1214.

Gallup, John L., Jeffrey D. Sachs, and Andrew D. Mellinger. 1998. "Geography and Economic Development." NBER Working Paper No. w6849.

Ganzach, Yoav. 2001. "Judging Risk and Return of Financial Assets." *Organizational Behavior and Human Decision Processes* 83:353–370.

Gardener, E.H. and W.R.M. Perraudin. 1992. "Asymmetry in the ERM: A Case Study of French and Germany Interest Rates Since Basle-Nyborg." IMF Working Paper No. 92/96.

Garrett, Geoffrey. 2004. "Globalization's Missing Middle." *Foreign Affairs* 83(6):84–96.

Garrett, Geoffrey and Barry Weingast. 1993. "Ideas, Interests, and Institutions: Constructing the European Community's Internal Market." In *Ideas and foreign policy*, ed. Judith Goldstein and Robert Keohane. Ithaca, NY: Cornell University Press, pp. 173–206.

Garriga, Marcelo and Pablo Sanguinetti. 1995. "The Determinants of Regional Exchange in Mercosur: Geography and Trade Liberalization." Working Paper No. 16, Universidad Torcuato Di Tella-Argentina.

Gaubatz, Kurt Taylor. 1996. "Democratic States and Commitment in International Relations." *International Organization* 50:109–139.

Gelos, Gaston R., Ratna Sahay, and Guido Sandleris. 2004. "Sovereign Borrowing by Developing Countries: What Determines Market Access?" IMF Working Paper.

Gheciu, Alexandria. 2005. "Security Institutions as Agents of Socialization? NATO and the 'New Europe'." *International Organization* 2005:973–1012.

Gilpin, Robert. 1987. *The Political Economy of International Relations*. Princeton, NJ: Princeton University Press.

Gleditsch, Kristian and Michael D. Ward. 2006. "Diffusion and the International Context of Democratization." *International Organization* 60:911–933.

Gleditsch, Kristian Skrede. 2007. "Transnational Dimensions of Civil War." *Journal of Peace Research* 44:293–209.

Glenn, John K. 2004. "From Nation-States to Member States: Accession Negotiations as an Instrument of Europeanization." *Comparative European Politics* 2(1): 3–28.

Glosten, L. and Paul Milgrom. 1984. "Bid, Ask and Transaction Prices in a Specialist Market with Heterogeneeously Informed Traders." *Journal of Financial Economics* 14:71–100.

Goertz, Gary and Kathleen Powers. 2012. "The Economic–Institutional Construction of Regions: Conceptualization and Operationalization." *Review of International Studies*, 37(5):2387–2415.

Goldstein, Judith O., Miles Kahler, Robert Keohane, and Ann-Marie Slaughter. 2000. *Legalization and World Politics*. Cambridge: Cambridge University Press.

González-Rozada, Martín and Eduardo Levy Yeyati. 2008. "Global Factors and Emerging Market Spreads." *The Economic Journal* 118:1917–1936.

Gosovic, Branislav and John Gerard Ruggie. 1976. "On the Creation of a New International Economic Order: Issue Linkage and the Seventh Special Session of the UN General Assembly." *International Organization* 30(2):309–345.

Gowa, Joanne and Soo Yeon Kim. 2005. "An Exclusive Country Club: The Effects of the GATT on Trade, 1950–1994." *World Politics*, 57(4):453–478.

Grabbe, Heather. 2002. "The Governance of the EU: Facing the Challenge of Enlargement." *New Economy* 9:113–117.

Gray, Julia. 2009. "International Organization as a Seal of Approval: European Union Accession and Investor Risk." *American Journal of Political Science* 53(4): 931–949.

Gray, Julia. 2014. "Domestic Capacity and the Implementation Gap in Regional Trade Agreements." Forthcoming, *Comparative Political Studies*.

Gray, Julia and Philip Potter. 2012. "Trade, Volatility, and Compensation at the Core and Periphery of the Global Economy." *International Studies Quarterly* 56(4): 793–800.

Gray, Julia and Jonathan B. Slapin. 2012. "How Effective are Preferential Trade Agreements? Ask the Experts." *Review of International Organizations* 7(3):309–333.

Gray, Julia and Jonathan Slapin. 2013. Forthcoming, *Political Science Research and Methods*.

Grief, Avner. 1993. "Contract Enforceability and Economic Institutions in Early Trade: the Maghribi Traders' Coalition." *American Economic Review* 83:525–548.

Grossman, Gene M. and Elhalan Helpmann. 1991. *Innovation and Growth in the Global Economy*. Cambridge, MA: MIT Press.

Guira, Jorge. 2005. *MERCOSUR: Trade and Investment Amid Financial Crisis*. London: Kluwer Law International.

Gwartney, James and Robert Lawson. 2004. "Economic Freedom of the World: 2004 Report." Fraser Institute.

Hafner-Burton, Emilie M. 2005. "Trading Human Rights: How Preferential Trade Agreements Influence Government Repression." *International Organization* 59(3): 593–629.

Hafner-Burton, Emilie and Alexander H. Montgomery. 2008. "Power or Plenty: Do International Trade Organizations Shape Economic Sanctions?" *Journal of Conflict Resolution* 52(2):213–242.

Haftel, Yoram. 2007. "Designing for Peace: Regional Integration Arrangements, Insitutional Variation, and Militarized Interstate Conflcit." *International Organization* 61(1):217–237.

Haftel, Yoram. 2012. *Regional Economic Institutions and Conflict Mitigation: Design, Implementation, and the Promise of Peace*. Ann Arbor, MI: University of Michigan Press.

Hallerberg, Mark and Guntram B. Wolff. 2008. "Fiscal Institutions, Fiscal Policy and Sovereign Risk Premia in EMU." *Public Choice* 136(3–4):379–396.

Halpern, Jennifer J. 1997. "Elements of a Script for Friendship in Transactions." *Journal of Conflict Resolution* 41:835–868.

Hanke, S.H. 1994. "Arbitrage in Argentina." *Forbes* 14:88.

Hardin, Russell. 1982. *Collective Action*. Baltimore, MD: Johns Hopkins University Press.

Harms, Philipp and Heinrich Ursprung. 2002. "Do Civil and Political Repression Really Boost Foreign Direct Investment?" *Economic Inquiry* 40(4):651–663.

Heckman, James. 1976. "The Common Structure of Statistical Models of Truncation, Sample Selection and Limited Dependent Variables and a Simple Estimator for Such Models." *Annals of Economic and Social Measurement* 5(4):475–492.

Henderson, Rebecca and Iain Cockburn. 1994. "Measuring Competence? Exploring Firm Effects in Pharmaceutical Research." *Strategic Management Journal* 15: 63–84.

Henisz, W. J., Bennet A. Zellner, and Mauro F. Guillen. 2005. "The Worldwide Diffusion of Market-Oriented Infrastructure Reform, 1977–1999." *American Sociological Review* 70:871–897.

Henisz, Witold J. and Bennet A. Zellner. 2006. "Interest Groups, Veto Points and Electricity Infrastructure Deployment." *International Organization* 60(1): 263–286.

Henisz, Witold Jerzy. 2004. "Political Institutions and Policy Volatility." *Economics and Politics* 16(1):1–27.

Higgins, Monica C. and Ranjay Gulati. 2003. "Getting Off to a Good Start: The Effects of Upper Echelon Affiliations on Underwriter Prestige." *Organization Science* 14:244–263.

Higgot, Richard. 1998. "The International Political Economy of Regionalism: Europe and Asia Compared." In *Regionalism and Global Economic Integration: Europe, Asia, and the Americas*, eds. W.D. Coleman and G.R.D Underhill. New York: Routledge, 42–67.

Hille, Peter and Christoph Knill. 2006. "'It's the Bureaucracy, Stupid': The Implementation of the Acquis Communautaire in EU Candidate Countries, 1999–2003." *European Union Politics* 7(4):531–552.

Hilscher, Jens and Yves Nosbusch. 2010. "Determinants of Sovereign Risk: Macroeconomic Fundamentals and the Pricing of Sovereign Debt." *Review of Finance* 14(2):235–262.

Hofhansel, Claus. 2001. "Germany, Multilateralism, and the Eastern Enlargement of the EU." Center for European Studies Program for the Study of Germany and Europe Working Paper No. 1.4.

Honaker, James, Gary King and Matt Blackwell. 2007. "Amelia II: A Program for Missing Data." http://gking.harvard.edu/cem/.

Honaker, Jamses, Gary King, Anne Joseph, and Kenneth Scheve. 2001. "Analyzing Incomplete Political Science Data: An Alternative Algorithm for Multiple Imputation." *American Political Science Review* 95(1):46–69.

Hooghe, Liesbet and Gary Marks. 2005. "Calculation, Community and Cues: Public Opinion on European Integration." *European Union Politics* 6(4):419–443.

Huckfeldt, Robert, Paul Allen Beck, Russell J. Dalton, and Jeffrey Levine. 1995. "Political Environments, Cohesive Social Groups, and the Communication of Public Opinion." *American Journal of Political Science* 39:1025–1054.

Hurd, Ian. 2005. "The Strategic Use of Liberal Internationalism: Libya and the UN Sanctions." *International Organization* 59(3):495–526.

Ikenberry, John G. 1988. "Institutions, Strategic Restraint, and the Persistence of American Postwar Order International Security." *International Security* 23(3): 43–78.

Ikenberry, John G. 2001. *After Victory: Institutions, Strategic Restrain, and the Rebuilding of Order after Major Wars*. Princeton: Princeton University Press.

Ikenberry, John G. and Charles A. Kupchan. 1990. "Socialization and Hegemonic Power." *International Organization* 44:283–315.

Jaimovich, Nir and Sergio Rebelo. 2005. "Can News about the Future Drive the Business Cycle?" National Bureau of Economic Research working paper.

Jensen, Christian B. 2007. "Implementing Europe: A Question of Oversight." *European Union Politics* 8(4):451–477.

Jensen, Nathan M. 2005. "Fiscal Federalism and International Capital." *Swiss Political Science Review* 11(4):77–95. Special Issue from the Economics and Politics Conference in Lugano, Switzerland.

Jensen, Nathan and Rene Lindstaedt. 2009. "Leaning Right and Learning from the Left: Diffusion of Corporate Tax Policy in the OECD." Working Paper Series.

Jensen, Nathan and Scott Schmith. 2005. "Market Responses to Politics: The Rise of Lula and the Decline of the Brazilian Stock Market." *Comparative Political Studies* 38(10):1245–1270.

Jo, Hyeran and Hyun Namgung. 2012. "Dispute Settlement Mechanisms in Preferential Trade Agreements: Democracy, Boilerplates, and the Multilateral Trade Regime." *Journal of Conflict Resolution* 56(6):1041–1068.

Johns, Leslie. 2008. "Endogenous Enforcement and Jurisdiction in International Adjudication." Working Paper.

Johns, Leslie and B. Peter Rosendorff. 2009. "Dispute Settlement, Compliance and Domestic Politics." In *Trade Disputes and the Dispute Settlement Understanding of the WTO: An Interdisciplinary Assessment.* Bingley, UK: Emerald Group Publishing, 139–163.

Johns, Leslie, Michael Gilligan, and B. Peter Rosendorff. 2009. "Strengthening International Courts and the Early Settlement of Disputes." Working Paper, NYU and UCLA.

Johnston, Alastair Iain. 2001. "Treating International Institutions as Social Environments." *International Studies Quarterly* 45:487–515.

Kahneman, Daniel and Amos Tversky. 1979. "Prospect Theory: An Analysis of Decision Under Risk." *Econometrica* 47(2):263–292.

Kaminsky, Graciela and Sergio L. Schmukler. 2002. "Emerging Market Instability: Do Sovereign Ratings Affect Country Risk and Stock Returns?" *World Bank Economic Review* 16:171–195.

Keefer, Philip and David Stasavage. 2002. "Checks and Balances, Private Information, and the Credibility of Monetary Commitments." *International Organization* 56(4):751–774.

Kelley, Judith. 2004. "International Actors on the Domestic Scene: Membership Conditionality and Socialization by International Institutions." *International Organization* 58(3):425–457.

Kelly, David L. 2006a. "Subsidies to Industry and the Environment." University of Miami Working Paper number 2006-2.

Kelley, Judith. 2006b. "New Wine in Old Wineskins: Promoting Political Reforms through the New European Neighbourhood Policy." *Journal of Common Market Studies* 44(1):29–55.

Keohane, Robert. 1984. *After Hegemony: Cooperation and Discord in the World Political Economy.* Princeton, NJ: Princeton University Press.

Keohane, Robert O., Stephen Macedo, and Andrew Moravcsik. 2009. "Democracing-Enhancing Multilateralism." *International Organization* 63:1–31.

Keohane, Robert, Andrew Moravsik, and Anne-Marie Slaughter. 2000. "Legalized Dispute Resolution: Interstate and Transnational." *International Organization* 54(3):457–488.

Keynes, John Maynard. 1936. *The General Theory of Employment, Interest and Money.* New York: Harcourt Brace.

Kim, Moonhawk. 2011. "Asymmetry in Relative Liberalization Commitments: Adjustment Costs and Commitments on the Rate and the Depth of Liberalization in PTAs." Working Paper. University of Colorado at Boulder.

Kim, Seok-Eun. 2005. "The Role of Trust in the Modern Administrative State: An Integrative Model." *Administration and Society* 37(5):611–635.

Kim, So-Yeoung. 2007. "Openness, External Risk, and Volatility: Implications for the Compensation Hypothesis." *International Organization* 61:181–216.

Kim, Soo Yeon and Raymond Hicks. 2012. "Reciprocal Trade Agreements in Asia: Credible Commitment to Trade Liberalization or Paper Tigers?" *Journal of East Asian Studies* 12(1):1–29.

Kindleberger, Charles P. 1986. *The World in Depression: 1929–1939.* Berkeley, CA: University of California Press.

Kindleberger, Charles P. 2005. *Manias, Panics, and Crashes: A History of Financial Crises* (5th edition). New York: Palgrave Macmillan.

Knafo, Samuel. 2005. "The Gold Standard and the Origins of the Modern International Monetary System." *Review of International Political Economy* 13(1):78–102.

Knauff, Markus, Claudia Budeck, Ann G. Wolf, and Kai Hamburger. 2010. "The Illogicality of Stock-Brokers: Psychological Experiments on the Effects of Prior Knowledge and Belief Biases on Logical Reasoning in Stock Trading." *Experimental Psychology and Cognitive Science* 18(5):134–183.

Konstantinidis, Nikitas. 2008. "Gradualism and Uncertainty in International Union Formation: The European Community's First Enlargement." *Review of International Organization* 3(4):399–433.

Koremenos, Barbara. 2001. "Loosening the Ties that Bind: A Learning Model of Agreement Flexibility." *International Organization* 55:289–325.

Koremenos, Barbara. 2005. "Contracting around International Certainty." *American Political Science Review* 99:549–565.

Koremenos, Barbara, Charles Lipson, and Duncan Snidal. 2001. "The Rational Design of International Institutions." *International Organization* 55:761–780.

Kostadinova, Petia A. 2004. "Initial Conditions and Economic Reform in the Postcommunist Countries." *East European Quarterly* 26(4):407–420.

Kostadinova, Petia. 2007. "Europeanization of Economic Policy in the New Member States." Working Paper. European Union Studies Association, Biennial Conference.

Krasner, Stephen. 1991. "Global Communications and National Power, Life on the Pareto Frontier." *World Politics* 43(3):336–366.

Kray, Aart and Vikram Nehru. 2004. "When Is External Debt Sustainable?" World Bank Policy Research Paper 3200.

Kuklinski, James H. and Normal L. Hurley. 1996. "It's A Matter of Interpretation." In *Political Persuasion and Attitude Change*, eds. Diana C. Mutz, Richard Brody, Paul Sriderma. Ann Arbor: University of Michigan Press, pp. 125–144.

Kurizaki, Shuhei. 2007. "Perception, Signaling, and War." Working Paper. Texas A & M University.

Kurscheidt, Markus and Bernd Rahmann. 2006. "Local Investment and National Impact: The Case of the Football World Cup 2006 in Germany." *The Economic Impact of Sport Events* 13(1):79–108.

Lacarte-Muro, J. and Petina Gappah. 2000. "Developing Countries and the WTO Legal and Dispute Settlement System: A View from the Bench." *Journal of International Economic Law* 3(3):395–401.

LaPorta, Rafael, Florencio Lopez de Silanes, Andrei Schleifer, and Robert W. Vishny. 1997. "Legal Determinants of External Finance." *Journal of Finance* 52:1131–1150.

LaPorta, Rafael, Florencio Lopez de Silanes, Andrei Schleifer, and Robert W. Vishny. 1998. "Law and Finance." *Journal of Political Economy* 106:1113–1155.

LaPorta, Rafael, Florencio Lopez de Silanes, Andrei Schleifer, and Robert Vishny. 2000. "Investor Protection and Corporate Governance." *Journal of Financial Economics* 58:3–27.

LaPorta, Rafael, Florencio Lopez de Silanes, Andrei Schleifer, and Robert Vishny. 2002. "Investor Protection and Corporate Valuation." *Journal of Finance* 57:1147–1170.

Lasas, Ainius. 2008. "Restituting Victims: EU and NATO Enlargements through the Lenses of Collective Guilt." *Journal of European Public Policy* 15(1):98–116.

Leblang, David and William Bernard. 2006. "Parliamentary Politics and Foreign Exchange Markets: The World According to GARCH." *International Studies Quarterly* 50:69–92.

Lebovic, James H. and Erik Voeten. 2006. "The Politics of Shame: The Condemnation of Country Human Rights Practices in the UNCHR." *International Studies Quarterly* 50:861–888.

Leeds, Brett Ashley, Jeffrey M. Ritter, Sara McLaughlin Mitchell, and Andrew G. Long. 2002. "Alliance Treaty Obligations and Provisions, 1815–1944." *International Interactions* 28:237–260.

Lei, Vivian, Charles N. Noussair, and Charles R. Plott. 2001. "Non-speculative Bubbles in Experimental Asset Markets: Lack of Common Knowledge of Rationality vs. Actual Irrationality." *Econometrica* 69:830–859.

Levine, R. and S. Zervos. 1998. "Stock Markets, Banks, and Economic Growth." *American Economic Review* 88:537–543.

Levitz, Philip and Grigore Pop-Eleches. 2010a. "Monitoring, Money, and Migrants: Countering Post-Accession Backsliding in Bulgaria and Romania." *Europe-Asia Studies* 62(3):461–479.

Levitz, Philip and Grigore Pop-Eleches. 2010b. "Why No Backsliding? The EU's Impact on Democracy and Governance Before and After Accession." *Comparative Political Studies* 43(4):457–485.

Lewis, Jeffrey. 2005. "The Janus Face of Brussels: Socialization and Everyday Decision Making in the European Union." *International Organization* 59(4):937–971.

Li, Quan and Adam Resnick. 2003. "Reversal of Fortunes: Democratic Institutions and Foreign Direct Investment Inflows to Developing Countries." *International Organization* 57:175–211.

Lo, Andrew W., Harry Mamayski, and Jiang Wang. 2004. "Asset Prices and Trading Volume under Fixed Transactions Costs." *Journal of Political Economy* 112:1054–1090.

Loayza, Norman V. and Raimundo Soto. 2003. "Market-Oriented Reforms: Definitions and Measurement." In *Understanding Market Reforms, Volume 1: Philosophy, Politics and Stakeholders*. New York: Palgrave Macmillan, pp. 78–112.

Lohmann, Susanne. 1992. "Optimal Commitment in Monetary Policy: Credibility versus Flexibility." *American Economic Review* 82(1):273–286.

Lucas, Robert E. 1998. "On the Mechanics of Economic Growth." *Journal of Monetary Economics* 22:3–42.

Lupia, Arthur. 1994. "Shortcuts versus Encyclopedias: Information and Voting Behavior in California Insurance Reform Elections." *American Political Science Review* 88:63–76.

Lupia, Arthur and Matthew Danial McCubbins. 1998. *The Democratic Dilemma: Can Citizens Learn What They Need to Know?* Chicago: Press Syndicate of the University of Chicago.

Lutz, E. and Kathryn Sikkink. 2001. "The Justice Cascade: The Evolution and Impact of Foreign Human Rights Trials in Latin America." *Chicago Journal of International Law* 21(2):1–33.

MacGregor, D.G., P. Slovic, D. Dreman, and M. Berry. 2000. "Imagery, Affect, and Financial Judgment." *Journal of Psychology and Financial Markets* 1(2):104–110.

Mansfield, Edward and Helen Milner. 1997. *The Political Economy of Regionalism.* New York: Columbia University Press.

Mansfield, Edward, Helen Milner, and Peter Rosendorf. 2000. "Free to Trade: Democracies, Autocracies and International Trade." *American Political Science Review* 94(2):305–321.

Mansfield, Edward and Jon Pevehouse. 2006. "Democratization and International Organization." *International Organization* 60(1):137–167.

Mansfield, Edward D. and Eric Reinhardt. 2008. "International Institutions and the Volatility of International Trade." *International Organization* 62:621–652.

Marin, Bernd and Renate Mayntz. 1992. *Policy Networks: Empirical Evidence and Theoretical Considerations.* Boulder: Westview.

Marinov, N. 2005. "Do Economic Sanctions Destabilize Country Leaders?" *American Journal of Political Science* 28:564–576.

Marsh, David and R.A.W. Rhodes, eds. 1992. *Policy Networks in British Government.* Oxford: Oxford University Press.

Martin, Lisa. 1997. "Legislative Influence and International Engagement." In *Liberalization and Foreign Policy*, ed. Miles Kahler. New York: Columbia University Press, pp. 67–104.

Martin, Lisa. 2005. "The President and International Commitments: Treaties as Signaling Devices." *Presidential Studies Quarterly* 35:440–465.

Mattli, Walter. 1999. *The Logic of Regional Integration: Europe and Beyond.* Cambridge: Cambridge University Press.

Maxfield, Sylvia. 1998. *Gatekeepers of Growth: The International Political Economy of Central Banking in Developing Countries.* Princeton, NJ: Princeton University Press.

Mayall, James. 1984. "The Sanctions Problem in International Economic Relations: Reflections in the Light of Recent Experience." *International Affairs* 60(4):631–642.

McCall Smith, James. 2000. "The Politics of Dispute Settlement Design: Explaining Legalism in Regional Trade Pacts." *International Organization* 54(1):137–180.

McGillivray, Fiona and Alastair Smith. 1998. "Cooperating Democrats, Deflecting Autocrats." Working Paper.

McGillivray, Fiona and Alastair Smith. 2000. "Trust and Cooperation through Agent-Specific Punishments." *International Organization* 54:809–824.

McGillivray, Fiona and Alastair Smith. 2004. "The Impact of Leadership Turnover on Trading Relations between States." *International Organization* 58:567–600.

Mead, George Herbert. 1934. *Mind, Self, and Society*. Chicago: University of Chicago Press.

Mearsheimer, John J. 1994. "The False Promise of International Institutions." *International Security* 19(3):5–49.

Mercer, Jonathan. 1996. *Reputation and International Politics*. Ithaca, NY: Cornell University Press.

Meseguer, Covadonga. 2002. *Bayesian Learning About Policies*. Madrid, Spain: Instituto Juan March de Estudios e Investigaciones.

Meseguer, Covadonga. 2006. "Learning and Economic Policy Choices." *Journal of Public Policy* 22:299–325.

Miers, Ann and T. Morgan. 2002. "Multilateral Sanctions and Foreign Policy Success: Can Too Many Cooks Spoil the Broth?" *International Interactions* 28(2):117–136.

Milgrom, Paul R., Douglass C. North, and Barry R. Weingast. 1990. "The Role of Institutions in the Revival of Trade: The Medieval Law Merchant, Private Judges, and the Champagne Fairs." *Economics and Politics* 2:1–23.

Milliken, Jennifer L. 2996. "Metaphors of Prestige and Reputation in American Foreign Policy and American Realism." In *Post-Realism: The Rhetorical Turn in International Relations*, eds. Francis A. Beer and Robert Harriman. Lansing, MI: Michigan State University Press, pp. 217–238.

Milner, Helen. 1998. "International Political Economy: Beyond Hegemonic Stability." *Foreign Policy* 110:112–123. Special Edition: Frontiers of Knowledge.

Min, Hong G. 1998. "Determinants of Emerging Market Bond Spread: Do Economic Fundamentals Matter?" Policy Research Working Paper No. WPS 1899, The World Bank.

Mintrom, Michael and Sandra Vergari. 1998. "Policy Networks and Innovation Diffusion: The Case of State Education Reforms." *Journal of Politics* 60:126–148.

Mitchener, Kris James and Marc D. Weidenmier. 2008. "Are Hard Pegs Credible in Emerging Markets? Lessons from the Classical Gold Standard." Working paper.

Moravcsik, Andrew. 1995. "Explaining International Human Rights Regimes: Liberal Theory and Western Europe." *European Journal of International Relations* 1(2):157–189.

Moravcsik, Andrew. 1997. "Taking Preferences Seriously: A Liberal Theory of International Politics." *International Organization* 51:513–553.

Morrow, James. 1987. "On the Theoretical Basis of a Measure of National Risk Attitudes." *International Studies Quarterly* 31(4):423–438.

Morrow, James. 1994. "Modeling the Forms of International Cooperation: Distribution Versus Information." *International Organization* 48(3):387–423.

Morrow, James D. 2002. "The Laws of War, Common Conjectures, and Legal Systems in International Politics." *Journal of Legal Studies* 31:S41–S60.

Mosley, Layna. 2000. "Room to Move: International Financial Markets and National Welfare States." *International Organization* 54(4):737–773.

Mosley, Layna. 2003. *Global Capital and National Governments*. New York: Cambridge University Press.

Mosley, Layna and Sarah Brooks. 2012. "Categories, Creditworthiness and Contagion: How Investors' Shortcuts Affect Sovereign Debt Markets." Working Paper.

Mosley, Layna and Iain Hardie. 2007. "Turkey's Convergence Tale: Market Pressures, Membership Conditionality, and EU Accession." Working Paper.

Mosley, Layna and David A. Singer. 2009. "The Global Financial Crisis: Lessons and Opportunities for International Political Economy." *International Interactions* 35(4):420–429.

Nooruddin, Irfan. 2002. "Modeling Selection Bias in Studies of Sanctions Efficacy International Interactions: Empirical and Theoretical Research." *International Relations* 28(1):564–576.

North, Douglass. 1990. *Institutions, Institutional Change and Economic Performance.* New York: Cambridge University Press.

North, Douglass C. and Barry R. Weingast. 1989. "Constitutions and Commitment: The Evolution of Institutional Governing Public Choice in Seventeenth-Century England." *Journal of Economic History* 49(4):803–832.

Oakes, P.J. 1987. "The Salience of Social Categories." In *Rediscovering the Social Group: A Self-Categorization.* Oxford: Blackwell, 117–141.

Oneal, John. 1994. "The Affinity of Foreign Investors for Authoritarian Regimes." *Political Research Quarterly* 47(3):565–588.

O'Neill, Barry. 2006. "Nuclear Weapons and National Prestige." Cowles Foundation Discussion Paper No. 1560.

Oppenheimer, Andrew. 2004. "West German Pacifism and the Ambivalence of Human Solidarity." *Peace and Change* 29(3):353–389.

Orenstein, Mitchell Alexander. 2003. "Mapping the Diffusion of Pension Innovation." In *Pension Reform in Europe: Process and Progress,* ed. Mitchell Alexander Orenstein, Robert Holzmann, and Michal Rutkowski. Washington, DC: The World Bank.

Orlowski, Lucjan and Kirsten Lommatzsch. 2005. "Bond Yield Compression in the Countries Converging to the Euro." William Davidson Institute Working Paper Series wp 799.

Pahre, Robert. 1997. "Endogenous Domestic Institutions in Two-Level Games and Parliamentary Oversight of the European Union." *Journal of Conflict Resolution* 41(1):147–174.

Perotti, Enrico C. and Pieter van Oijen. 2001. "Privatization, Political Risk and Stock Market Development in Emerging Economies." *Journal of International Money and Finance* 20:43–69.

Perron, Pierre. 1989. "Testing for a Unit Root in a Time Series with a Changing Mean." *Journal of Business and Economic Statistics* 8:153–162.

Pevehouse, Jon. 2002. "With a Little Help from My Friends? Regional Organizations and the Consolidation of Democracy." *American Journal of Political Science* 46(3):611–626.

Plaza, L. De La and S. Sirtaine. 2005. "An Analysis of the 2002 Uruguayan Banking Crises." World Bank Policy Research Working Paper.

Plümper, Thomas, Christina Schneider, and Vera Troeger. 2005. "Regulatory Conditionality and Membership Selection in the EU, Evidence from a Heckman Selection Model." *British Journal of Political Science* 36:17–38.

Plumper, Thomas and Walter Mattli. 2002. "The Demand-Side Politics of EU Enlargement: Democracy and the Application for EU Membership." *Journal of European Public Policy* 9:550–574.

Podolny, Joel M. 1994. "Market Uncertainty and the Social Character of Economic Exchange." *Administrative Science Quarterly* 39:458–483.

Posen, Adam. 1995. "Declarations Are Not Enough: Financial Sector Sources of Central Bank Independence." *NBER Macroeconomics Annual* 10:251–274.

Potter, Phil. 2008. "Soft Interdependence and International Conflict." UCLA Dissertation.

Przeworski, Adam. 2004. "Institutions Matter?" *Government and Opposition* 39(4):527–540.

Putnam, Robert. 1988. "Diplomacy and Domestic Politics." *International Organization* 42(3):427–461.

Putterman, Louis, ed. 1986. *The Economic Nature of the Firm: A Reader*. New York: Cambridge University Press.

Rajan, Raghuram G. and Luigi Zingales. 1998. "Power in a Theory of the Firm." *The Quarterly Journal of Economics* 113:387–432.

Rao, Hayagreeva. 1994. "The Social Construction of Reputation: Certification Contests, Legitimation, and the Survival of Organizations in the American Automobile Industry: 1895–1912." *Strategic Management Journal* 15:29–44.

Ravenhill, John. 2008. "Fighting Irrelevance: An Economic Community 'with ASEAN Characteristics'." *The Pacific Review* 21(4):469–488.

Reicher, S.D., R. Spears, and T. Postmes. 1995. "A Social Identity Model of Deindividuation Phenomena." *European Review of Social Psychology* 6:161–198.

Reinhart, Carmen and Ken Rogoff. 2009. *This Time Is Different: Eight Centuries of Financial Folly*. Princeton: Princeton University Press.

Rindova, V., I. Williamson, A. Petkova, and J. Sever. 2005. "Being Good or Being Known: An Empirical Examination of the Dimensions, Antecedents, and Consequences of Organizational Reputation." *Academy of Management Journal* 48:1033–1050.

Risse, Thomas, Stephen C. Ropp, and Kathryn Sikkink. 1999. *The Power of Human Rights: International Norms and Domestic Change*. Boston: Cambridge University Press.

Roberts, Tyson. 2005. "Political Institutions and Foreign Direct Investment in Developing Countries: Do Veto Players Mean More to Investors than Democracy or Property Rights?" Working Paper.

Robin, Corey. 2002. "Reflections on Fear: Montesquieu in Retrieval." *American Political Science Review* 94:347–360.

Rodrik, Dani. 1989. "Policy Uncertainty and Private Investment in Developing Countries." NBER Working Papers 2999.

Rodrik, Dani. 1991. "Policy Uncertainty and Private Investment in Developing Countries." *Journal of Development Economics* 36:229–242.

Rodrik, Dani. 1997. *Has Globalization Gone Too Far?* Washington, DC: Institute for International Economics.

Rodrik, Dani. 1998. "Why Do More Open Economies Have Bigger Governments?" *Journal of Political Economy* 106:997–1032.

Rodrik, Dani. 2003. "Institutions, Integration, and Geography: In Search of the Deep Determinants of Economic Growth." In *In Search of Prosperity: Analytic Country Studies on Growth*, ed. Dani Rodrik. Princeton: Princeton University Press.

Rogers, Everett M. 1962. *Diffusion of Innovations*. New York: Free Press.

Root, Hilton L. 2005. *Capital and Collusion: The Politics of Risk and Uncertainty in Economic Development*. Princeton: Princeton University Press.

Rose, Andrew K. 2002. "One Reason Countries Repay Their Debts: Renegotiation and International Trade." NBER Working Paper no. 8853.

Rose, Andrew and Mark M. Spiegel. 2002. "A Gravity Model of Sovereign Lending: Trade, Default, and Credit." NBER Working Paper 9285.

Rosendorff, B. Peter. 2005. "Stability and Rigidity: The Dispute Resolution Mechanism at the WTO." *American Political Science Review* 99:389–400.

Rosendorff, B. Peter and Helen Milner. 2005. "The Optimal Design of International Trade Institutions: Uncertainty and Escape." *International Organization* 55:829–857.

Rosenthal, Howard and Erik Voeten. 2007. "Measuring Legal Systems." *Journal of Comparative Economics* 35(4):711–728.

Rowland, Peter and José L. Torres. 2004. "Determinants of Spread and Creditworthiness for Emerging Market Sovereign Debt: A Panel Data Study." Working Paper.

Sachs, Jeffrey and Andrew Warner. 1996. "Achieving Rapid Growth in the Transition Economies of Central Europe." HIID Development Discussion Paper No. 544.

Sachs, Jeffrey D. and Andrew M. Warner. 1995. "Economic Convergence and Economic Policies." NBER Working Paper No. 5039.

Saiegh, Sebastian. 2005. "Do Countries Have a Democratic Advantage?" *Comparative Political Studies* 38:366–387.

Sakwa, Richard and Mark Webber. 1999. "The Commonwealth of Independent States, 1991–1998: Stagnation and Survival." *Europe-Asia Studies* 51(3):379–415.

Santos, Manuel S. and Michael Woodford. 1997. "Rational Asset Pricing Bubbles." *Econometrica* 65:19–57.

Sanya, Sarah O. and Montfort Mlachila. 2010. "Post-Crisis Bank Behavior: Lessons from Mercosur." IMF Working Paper.

Sartori, Giovanni. 2004. "Where Is Political Science Going?" *Political Science and Politics* 37:785–787.

Scharfstein, David S. and Jeremy C. Stein. 1990. "Herd Behavior and Investment." *American Economic Review* 80(3):465–479.

Scheff, T.J. 1966. *Being Mentally Ill: A Sociological Theory.* Chicago: Aldine.

Schimmelfennig, Frank and Ulrich Sedelmeier. 2005. *The Europeanization of Central and Eastern Europe.* Ithaca: Cornell University Press.

Schindler, Mark. 2007. *Rumors in Financial Markets.* Sussex: John Wiley and sons.

Schneider, Christina. 2009. *Conflict, Negotiation and EU Enlargement.* New York: Cambridge University Press.

Schneider, Christina and Johannes Urpelainen. 2012. "Accession Rules for International Institutions: A Legitimacy/Efficacy Trade-off?" Working Paper.

Schultz, Kenneth A. 2001. *Democracy and Coercive Diplomacy.* Cambridge, New York: Cambridge University Press.

Schultz, Kenneth A. and Barry R. Weingast. 2003. "The Democratic Advantage: Institutional Foundations of Financial Power in International Competition." *International Organization* 57(1):3–42.

Serra, M.I., M.F. Pazmino, G. Lindow, B. Sutton, and G. Ramirez. 2006. "Regional Convergence in Latin America." IMF Working Paper.

Shleifer, Andrei. 2000. *Inefficient Markets: An Introduction to Behavioral Finance.* Oxford: Oxford University Press.

Shleifer, Andrei and R.W. Vishny. 1997. "The Limits of Arbitrage." *Journal of Finance* 52(1):35–55.

Shubik, Martin. 1970. "Voting, or a Price System in a Competitive Market Structure." *American Political Science Review* 64(1):179–181.

Sikkink, Kathryn and Carrie Booth Walling. 2005. "Errors about Trials: The Political Reality of the Justice Cascade and Its Impact." Presented to the annual meeting of the American Political Science Association. Washington, DC, September 1.

Simmons, Belt. 1996. "Rulers of the Game: Central Bank Independence during the Interwar Years." *International Organization* 50(3):407–443.

Simmons, Beth. 2000a. "International Law and State Behavior: Commitment and Compliance in International Monetary Affairs." *American Political Science Review* 94(4):819–835.

Simmons, Beth. 2000b. "The Legalization of International Monetary Affairs." *International Organization* 54(3):573–602.

Simmons, Beth A. 2001. "The International Politics of Harmonization: The Case of Capital Market Regulation." *International Organization* 55:589–620.

Simmons, Beth and Zach Elkins. 2004. "The Globalization of Liberalization: Policy Diffusion in the International Political Economy." *American Political Science Review* 98(1):171–189.

Sinclair, Peter. 2003. "The Optimum Rate of Inflation: an Academic Perspective." *Bank of England Quarterly Bulletin* 43:343–351.

Slapin, Jonathan. 2006. "Who Is Powerful? Examining Preferences and Testing Sources of Bargaining Strength at European Intergovernmental Conferences." *European Union Politics* 7(1):171–189.

Slaughter, Matthew J. 1995. "The Antebellum Transportation Revolution and Factor-Price Convergence." NBER Working Paper No. 5303.

Smith, Karen. 2005. "The Outsiders: The European Neighborhood Policy." *International Affairs* 81(4):757–773.

Snidal, Duncan. 1985. "Coordination versus Prisoners' Dilemma: Implications for International Cooperation and Regimes." *American Political Science Review* 79:923–942.

Snidal, Duncan. 1994. "The Politics of Scope: Endogenous Actors, Heterogeneity and Institutions." *Journal of Theoretical Politics* 6(4):449–472.

Söderbaum, Fredrick. 2005. ""With a Little Help From My Friends": How Regional Organizations in Africa Sustain Clientelism, Corruption and Discrimination." Working Paper.

Solingen, Etel. 1998. Regional Orders at Century's Dawn: Global and Domestic Influences on Grand Strategy. Princeton, NJ: Princeton University Press.

Solow, Robert M. 1956. "A Contribution to the Theory of Economic Growth." *Quarterly Journal of Economics* 70:65–94.

Soydemir, Gökçe. 2000. "International Transmission Mechanism of Stock Market Movements: Evidence from Emerging Equity Markets." *Journal of Forecasting* 19:149–176.

Spence, Michael. 1973. "Job Market Signaling." *Quarterly Journal of Economics* 87(3):355–374.

Stallings, Barbara. 1992. "International Influence on Economic Policy: Debt, Stabilization, and Structural Reform." In *The Politics of Economic Adjustment: International Constraints, Distributive Conflicts and the State*, ed. Stephen Haggard and Robert R. Kaufman. Princeton: Princeton University Press, pp. 41–88.

Stasavage, David. 2002. "Private Investment and Political Institutions." *Economics and Politics* 14(1):41–63.

Stasavage, David. 2004. "Open-Door or Closed-Door? Transparency in Domestic and International Bargaining." *International Organization* 58(3):667–703.

Stasavage, David. 2007. "Cities, Constitutions, and Sovereign Borrowing in Europe, 1274–1785." *International Organization* 61:489–525.

Steneri, Carlo. 2004. "Uruguay Debt Reprofiling: Lessons from Experience." *Georgetown Journal of International Law* 35(4):731–754.

Stinnett, Doug. 2007. "Depth, Compliance, and the Design of Regional Trade Institutions." Midwest Political Science conference paper.

Stone, Randall. 2002. *Lending Credibility: The International Monetary Fund and the Post-Communist Transition.* Princeton, NJ: Princeton University Press.

Stone, Randall, Branislav Slantchev, and Tamar London. 2008. "Choosing How to Cooperate: A Public Goods Model of International Relations." *International Studies Quarterly* 52(4):335–362.

Stuart, Toby E., Ha Hoang, and Ralph Hybels. 1999. "Interorganizational Endorsements and the Performance of Entrepreneurial Ventures." *Administrative Science Quarterly* 44:315–349.

Sturzenegger, Frederico and Jeromin Zettelmeyer. 2005. "Haircuts: Estimating Investor Losses in Sovereign Debt Restructurings, 1998–2005." IMF Working Paper 05-137.

Subramanian, Arvind. 2007. "Behavioural Finance: A Review and Synthesis." *European Economic Management* 1:12–29.

Subramanian, Arvind and Shan-Jin Wei. 2007. "The WTO Promotes Trade, Strongly but Unevenly." *Journal of International Economics* 72(1):151–175.

Summers, Lawrence. 1990. "What Is the Social Rate of Return to Capital Investment?" In *Essays in Honor of Robert Solow*, ed. Peter Diamond. Cambridge, MA: MIT Press.

Sushil, Bikchandi, David Hirshleifer, and Ivo Welch. 1992. "A Theory of Fads, Fashion, Custom, and Cultural Change as Informational Cascades." *Journal of Political Economy* 100:83–97.

Sussman, Nathan and Yishay Yafeh. 2000. "Institutions, Reforms, and Country Risk: Lessons from Japanese Government Debt in the Meiji Period." *Journal of Economic History* 60:442–467.

Svejnar, Jan. 2002. "Transition Economies: Performance and Challenges." *Journal of Economic Perspectives* 16:3–28.

Tajfel, Henri. 1978. "Social Psychology of Intergroup Relations." *Annual Review of Psychology* 33:1–39.

Tajfel, Henri and Jonathan H. Turner. 1979. *Differentiation between Social Groups: Studies in the Social Psychology of Intergroup Relations.* European Association of Experimental Social Psychology by Academic Press chapter "An integrative theory of intergroup conflict."

Taylor, John B. 2007. "The 2002 Uruguayan Financial Crisis: Five Years Later." Conference on the 2002 Uruguayan Financial Crisis and Its Aftermath, Motevideo, Uruguay, May 29, 2007.

Thaler, Richard H. 1993. *Advances in Behavioral Finance.* New York: Russell Sage Foundation.

Thaler, Richard H. 1994. *Quasi Rational Economics.* New York: Russell Sage Foundation.

Thompson, Alexander. 2006. "Management under Anarchy: The International Politics of Climate Change." *Climate Change* 78(1):7–29.

Tichy, Noel M., Michael L. Tushman, and Charles Fombrun. 1979. "Social Network Analysis in Organizational Settings." *Academy of Management Review* 4:507–519.

Tomz, Michael. 2007. *A Reputational Thery of Sovereign Debt*. Princeton: Princeton University Press.

Tomz, Michael. 2008. "Reputation and the Effect of International Law on Preferences and Beliefs." Stanford University manuscript, available at: http://www.stanford.edu/tomz/working/working.shtml.

Tomz, Michael, Judith Goldstein, and Douglas Rivers. 2007. "Do We Really Know That the WTO Increases Trade? Comment." *American Economic Review* 97(5):2005–2018.

Tomz, Michael, Jason Wittenberg, and Gary King. 2003. "Software for Interpreting and Presenting Statistical Results, Version 2.1." Stanford University, University of Wisconsin, and Harvard University. January 5, Available at: http://gking.harvard.edu/.

Treisman, Daniel. 2002. "Decentralization and the Quality of Government." UCLA Department of Political Science manuscript.

Tsebelis, George. 2002. *Veto Players: How Political Institutions Work*. Princeton: Princeton University Press.

Tucker, Robert R., Ella Mae Matsumura, and K.R. Subramanyam. 2003. "Going-Concern Judgments: An Experimental Test of the Self-Fulfilling Prophecy and Forecast Accuracy." *Journal of Accounting and Public Policy* 22(5):401–432.

Turner, J.C., M.A. Hogg, P.J. Reicher, and M. Wetherell. 1987. *Rediscovering the Social Group: A Self-Categorization Theory*. Oxford, UK: Basil Blackwell.

Underdal, Arild. 1998. "Explaining Compliance and Defection: Three Models." *European Journal of International Relations* 4(1):5–30.

Vachudová, Milada. 2002. "The Leverage of International Institutions on Democratizing States: The European Union and Eastern Europe." Paper provided by European University Institute (EUI), Robert Schuman Centre of Advanced Studies (RSCAS) in its series EUI-RSCAS Working Papers with number 33.

Vachudová, Milada Anna. 2005. *Europe Undivided: Democracy, Leverage, and Integration After Communism*. Oxford: Oxford University Press.

Vachudová, Milada Anna. 2006. "EU Leverage in the Western Balkans." *New Europe Review* 3(1):1–26.

Vaillant, Marcel. 2007. "Why Does Uruguay Need to Negotiate with the United States?" *Cuadernos del CLAEH* 3:92–120.

Valley, K.L., J. Moag, and M.H. Bazerman. 1998. "'A Matter of Trust': Effects of Communication on the Efficiency and Distribution of Outcomes." *Journal of Economic Behavior and Organization* 34(2):211–238.

van Ham, Peter. 2001. "Security and Culture, or, Why NATO Won't Last." *Security Dialogue* 32:393–406.

Vaugirard, Victor. 2005. "Beliefs, Bailouts and Spread of Bank Panics." *Bulletin of Economic Research* 57(1):93–107.

Ventura, Jaume. 1997. "Growth and Interdependence." *The Quarterly Journal of Economics* 112:57–84.

Volden, Craig and Charles R. Shipan. 2007. "When the Smoke Clears: Interstate vs. Intrastate Diffusion of Youth Access Policies." Prepared for presentation at 2007 Annual Meeting of the American Political Science Association, Chicago.

von Stein, Jana. 2005. "Do Treaties Constrain or Screen? Selection Bias and Treaty Compliance." *American Political Science Review* 99:611–622.

Vreeland, James Raymond. 2001. "Institutional Determinants of IMF Agreements." Working Paper, New Haven: Department of Political Science, Yale University.

Vreeland, James Raymond. 2003. *The IMF and Economic Development.* New York: Cambridge University Press.

Wang, Yong. 1993. "Near-Rational Behaviour and Financial Market Fluctuations." *The Economic Journal* 103(421):1462–1478.

Weyland, Kurt. 2005. "Theories of Political Diffusion: Lessons from Latin American Pension Reform." *World Politics* 57:262–295.

Wheeler, Katherine Hancy. 2007. "Uruguay Signs a TIFA with the U.S.: Will This Mean an Unraveling of Mercosur or Is Montevideo Maneuvering to Be Left Out in the Cold?" Council on Hemispheric Affairs Working Paper.

Willerton, John P., Gary Goertz, and Michael O. Slobodchikoff. 2012. "Mistrust and Hegemony: Regional Institutional Design, the CIS, and Russia." Working Paper.

Williamson, Oliver E. 1985. *The Economic Institutions of Capitalism.* New York: Free Press.

Wilson, Sven and Dan Butler. 2002. "Too Good to Be True? The Promise and Peril of Panel Data in Political Science." Working Paper, Brigham Young University.

Winters, L. Alan and Zhen Kun Wang. 1994. *Eastern Europe's International Trade.* Manchester: Manchester University Press.

Wolford, W. 2008. "Global Shadows: Africa in the Neoliberal World Order." *Singapore Journal of Tropical Geography* 29:266–269.

Wright, M.L.J. 2005. "Coordinating Creditors." *The American Economic Review* 95:388–392.

Young, Alwyn. 1991. "Learning by Doing and the Dynamic Effects of International Trade." *Quarterly Journal of Economics* 106:369–405.

Zuckerman, E.W. 2004. "Structural incoherence and stock market activity." *American Sociological Review* 69(3):405–432.

Zürn, Michael and Jeffrey T. Checkel. 2005. "Getting Socialized to Build Bridges: Constructivism and Rational Choice, Europe and the Nation-State." *International Organization* 59:1045–1079.

Index

Ability to repay debt, 8, 16, 18, 28–30, 42–43, 52, 55, 60, 63, 122, 170, 173, 178
indicators for, 20, 21
ACU. *See* Asian Currency Unit
Accession to international organizations. *See* International organization enlargement, European Union enlargement
Affiliations and reputation, 17–18, 33–36, 38, 42–43, 157, 177
impact on risk levels of assets, 30, 31
influential third parties, 30–31
effects for new borrowers, 30
in pharmaceutical research, 30
African-Caribbean-Pacific (ACP) countries, 155
African countries
EPAs and, 155
RTAs and, 157
sovereign bonds, 156
Namibia. *See* Namibia
Tanzania. *See* Tanzania
South Africa. *See* South Africa
ALBA, 2, 14, 36, 39, 41, 70, 126, 150, 160, 190, 193, 195
benchmark ideology of, 131–132
comparison with CAFTA, 132–133
Cuba role in foundation of, 134
Dmitri Medvedev participation in, 131
El Salvador's refusal to sign onto, 124, 141–145
expansions of, 131
founding members of, 133–134
Haiti's possible entry into, 133

international media's views on, 132
investor perception of, 126–127, 133–135
SUCRE currency of, 132
membership, 126, 131, 139, 144–145
of Bolivia, 134–135
of Dominica, 133–134
economic benefits of, 126, 133
of Ecuador. *See* Ecuador, ALBA membership of
of Honduras. *See* Honduras, ALBA membership of
of Nicaragua, 134
Andean Community, 55, 78, 130, 195
Chile's exit from, 153
political content of, 153
Venezuela's exit from, 140, 153
Argentina, 20, 54, 82, 130, 139, 170, 191–192, 196
and Venezuela, close relations between, 182
bonds, 54, 82, 181–182
Argentine default of 2001, 48, 130–134, 175, 176–178
effect on Mercosur members, 176
causes of, 175
and debt restructuring, 182
Association of Southeast Asian Nations (ASEAN) 41, 58, 197, 199
credibility of, 41
China's FTA with, 158–159
Expansion, 164
proposal for Asian common bond market, 197
Asian Currency Unit, 196